VICTORIAN VALUES

VICTORIAN VALUES
Secularism and the size of families

J. A. BANKS

ROUTLEDGE & KEGAN PAUL
London, Boston and Henley

First published in 1981
by Routledge & Kegan Paul Ltd
39 Store Street, London WC1E 7DD,
9 Park Street, Boston, Mass. 02108, USA and
Broadway House, Newtown Road,
Henley-on-Thames, Oxon RG9 1EN
Printed in Great Britain by
Billing & Sons Ltd
Guildford, London, Oxford and Worcester

Library of Congress Cataloguing in Publication Data

Banks, Joseph Ambrose.
Victorian values.

Including bibliographical references and indexes.
1. Family size - Great Britain - Moral and
religious aspects - History - 19th century. 2. Birth
control - Great Britain - Moral and religious aspects
- History - 19th century. 3. Secularism - Great
Britain - History - 19th century. 4. Great Britain
- Social conditions - 19th century. I. Title.

HQ614.B44   304.6'3   81-8604

ISBN 0 7100 0807 4   AACR2

TO THE MEMORY OF DAVID GLASS

CONTENTS

TABLES

1 FERTILITY AND THE DECLINE IN RELIGIOUS BELIEF

Precise statistics of the growth of human population have been kept only in recent times and even today the figures published for some countries are rarely as accurate as they might be. Nevertheless, it is possible to make some reasonably cogent comparisons with the past. From these estimates it appears that never in the recorded history of mankind has the number of people on the earth increased so fast as at present. From the evidence at our disposal it would seem that it took 200,000 years for the world's population to reach the 2,500 million mark. Yet the last 800 millions of these were added between 1900 and 1950,[1] and during the following twenty years the world rate of increase was reckoned to be about 1.9 per cent per annum, so that in the general demographic conditions of 1950-70 the officers of the United Nations concluded that for the rest of this century the rate could rise to become as high as 2.3 per cent per annum, although the more likely figure was 2.0 per cent. As compared with the period 1750-1800 - the earliest for which there is reasonably reliable information and in which the rate of increase was 0.4 per cent[2] - the present is remarkable for the growth of numbers of human beings on the earth; and there are not many signs that this growth is slackening off much, save in a few countries. Thus, between 1950 and 1965 a further 800 millions were added to the world's total.[3]

Faced with the requirement to comment on this situation, population experts have asserted that they believe it inconceivable for an increase of this magnitude to be maintained. 'With the present rate of growth, it can be calculated that in 600 years there will be only one square metre for each to live on. It goes without saying that this can never take place; something will happen to prevent it.'[4] The question that has most concerned them in this context, therefore, has been the forms that this 'something' might take; and the 1950s and 1960s were marked, especially in those areas of the world under European cultural influence, by the strong feeling that what were often referred to as 'dangerous population pressures'[5] were rapidly building up, particularly in those economically less developed territories where the most unprecedented rates of growth were occurring. Already by 1957 the United Nations Organization specifically advised that measures for dealing with population problems of all kinds should be included in the social and economic programmes of such areas.[6]

Since that time not every country has attempted to develop a

population policy, let alone a programme, and some of the less
well developed territories have been suspicious about Western
obsession with population control,[7] while others have favoured
the continuation of high rates of population growth.[8] For those
relatively few countries, which had inaugurated family planning
programmes by the 1970s,[9] it was not altogether certain that
their assumptions about the possibility of controlling population
growth through state action was properly justified. Indeed,
there is no clear indication to this day that population planners
in fact possess that kind of knowledge of the dynamics of
population control which their programmes require. Nor is it
certain that they have come to realize this. In the case of Puerto
Rico in the 1950s, for example, where 'since 1939 a network of
government-sponsored birth-control clinics has provided
information and free materials to all those who desire and need
them' and where, 'despite this fact there has been little appreciable change in the crude birth-rate' there is little sign that
the government has come to realize that an alternative approach
might be necessary. Nor is it likely that the efforts of that
government have been unappreciated by the public, for the
contents of Puerto Rican newspapers from the beginning of 1949
to the end of 1951 demonstrates that 'regardless of their stand
on the issues, it is clear that such a heavy amount of newspaper coverage on population, birth control and sterilization
is sure to alert some readers to the fact that there are means
available to limit conception'.[10] The real problem for the
government, or for the population experts working on its
behalf, was indeed 'the discovery of factors accounting for the
success of *some* and the failure of *most* Puerto Ricans to contain
their fertility in line with their stated goals for family size'.[11]
    In India, similarly, the government has been actively con-
cerned to promote a birth-control programme since 1946,
although in this instance it was aware of the considerable difficulties which it had to face.[12] Some favourable response was
reported over the first ten years of the establishment of family
planning clinics,[13] but the net impact on the birth-rate since
has not been at all impressive.[14] Moreover, in Japan where
population growth was rapidly decreased in the post-war years,
the method most employed was abortion, in direct antagonism to
the government policy which favoured contraception.[15] The
evidence, in brief, supports the argument that effective population policies cannot be based simply on the assumption that
people will be 'rational' in the long run, in the sense that they
will appreciate the population question in the way in which
government experts understand it;[16] and this leads in turn to
the reconsideration of Joseph Stycos's assertion that whether
or not propaganda will succeed depends on the extent to which
the sentiments it expresses are consonant with what he called
the 'fertility belief system'[17] of the couples to whom such propaganda is addressed. An essential prerequisite of any attempt
by government action to control population trends, from this

point of view, is knowledge of the ramifications of such belief systems within the population; and it is almost axiomatic among sociologists that such knowledge is rather more difficult to obtain than has apparently been usually believed.

For example, it is quite common in Roman Catholic polemics on the fertility question to find authors asserting such claims as that 'under-sized families are dangerous'.[18] It is also well known among demographers that Roman Catholic families are on average larger than those of other groups in an otherwise comparable population. Is it valid to assume that these two facts are related in the simple fashion that Roman Catholics have larger families because they adhere to a family belief system which emphasizes the harmful effects of smaller families? Empirical enquiry leads to the conclusion that this relationship, where it holds at all, is rather more complicated than at first sight appears. Amongst all the religious groups studied by Gerhard Lenski, for example, those who attended their churches regularly had larger families than those who did not. Similarly, those who in interview expressed themselves in a doctrinally orthodox fashion also tended to have larger families than those who did not, irrespective of denomination;[19] and amongst Catholics alone, those who had had a Catholic education had larger families than those who had had a public education.[20] Clearly, the simple designation of a population, or a section of a population, as Roman Catholic, does not mean that the family belief system of such a group will unambiguously demonstrate what is generally understood to be the Catholic view in this respect. In practice there will be variations within the group, and some more satisfactory method than readily accepting the officially proclaimed dogma must be employed to obtain details about what the family belief system of any Catholic group is.

Nor is this all. During the last half-century techniques of social enquiry have been developed which now make it possible for 'samples' of a population to be interviewed for accurate information on the kinds of opinions, attitudes and habits of mind which constitute such belief systems. Studies such as the Indianapolis Fertility Survey[21] and, more recently, the Growth of American Families Studies in America and those by the Population Investigation Committee, the Institute of Community Studies, Aberdeen University, and the Office of Population Censuses and Surveys in Britain[22] - to mention but a few - have demonstrated the extent to which a research organization can obtain reasonably reliable information of the sort required for population forecasting and policy formulation by any government which is willing to use some of its resources intelligently for this purpose. Yet, knowledge of the content of the family belief systems which prevail in a community, and even of the variations on such beliefs which occur between different geographical regions, different social groups, different generations of parents and would-be parents, and so forth, is not enough. If a programme of fertility control pro-

paganda is to be devised with confidence that it will be likely
to succeed, it is also necessary for those who are preparing it
to know how opinions, attitudes and states of mind about
families may be made to change; and such knowledge is so far
in a very rudimentary stage. This does not mean that research
into, say, mass communications has nothing to contribute to
this problem: in particular, the general importance of 'opinion
leaders' might very well be relevant here; but up to the present
the systematic analysis of findings from the field of communication research has not been applied successfully to effective
policy-making.

Indeed - to change the emphasis - little enough is known
about those spontaneous changes in family belief systems which
have already occurred, without introducing further complications
in the form of attempts deliberately to induce them in the
future. Hence it is not unreasonable to argue that an investigation of the factors responsible for spontaneous changes in
attitudes towards the size of families is as much relevant to
contemporary population planning as is a knowledge of the
techniques of persuasion by which population policies may be
implemented. In this sense the argument implies that nations
which are hurriedly struggling to achieve control over their
population growth need not necessarily start from a 'clean
slate'. There is 'background material from the past' and demographic information from the histories of those countries which,
as David Glass put it, 'have succeeded -- often in the face of
considerable institutionalized hostility -- in achieving just that
kind of reduction in fertility which is now being pressed for
elsewhere',[23] which may be used for the purpose. The main
issue in question, that is to say, is how these historical data
may be used. Of course, in many instances there is one fundamental feature of difference between this historical experience
and the present situation, namely, active government support
of birth-control movements,[24] which in the past had to struggle
not only for official recognition but for survival in the face of
official hostility; but unless it is assumed that this factor
outweighs all the others together in importance, it is reasonable
to suppose that those other factors which operated in the West
in the past may also be operative elsewhere today. That, at
any rate, is the presupposition on which this book is based to
justify the submission of a study of nineteenth-century
England as a contribution to our understanding of twentieth-
century world population problems.

What this amounts to, in effect, is the assertion that to a
limited extent, at least, it is now possible to provide a systematic examination of some of the proposed explanations for the
decline in the fertility of the populations of economically
developed countries, which is relevant for predicting what is
likely to occur elsewhere. At a superficial level 'explanations'
of this general form, but without systematic corroboration,
have been a commonplace for some time. Most sociologists and

demographers, for example, are said to be agreed that:[25]
> the basic causes of the general decline are: (a) a major shift
> in functions from the family to other specialized institutions,
> so that there was a decrease in the number of children
> required to achieve socially valued goals, and (b) a sharp
> reduction in mortality which reduced the number of births
> necessary to have any desired number of children.

But this reference to undisputed social and demographic fact
remains relatively superficial so long as no satisfactory accounts
are given for why there should have occurred such a 'major
shift of functions' or why there should have been such a time-
lag as there was between the onset of the decline of mortality
and that of fertility. Moreover, commonplaces such as these
come perilously close to committing the fallacy of ignotum per
ignotius; for the permanence of these 'socially valued goals',
presumably so fundamental that changes in fertility belief
systems automatically occur in order to maintain them, is not
accounted for at all.[26] 'Explanations' at such a very general
level of abstraction, that is to say, can be of very little use
for the development of valid population policy and it is necessary, therefore, for more specific explanatory hypotheses to
be both formulated and tested.

The emphasis here, it should be understood, is on confirma-
tion by evidence as much as on formulation. Thus, a classic
study of the history of family planning advanced a fairly
comprehensive list of social, economic and intellectual changes
which were said to have 'paved the way for widespread adoption
of contraceptive practices',[27] but nowhere did this author,
Norman Himes, submit his list to anything but cursory examination; and it is difficult to imagine how he could have done so
in a single volume, ranging from the beginning of written
history to the 1930s. As a later authority admitted -- after
having produced another list which contained only five of
Hime's ten 'causes of the Vital Revolution' and proffered four
different ones[28] -- 'it would be exceedingly difficult to trace
how they acted and reacted on each other or to assess their
relative importance'. Accordingly, it made no attempt to carry
out such a detailed study itself, but remained content with
sketching briefly what it described as how these causes
'severally contributed to the movement for smaller families'. The
danger here is that any author, who assumes this approach to
be satisfactory, may list from everything that is known to
have occurred in the history of Western Europe since the end
of the Middle Ages anything which strikes his fancy as in some
sense contributing to the growth of family planning. What the
policy-maker wants to know is which of the events have been
most significant and influential, so that he can decide whether
they are still operating now, and if not, what he can do to
induce them to occur.

In the context of the present discussion this can only imply
a detailed historical study in order to disentangle the relative

effects of the several factors thought to have been at work.
Each of the 'possible' influences in lists like those of Himes or
of the Royal Commission on Population should have been treated
as a hypothesis. As such it should have been analysed meticu-
lously to ascertain the nature of the events to which it con-
ceptually refers, and the recorded data about events themselves scrutinized in terms of their relevance to this analysis,
that is, in terms of their temporal sequence and of their
evident relationship to the onset of family planning practices
on the part of different sections of the population at different
points in time. Far too often in writing about demographic
transitions writers fall into the fallacy of post hoc ergo propter
hoc because they do not bother to look for evidence of connection between the events they assume to be related. Sometimes
they even commit the fault of propter hoc quamquam ante hoc,
because they do not take the trouble to set out the events, to
which they often only vaguely refer, in their correct sequence
in time. Thus, a technological revolution in the vulcanization of
rubber and in the manufacture of caps and condoms has sometimes been said to be the operative factor in the fall in family
size, presumably on the implied ground that 'once given reliable means, Western woman was certain to practise contraception whether she was prosperous or poor.'[29] Even Himes at one
point in his history asserted that 'the cheap manufacture of
condoms, cervical caps and vaginal diaphragms of the Mensinga
type' was a fundamental.[30] Yet the evidence he presented on
this point was all for the late nineteenth century when the
decline of family size amongst the English middle classes was
already well under way[31] and when the decline in the crude
birth-rate in France had been in operation for about a hundred
years.[32] All the evidence available, indeed, suggests that the
means employed by family planners in the first historical
instance is that of coitus interruptus, a technique which has
been known, and used, for a very long time and requires no
technical apparatus. In this sense it is true that the means of
population control through family limitation have always been
available and that artificial aids to contraception even are older
than history -- 'the medical history of conception control is
much older than the social movement.'[33] What has to be explained,
therefore, is what Himes referred to as the 'democratizing
revolution',[34] the widespread decision to limit the size of
families, which is largely a nineteenth-century phenomenon
and precedes the technological revolution in the manufacture
of contraceptive devices.

Or again, to take another example -- as one of the quotations
in the last paragraph implies and other authors assert -- the
adoption of family planning closely coincides in time, in Britain
and America at any rate, with the emergence of women from
domination by their fathers and husbands. Hence the emancipation of women and the feminism of feminist movements are
usually listed among the 'causes' of fertility decline and have

been accorded pride of place by at least one author.[35] Yet a careful chronological examination of the actual achievements of the English feminists shows that this occurred after the middle-class birth-rate began to fall. Emancipation, if understood in the feminist sense of a struggle of the underprivileged female against the privileged male, was not a causal factor. Middle-class husbands in the 1860s and 1870s were willing partners, if not in fact the initiators, in the decision to limit the size of their families.[36] Looked at from the point of view of the demo-cratization of birth control, this was emancipation by consent. Then why did the goals of the feminists, who, incidentally, did not include the right of women to control their own fertility amongst their expressed aims, have to be fought for every step of the way for the rest of the century? The reasonable answer seems to be that the two types of event were not connected; but only detailed analysis of what was involved makes this plain.

The valid sociological study of the onset of family limitation thus demands the empirical testing of hypotheses formulated to be likely explanations for the phenomena under discussion; and this raises the further methodological issue of how such research is to be conducted. If only a single causal factor is investigated at a time the task is manageable. But single-factor theories of social change have been shown regularly to be exaggerations, even though some authors continue to employ them in disguise, listing many factors and referring to one of them as 'pre-eminent' or 'dominant'. Himes, for example, ended his list with 'the widespread desire for self-advancement economically' which at the same time he said was 'no doubt fundamental'.[37] Among more recent lists an overemphasis on urbanism is common, with the implication that other factors fit plausibly in to reinforce the operation of this 'more basic force' in social change.[38] Yet multiple-factor theories, which are the logical alternative, are rendered almost beyond testing, since multiple-factor methodologies are extremely difficult to manipu-late, especially on an historical plane; for, while mathematical techniques exist, usually involving the use of computers, to deal with multiple-factor analysis of contemporary social survey data, comparable techniques for handling non-numerical data over time are at best rudimentary. The carrying along of many factors in a single example of comparative historical investiga-tion usually results in the methodology becoming too compli-cated to follow, and it is hardly surprising to find that in practice the analysis quickly degenerates into the mere asser-tion that many factors have been responsible for the given instance of social change, without systematic proof in the form of relevant evidence to support all or any of them.

The alternative, which needless to say is favoured here, is to proceed seriatim, taking one hypothesis at a time and test-ing it, not only by reference to the sequence of events in population control but also by reference to what has been

discovered in support, or rejection, of an hypothesis studied
previously. Thus the study of feminism, mentioned above,
was conceived as a sequel to an earlier study of the relationship between family planning and the middle-class conception
of the standard of living in nineteenth-century England. That
investigation had concluded that the increase in the actual
well-being of a category of people (their level of living) and
the expansion in the range of satisfactions which they considered appropriate for a civilized existence (their standard
of living) formed a necessary but not a sufficient condition for
the advent of family planning on a widespread scale amongst
them.[39] The further study, 'Feminism and Family Planning',
subsequently showed that feminism was not a causative influence
at all in these events and also that those aspects of woman's
emancipation which might possibly be believed to be connected
with the desire to restrict the size of the family -- such as
freedom from the chores of the domestic routine -- were themselves produced by the 'spread of gentility' amongst the
middle classes.[40] In this way the importance of the rising standard of living as a causal factor in fertility decline is strengthened, not merely because an alternative hypothesis has been
discredited, but because the events to which that hypothesis
refers may be subsumed in this instance under the rubric of
the standard of living. Thus, whatever may be the eventual
fate of the argument about the implications of rising expectations on the attitudes of middle-class parents towards the
size of their families, the influence of these expectations on
the development of new attitudes on the part of middle-class
husbands towards their wives can hardly be denied; and it is
this by-product of the more central preoccupation which
demonstrates an additional advantage of the piecemeal, factor
by factor, research procedure.

The strategy pursued in the present study may be understood to follow from these observations. A further hypothesis
to account for the decline in fertility amongst the Victorian
middle classes -- the spread of secularism and the decline in
religious belief and observance -- is examined in terms of the
kinds of data which are necessary to test its validity, that is,
in terms of the relationship between those belief systems which
are consonant with such apostasy and those which refer to
the middle-class conception of parenthood. At the same time
these same beliefs about secularism and Christian morality are
related to what is already known about the middle-class standard and level of living throughout the period, and to the
position of middle-class women in the family at this time. It may
at first sight appear that this last consideration is unnecessary,
since the emancipation of women and feminism seem to have
been disposed of in the previous research; but, as has already
been mentioned, sociological research using historical evidence
is very far from precise -- it nowhere approaches the rigour
at present attainable in social research into contemporary

issues -- so that it seems a reasonable precaution to include this aspect of the relationship between the decline in religious adherence and the emancipation of women as a further test of the validity of what has been concluded so far. If a relationship is found which points to the same general conclusion as 'Feminism and Family Planning', confidence in the results of that study is enhanced.

Nevertheless, it is pertinent to consider why these particular issues -- the spread of secularism and the decline of religious belief -- as possible causal factors in the democratization of family planning, have been selected for study, quite apart from the fact that they are so often listed amongst the presumed relevant influences. One of the main reasons why the first study, 'Prosperity and Parenthood', concluded that the rise in the standard of living was not a sufficient, although a necessary, cause was that it did not, on the basis of the data presented, explain how it had come about that the age-old tradition, which judged interference with 'the intentions' of providence in the matter of births to be morally indefensible, should have withered in the face of the growing appeal of the middle-class level of living. 'Unless it can be shown', it was argued,[41]

> that the failing hold of religion in this period was *directly* related to the changing real income structure and to the greater opportunities made available for the consumption and enjoyment of an ever-growing number of man's worldly goods, the argument that the rising standard of living was the *major* factor in the spread of family limitation, although strongly supported by a plausible array of evidence, must remain something of a *non sequitur*.

Logically, the decline of religious belief amongst the middle classes was the next hypothesis obviously to be tested, and it was for extraneous reasons, such as the intrinsic attraction of investigating a subject about which so much had been written and so little of sociological value had been said,[42] that feminism and the emancipation of women had been allowed to intrude between.

Moreover, the study of the possible influence of the decline of religious belief may be justified on other grounds. Most of the likely factors, favoured by authors such as Himes, refer to influences which are connected in one way or another with the industrial revolution; but the decline in family size in France appears to have occurred in the eighteenth century, when these changes were in their infancy, and the weakening hold of religion there in that century has been suggested as the main factor.[43] Unfortunately, the data to justify this conclusion have not been put together. The argument is rudimentary, and in many respects is likely to continue to remain so, since the documentary evidence for that century is quite sparse, especially when compared with what is available for the nineteenth. This, incidentally, is one very good reason for continuing to work on the English, rather than on the French, middle class. To be sure, contemporary surveys also emphasize the importance of religious belief in differential fertility, but this point should not be given much weight because it is clear that over the last hundred years or so official religious dogma on contraception and other forms of family planning has experienced changes,[44] even if apparently after the event and not as a causal factor. What this means is that middle-class apostasy has a very special relevance because it constituted in this connection a revision of the family belief system of a section of the population in the face of the opposition of religious leaders of the day to whom it appears to have nevertheless deferred in other matters -- a revision in practice which later churchmen came eventually to accept themselves.

The term, 'apostasy' is used advisedly here in the conviction that the behaviour of these middle-class parents represented a turning away on their part from a previously accepted religious doctrine. This 'decline' in religious belief was quite distinct from the contemporaneous indifference to religion demonstrated by sections of the working class, who by the time of the 1851 Census of Religious Worship, were said to be 'thoroughly estranged from our religious institutions', although not because they had made an intellectual examination of Christianity and had decided upon infidelity in the manner of the secularists. Rather was it that they had drifted into 'unconscious' secularism, 'engrossed by the demands, the trials or the pleasures of the passing hour, and ignorance of the future'.[45] The compilers of the Census believed that the main cause of this occurrence was 'spiritual destitution',[46] that is, 'the grievous lack of accommodation for the *masses* of our civic population',[47] but, it should be emphasized that, whatever the cause, this 'unconscious' secularism did not result in any obvious change in the family belief systems of the working class on a scale comparable to that of the middle class. For them, the flight from parenthood took place much later, after the middle class had developed its own new conception of parenthood, although it is open to question whether this later change was simply a matter of copying a middle-class fashion or had a different causal explanation.[48] Moreover, during the crucial period up to 1851, church accommodation for middle-class believers had apparently been increasing,[49] so that their turning away from the doctrines of their fathers constituted a rather more complicated process of the re-interpretation of Christian teaching on the responsibilities of parents than the simple failure on their part to attend church and to be exposed to sermons on their obligations. This is why it is necessary to begin this account with an examination of the orthodox position on these matters, from which the change in the middle-class fertility belief system took its point of departure. What were the particular religious principles which middle-class couples began to abandon after the middle of the century?

How had their parental obligations been defined when the population controversy raged in the earlier part of the century? And how was this definition related to the attacks on Christian morality made by the secularists? The following chapters are concerned to answer these questions in some detail.

2 THE RELIGIOUS ROOTS OF THE MALTHUSIAN CONTROVERSY

The population controversy, which dominated economic thinking for the first twenty years or so of the nineteenth century,
was in part a reaction against the ideas of the French Revolution, as these were popularly conceived. When Thomas Malthus
published the first edition of his famous essay in 1798, his
aim was to refute what were commonly regarded as the Jacobin
notions that imperfect social institutions were the cause of
human misery and that therefore a transformation in social
relationships, by force if necessary, was essential if human
beings were ever to move closer to perfection. These notions,
especially in the forms given to them by Marie Jean Caritat,
Marquis de Condorcet and William Godwin, were rejected out of
hand by Malthus as based on a simple misconception. The cause
of human misery, he asserted, lay in men themselves. Although
a change in social institutions could have a short-run effect
in improving the conditions of some people, in the long-run
such improvement would prove to be negligible; for, the
tremendous growth in population, that would inevitably result,
would re-introduce the misery and vice which the changes had
been inaugurated to abolish.

The Malthusian counter-argument, it should be understood,
rested on the proposition that the 'law of nature which makes
food necessary to the life of man' does not include any exemp-
tion from the restraints which confine animal and vegetable
populations alike.[1]

The race of plants, and the race of animals shrink under this
great restrictive law. And the race of man cannot, by any
efforts of reason, escape from it. Among plants and animals
its effects are a waste of seed, sickness, and premature death.
Among mankind, misery and vice. The former; misery is an
absolutely necessary consequence of it. Vice is a highly probable consequence, and we therefore see it abundantly prevail.

However, Malthus, although 'melancholy',[2] was not quite the
pessimist and reactionary he has often been thought to be.
The advocates of 'the present order of things' he regarded as
being equally short-sighted and mistaken as the advocates
of 'the perfectibility of man and of society'.[3] What the 'Essay
on the Principle of Population' was manifestly intended to
demonstrate was the genuine possibility of progress, albeit in
a very different way from that proposed by the revolutionaries.
Thus, the reference to vice abundantly prevailing, quoted

12

above, is incomplete. In the original it concluded with a comma,
not a full-stop, and it then continued: 'but it ought not,
perhaps, to be called an absolutely necessary consequence. The
ordeal of virtue is to resist all temptation to evil.'[4] The individual, that is to say, was seen by Malthus as capable of aspiring to perfection in himself; and to the degree that a growing
number of people chose virtue to vice, to that degree the
human race moved onwards and upwards.

To understand this particular notion of progress it is necessary to realize that Malthus did not think of the world as 'a
state of trial and school of virtue preparatory to a superior
state of happiness'.[5] Rather did he interpret it as the setting[6]

for the creation and formation of mind, a process necessary
to awaken inert, chaotic matter into spirit, to sublimate the
dust of the earth into soul, to elicit an ethereal spark from
the clod of clay. And in this view of the subject, the various
impressions and excitements which man receives through life
may be considered as the forming hand of his Creator, act-
ing by general laws, and awakening his sluggish existence,
by the animating touches of the Divinity, into a capacity of
superior enjoyment.

The curate of Okewood, ordained in 1798,[7] firmly set his first
attempt at expounding the principle of population in a religious
tradition of the eighteenth century - one most usually associated
with the name of William Paley, although it is possible that
Malthus, like Paley, was directly influenced by the philosopher,
Abraham Tucker, whose 'Light of Nature Pursued', published
over the pseudonym of Edward Search, had appeared in 1768.[8]

God, according to Tucker, was to the universe as the clock-
maker to 'am immense clock'.[9] Having laid down the foundations
of nature with intrinsic powers 'to repair the constant decays
of motion, and keep the material clock-work regularly wound
up',[10] the Creator 'rested from his works, and having once
made us, retained, as I may say, no longer any concern with us,
but delivered us over to that Providence which governs and
disposes the things already created, exercises the capacities,
and employs the qualities already assigned'.[11] As Leslie Stephen
later paraphrased Tucker, God[12]

does not remain with us as a guide, nor leave any supernatural monitor within our breasts to warn us of what is
pleasing to him. Our own natural instincts are sufficient to
lead us, as the force of gravity is sufficient to keep the
stars in their courses without further interference. And thus
morality, like everything else, is merely the product of
natural forces.

Or, in Tucker's own words,[13]

God gives to every man the talents, the opportunities, the
lights, sufficient for the work whereto he calls him: it is
the creature's business to answer the call, whether coming
by the voice of his own reason, or the general recommendation of the judicious, or the admonitions of his moral sense,

or whatever other channel of conveyance his best judgment
shall satisfy him brings it genuine. For by following steddily
[sic!] the best guidance he can get against the opposition of
passion, danger, pain and affliction, he shall become an
object of the Divine favour.
And, in any case, 'each man's own happiness is the proper
foundation whereon all his schemes of conduct are to be ultimately placed'.[14]

For his part, Malthus devoted two whole chapters in a short
book of nineteen chapters to this utilitarian derivative of
natural theology. The 'wants of the body' – a topic which he
originally intended to develop as 'a kind of second part to the
essay' – 'rouse man into action, and form his mind to reason'.[15]
All appearances to the contrary, 'we have every reason to think
that there is no more evil in the world than what is absolutely
necessary as one of the ingredients in the mighty process'.[16]
The principle of population, from this point of view, was no
more than a condition for the guarantee of progress. 'Evil exists
in the world not to create despair but activity. We are not
patiently to submit to it, but to exert ourselves to avoid it.'[17]

In his eagerness to·argue that Godwin had put too much
weight on the influence of social institutions, Malthus failed to
apply his theological reasoning consistently to the problem in
hand. Let us suppose, he argued, that a perfect society already
existed. In such a society all the restraints on intercourse
between the sexes would be removed and 'extraordinary
encouragements' would thus be given to population growth.
Such a society, to be sure, would also encourage a marked
increase in the supply of food; but, he argued, in less than
two generations the number of people would be spilling over
into the less naturally fertile areas, so that very rapidly 'the
spirit of benevolence, cherished and invigorated by plenty'
would be 'repressed by the chilling breath of want'. Within
fifty years there would return 'violence, oppression, falsehood,
misery, every hateful vice, and every form of distress, which
degrade and sadden the present state of society' and all this
because of 'laws inherent in the nature of man, and absolutely
independent of all human regulations'.[18] The possibility that
the people of such a society might not patiently submit to their
numbers increasing beyond this critical point and instead might
exert themselves to avoid it by some form of population control,
does not seem to have occurred to him, in spite of the fact
that in 'Political Justice' Godwin had cited the 'exposing of
children', 'the art of procuring abortion', 'promiscuous intercourse of the sexes' and 'a systematical abstinence', as examples
of such control used at different times in human history.[19]

Of course, all these – even including the last because of its
reference to monastic life – were abhorrent to Malthus's
Anglican turn of mind and it is possible that in 1798 he had been
unable to see their implications for this reason. Certainly he
did not immediately appreciate the significance of what Godwin

meant by the operation of human reason in this context; for he
replied to a letter from him:[20]

The prudence which you speak of as a check to population
implies a foresight of difficulties: and this foresight of difficulties almost necessarily implies a desire to remove them.
Can you give me an adequate reason why the natural and
general desire to remove these difficulties would not cause
such a competition as would destroy all chance of an equal
division of the necessary labour of society, and produce such
a state of things as I have described?

Godwin's position, in fact, was characteristically simple. 'If I
look to the future,' he wrote in 1801, 'I cannot so despair of
the virtues of man to submit to the most obvious rules of
prudence, or of the facilities of man to strike out remedies as
yet unknown.'[21] On this occasion the point was well taken.
Malthus so restructured his *Essay* that the second edition
became in many aspects a different book. Moral restraint from
early marriages, which Godwin had referred to, was accepted
and explicitly acknowledged.[22] It was also elevated to become
one of the chief sources of population control which Malthus had
in mind whenever he departed from the empirical data in support
of his thesis and ascended the pulpit.

In passing it should be noted that the second, and subsequent, editions of the 'Essay' omitted the two chapters on
natural theology entirely. The plan of this edition, Malthus
wrote, was different from that of the original essay and certain
matters had been left out 'not because I thought them all of
less value than what has been inserted, but because they did
not suit the different plan of treating the subject which I had
adopted'.[23] What this plan was, is not altogether clear, inasmuch
as it resulted in the omission of the substantial theological
argument and its replacement by intermittent references to the
apparent objects of the Creator.[24] In the light of his earlier
avowed intent to write even more than he had on the relationship between necessity and invention, this abandonment of the
theological underpinning of his argument is curious. Unfortunately, no information exists on why there was such a change
of plan, although James Bonar's comment that 'in the controversy that followed the essay there are few references' to
Malthus's treatment of the problem of evil,[25] may indicate one
possibility. However, it is known that the two converts to his
version of the principle of population of whom Malthus was most
proud, were William Pitt and William Paley,[26] and Paley published his 'Natural Theology' in 1802. Did Malthus know, while
he was preparing his second edition, that Paley had changed
his mind and had worked the Malthusian argument into his
treatment of the goodness of God, as part of a most elaborate
contribution to utilitarian natural theology? So far as is known,
no evidence exists which can illuminate this question.

In 1796 Malthus had written:[27]

I cannot agree with Archdeacon Paley, who says, that the

quantity of happiness in any country is best measured by
the number of people. Increasing population is the most
certain possible sign of the happiness and prosperity of a
state, but the actual population may be only a sign of the
happiness that is past.

Paley's position at that time was that although in principle
'the population of a country must stop when the country can
maintain no more, that is, when the inhabitants are already so
numerous as to exhaust all the provision which the soil can be
made to produce', in practice,[28]

the number of people have seldom, in any country, arrived
at this limit, or even approached to it. The fertility of the
ground, in temperate regions, is capable of being improved
by cultivation to an extent which is unknown .... The two
principles, therefore, upon which population seems primarily
to depend, the fecundity of the species, and the capacity of
the soil, would in most, perhaps in all countries, enable it
to proceed much further than it has yet advanced.

But by 1802 his argument had become pure Malthusian.[29]

Mankind will in every country breed up to a certain point of
distress. That point may be different in different countries
or ages, according to the established usage of life in each.
It will also shift upon the scale, so as to admit of a greater
or less number of inhabitants, according as the quantity of
provision, which is either produced in the country, or supplied to it from other countries, may happen to vary. But
there must always be such a point and the species will always
breed up to it. The order of generation proceeds by something like a geometrical progression. The increase of provision, under circumstances even the most advantageous, can
only assume the form of an arithmetic series. Whence it follows, that the population will always overtake the provision,
will pass beyond the line of plenty, and will continue to
increase till checked by the difficulty of procuring subsistence.

Paley was fifty-nine at this time, with only three more years
to live. Possibly this is why he never revised his chapter, 'on
population and provision; and of agriculture and commerce, as
subservient thereto' in the 'Principles'. The two contradictory
statements of his position on population, accordingly, went
down together into the nineteenth century,[30] although there
can hardly be any doubt but that his *Natural Theology* more
accurately represents his last view on the subject.[31]

Malthus nowhere mentioned Paley's 'Natural Theology' in
the revised versions of his 'Essay on Population'. In the fifth
edition, however, he responded warmly to John Sumner's
Treatise on the *Records of Creation*,[32] which covered very much
the same ground, and which he spoke of thereafter as having
ably fought 'the religious part of the battle'.[33] There was, to
be sure, one curious feature of this new assessment of utilitarian
natural theology which deserves comment. 'Some have argued,'

wrote Sumner, 'that the principle of population leads inevitably to misery, and hence impeaches the wisdom of the Creator.
Concessions must be made to this point of view, but since this
world is merely a preparation for the hereafter, the principle
of population may be seen as a species of trial.'[34] Malthus
applauded. 'I have always considered the principle of population,' he wrote, 'as a law peculiarly suited to a state of discipline and trial.'[35] No doubt he had forgotten what he had
written in the first edition, nearly twenty years earlier. Perhaps he had not the kind of mind which is required for consistent theological reasoning. Nevertheless, his purpose throughout seems plain. The principle of population in his hands was
meant to be centrally located in the dominant Anglican doctrines
of his time. Hence when it was objected to him in conversation
that his principles contradicted 'the original command of the
Creator, to increase and multiply and replenish the earth',[36] he
replied: 'I believe that it is the intention of the Creator that
the earth should be replenished, but certainly with a healthy,
virtuous, and happy population, not an unhealthy, vicious
and miserable one.'[37] 'Every express command given to man by
his Creator is given in subordination to those great and uniform
laws of nature, which he had previously established.'[38] For his
part, Sumner added that the empirical part of Malthus's work
showed that 'mankind have uniformly increased and multiplied,
in conformity with the command of their Creator, and also
that, agreeably to the same Creator's denunciation, they have
always been condemned to acquire their subsistence by painful
and continual labour'.[39] Utilitarian natural theology was sufficiently broad to encompass the Malthusian reasoning within
the bounds of its scope.

  The religious objections to Malthus, including the occasional
assertion that he was an atheist, may therefore be fairly interpreted as part of the continuing theological controversy inside
the Christian church of the time, rather than more generally
as part of a defence against that kind of agnostic apostasy which
characterized the literary career of Godwin.[40] The anonymous
conclusion of 1807, for example, that 'it is evident to anyone
who attentively reads the 'Essay on Population' that its author
does not believe in the existence of God, but substitutes for
Him sometimes the principle of Population, sometimes that of
Necessity',[41] may be justified only on the ground that the
particular brand of theology, shared by Tucker, Paley, Malthus
and Sumner, and of course, other Cambridge metaphysicians
influenced by Paley's writings, reduced the transcendent deity,
not so much perhaps to a First Cause merely, but to a scientist
who interfered in human affairs but rarely and always on fixed
principles.[42] From this point of view God seemed to be a part
almost of the universe rather than something standing outside
or above it, and it was only by emphasizing the occurrence of
miracles as a form of revelation, that Paley was able to anchor
his brand of Christianity in divine authorization.[43] The problem

of evil was in this sense dismissed. The ways of God were
accepted as beyond understanding, except that mankind had to
live with evil, and embrace it as a form of trial for the hereafter, or as a divine means for ensuring the development of a
virtuous character in an individual endowed with free will.
Thus Malthusianism could be seen as a way of scrutinizing
nature, and man's place in it, for signs that human happiness
was attainable as a result of following certain defined lines of
conduct. Religious obedience, in consequence, might be said
to have become 'formal, rational, cold and prudentially calculat-
ing'.[44]

Central to this Malthusian conception of the possibility of the
individual achieving perfection was 'moral restraint', and this
had its roots in the Christian ideals of premarital and extra-
marital chastity. Although he always wrote of restraint itself
in terms of 'abstinence from marriage, either for a time or
permanently',[45] Malthus nevertheless had in mind the exercise
of control by reason over a 'dictate of nature' - namely, 'an
early attachment to one woman'.[46] Hence 'promiscuous intercourse, unnatural passions, violations of the marriage bed, and
improper arts to conceal the consequences of irregular con-
nexions', he listed as preventive checks that 'clearly come
under the head of vice'. Moral restraint, or that form of
abstinence from marriage 'which is not followed by irregular
gratifications',[47] was the only preventive check which could be
acceptable to a devout Christian as consistent with virtue. Of
course, Malthus was very well aware that postponement of
marriage 'from prudential motives, with a conduct strictly moral
during the period of restraint'[48] was not at all an easy path to
follow; but, he argued,[49]

the Christian cannot consider the difficulty of moral restraint
as any argument against its being his duty; since, in almost
every page of the sacred writings, man is described as
encompassed on all sides by temptations, which it is extremely
difficult to resist; and though no duties are enjoined which
do not contribute to his happiness on earth as well as in a
future state, yet an undeviating obedience is never represented as an easy task.

It was, indeed, a measure of Malthus's Anglicanism that he
never recommended celibacy as the highest virtue. On the
contrary, his approach to marriage was almost purely Pauline,
if by this is understood that he could not altogether hide his
misgivings about sexual relationships and, like St Paul, desired
to keep them 'within very strict limits, in order to avoid find-
ing the sex instinct too strong a competitor with the religious
interest'.[50] In Malthus's terms this meant approaching marriage
as a device which was virtuous only if prudential. 'Without
entering minutely into the subject, which would evidently lead
us too far,' he wrote, 'I think it will be admitted, that, if we
apply the spirit of St Paul's declarations respecting marriage,
to the present state of society, and the known constitution

of our nature, the natural inference seems to be, that, when marriage does not interfere with higher duties it is right, when it does, it is wrong.'[51] Thus, the question for Christians of Malthus's persuasion was how they were to know when marriage did, or did not, interfere with higher duties; and the answer which he gave was for them to make reference to the Paleyan principle of utility.[52]

There are perhaps few actions that tend so directly to diminish the general happiness, as to marry without the means of supporting children. He who commits this act, therefore, clearly offends against the will of God; and having become a burden on the society in which he lives, and plunged himself and family into a situation, in which virtuous habits are preserved with more difficulty than in any other, he appears to have violated his duty to his neighbours and to himself, and thus to have listened to the voice of passion in opposition to his higher obligations.

Malthus, it should be understood, also believed that couples should exercise moral restraint within marriage. Although he appears never to have asserted this categorically, there is clear evidence in the 'Essay' that for him a man's prime reproductive duty, which he thought was 'intelligible to the humblest capacity' was 'not to bring beings into the world for whom he cannot find the means of supporting'.[53] This belief underlay Malthus's policy for the abolition of poverty through the amendment of the Poor Laws; for, he proposed that 'no child born from any marriage, taking place after the expiration of a year from the date of the law, and no illegitimate child born two years from the same date, should ever be entitled to parish assistance',[54] on the assumption that such a measure would deter the virtuous poor from reckless breeding. Of course, the efficacy of his proposal also turned on the accuracy of his conviction that the wages of labour were 'regulated by the proportion of the supply to the demand',[55] so that a higher level of living would accrue to a smaller number of labourers. To maintain the morality of the 'restraint', moreover, which might be presumed to result from the lack of public assistance in such cases, it was necessary that married couples should not practise birth control by means of contraceptive devices. In flat contradiction to James Grahame's misrepresentation of his views,[56] Malthus vigorously asserted that he had 'never adverted to the check suggested by Condorcet without the most marked disapprobation'. Indeed, he continued,[57]

I should always particularly reprobate any artificial and unnatural modes of checking population, both on account of their immorality and their tendency to remove a necessary stimulus to industry. If it were possible for each married couple to limit by a wish the number of their children, there is certainly reason to fear that the indolence of the human race would be very greatly increased; and that neither the population of individual countries, nor of the whole earth, would ever reach its natural and proper extent. But the restraints which I have recommended are quite of a different character. They are not only pointed out by reason and sanctioned by religion, but tend in the most marked manner to stimulate industry. It is not easy to conceive a more powerful encouragement to exertion and good conduct than the looking forward to marriage as a state peculiarly desirable; but only to be enjoyed in comfort, by the acquisition of habits of industry, economy and prudence. And it is in this light that I have always wished to place it.

It can hardly be doubted that Malthus was expressing here the dominant strand in the conventional moral wisdom of his time. For all that Francis Place tried to urge that it was 'not disreputable for married persons to avail themselves of such precautionary measures as would, without being injurious to health, or destructive of female delicacy, prevent conception',[58] public opinion went on record that disreputable it was, and the advocates of contraceptive birth control in the 1820s and 1830s found themselves arousing bitter abhorrence amongst the publicists from the middle and the working classes alike. For the remainder of his life, for example, the name of Francis Place was 'hardly ever mentioned in print without some reference, deprecatory or abusive, to his notorious opinions. Good men refused to be introduced to him, and, in 1834, his help was declined on this ground alone by the strongly liberal "Society for the Promotion of Useful Knowledge".[59] Richard Carlile, the author of 'Every Woman's Book; or, What is Love?'. a birth-control pamphlet, published in 1826, was shouted down while lecturing in Bath, his pamphlet publicly burned, and he himself 'run out of town'.[60] Only in freethinking and secularist circles did birth-control propaganda flourish, and it was in these circles that it became so much a part of the general philosophy of life without religion that the two movements seem to have become identified in the public mind. This raises the possibility that during what is usually known as the period of 'quiet percolation' of the practice of family limitation,[61] more open discussion of the subject was inhibited by the fear that those who engaged in it would be branded as adherents to that kind of militant, anti-Christian scepticism associated with the names of Carlile and Place, whom 'Fraser's Magazine' had dubbed the 'Moses of the Preventive Check',[62] and of course, at a later date with that of the supreme militant of both movements, Charles Bradlaugh. Although there was hardly anything in the dominant Anglican doctrine of the time to inhibit family limitation as such, the advocacy of artificial aids to birth control by the secularists meant that anyone who supported such claims would necessarily be open to the suspicion that they accepted the secularist case for birth control because they were well on the way to becoming secularists themselves. The significance of this association of ideas for the trend towards the smaller family becomes clearer when the secularist case is more closely examined.

3 THE SECULARIST CASE FOR BIRTH CONTROL

'Secularism,' wrote George Jacob Holyoake in 1854,[1]
is a development of freethinking, including its *positive* as
well as its *negative* side. Secularists consider freethinking
as a *double* protest – a protest against specific speculative
error, and in favour of specific moral truth. The term
Secularism has not been chosen as a concealment, or a disguise, or as an apology for free enquiry, but as expressing
a certain positive and ethical element, which the terms
'Infidel', 'Sceptic', 'Atheist' do not express .... A Secularist
is one who gives primary attention to those speculations the
issues of which can be tested by the experiences of this
life .... Its *moral basis* is, that *Justification by Conduct* is
a higher and more reliable truth than 'Justification by Faith
in Christ'.
Critics who regarded secularism as 'the old black crow of infidel
negation disguised in the stolen peacock plumes of positive
philosophy'[2] failed to appreciate that the positive side of secularism was intended to be much more significant than the negative. It was, indeed, no accident that Holyoake graced the title
page of his pamplet with a quotation from Auguste Comte's
'Positive Philosophy': 'Each of us is aware, if he looks back
on his own history, that he was a theologian in childhood, a
metaphysician in his youth, and a natural philosopher in his
manhood.' The message of secularism was an appeal to give up
adolescent speculation about the nature of life after death, to
abandon the Bible as a source of morality, divinely ordained,
and to proceed with the building of a new moral order, based
upon the natural brotherhood of men and on a social science
which did not need to assume a Father in Heaven, 'to make the
relationship perfect',[3] as Christians did.
    In his time Holyoake had been a Social Missionary, that is,
an organizer, lecturer and debater, employed by the Owenites
to propagate the millennial doctrines of the Social Father,
Robert Owen himself.[4] Like Owen he was probably a deist or
even an agnostic, more concerned with revolting against the
influence and authority of the church than with attempting to
explain the universe and the meaning of life, more concerned
with this life than with preparing himself for the next. The
positive side of his this-worldly, mundane philosophy was thus
rooted in the 'world-making'[5] schemes of the Owenites, co-
operators and community-builders. Secularism was a doctrine,
designed to promote 'that development and culture of free

humanity trained by disciplined conscience', as Sophia Collet
put it to him at about this time,[6] and to this extent it constituted a re-affirmation of the doctrine of the perfectibility of
man which had caused Malthus to write his 'Essay' in refutation
of Godwin nearly sixty years before.

The Owenites were, of course, aware of the Malthusian argument against the possible success of their co-operative communities. In a letter to a London newspaper, published on 25
July 1817, Owen had affirmed that he had:[7]

> no apprehension whatever on this ground. Every agriculturist
> knows that each labourer now employed in agriculture can
> produce five or six times more food than he can eat; and,
> therefore, even if no other facilities were given to him than
> those he now possesses, there is no necessity in nature for
> 'the population to press against subsistence', until the earth
> is fully cultivated. There can be no doubt it is the artificial
> law of supply and demand, arising from the principles of
> individual gain in opposition to the general well-being of
> society, which has hitherto compelled population to press
> upon subsistence.

Other co-operators, however, were not so certain that the
problem was not rather more immediate. Owen's son, Robert
Dale Owen, published a book in New York on the population
question generally in which he recommended coitus interruptus
as a remedy for the vice and misery which was, without
recourse to birth control, the inevitable consequence of 'animal
impulse', the 'unreasoning instinct, which men, in the mass,
have not learnt either to resist or control'.[8] He did not mention
the community-builders in this connection, possibly because
of the conviction that these communities themselves would also
be a solution to vice and misery, exemplifying that degree of
rationality which men in the mass had not attained. Just as
there would be rational planning of agricultural production and
animal breeding in these communities, so the increase of human
numbers would not be left to blind caprice.[9]

For his part, Holyoake may never have believed that birth
control was necessary, although he sold pamphlets on the subject in the 1850s.[10] Publicly he never expressed himself as a
Malthusian, claiming indeed that 'when Malthus some years ago
issued notice that mothers were no longer wanted in England,
he seriously lowered the domestic morality of this country'.[11]
Perhaps he believed that the open advocacy of contraception
by secularists would lose their cause public support. 'On a
question such as family limitation,' he wrote half-a-century
later, 'delicacy of phrase and purity of taste are everything.
They are themselves safeguards of morality. Foolishness of
thought, coarseness of illustration, deter from acts of the
highest prudence and repel instead of attracting serious attention.'[12] This seems to represent a consistently held view.
Certainly he is known in the 1850s to have expressed the
opinion that the Bible was 'a mischievous book', possibly

because some of the passages in it were immoral if not actually
obscene,[13] and in his autobiography he claimed that he had been
instrumental in persuading George Drysdale to change the
'disagreeable' title of his book on physiology, political economy
and the population question to 'Elements of Social Science'.[14]

'Physical, Sexual and Natural Religion' by a Student of
Medicine was published in 1855,[15] anonymously 'from the fear
of causing pain to a relation'.[16] It was re-issued in 1857 as
'The Elements of Social Science, or Physical, Sexual and Natural
Religion, with the Solution of the Social Problem, containing
an exposition of the true cause and only cure of the three
primary social evils - poverty, prostitution and celibacy', by
a student of medicine;[17] but, of course, the message, although
now longer, was exactly the same. What Drysdale had set out
to achieve was to provide an alternative 'religion' to Christianity which would endow its followers with a sense of
reverence for the human body, replacing the Christian preoccupation with the soul. 'The question,' he wrote,[18]

is no longer whether a man have or have not a *deep and
settled religious* belief, but whether he believe in supernatural religion or in Nature. Those who believe in the
supernatural, deny the adequacy of the powers of Nature,
and dethrone her from her sovereign sway over the universe
and our hearts; which Natural Religion, on the other hand,
devoutly acknowledges. Let us not deceive ourselves; we
cannot serve two masters. *Belief in God is disbelief in Nature.*

Drysdale preferred the term, 'natural religion' because he
thought that there was:[19]

something cold and uninviting in the words Rationalism and
Secularism ... the word 'Religion' is inwardly dear to all of
us; it is a name to which the noblest feelings of humanity
have been consecrated; which has been hallowed by the virtues, the pious lives, and heroic deaths, of many of the
most glorious characters in history; which has filled men's
breasts with that heroic self-devotion that makes them under-
go all trials and privations, to do that which their conscience
tells them is right; which sends men to the wilderness to
convert the heathen, and to the death bed, and the haunts
of crime and pestilence, to succour and console their suffering fellow-beings - oh may this name and all the devout,
earnest, and loving feelings it breathes, sink into the minds
of all of us, and may the followers of Natural Religion be
animated by a no less exalted enthusiasm. The name of
Natural Religion expresses, that the beliefs it represents
are but a continuation of the religious progress of the race;
a progress which has been going on ever since the birth of
history, and will advance till the end.

From this point of view, the Christian emphasis on the soul
was an obstacle to progress since it prevented the believer
from concerning himself positively with the pursuit of physical
and, therefore, mental health. 'Sad it is indeed', exclaimed

Drysdale, 'to look back on the fate of the apostles of the body! ... the clergyman, who has the cure of souls, has been for ages held in much higher esteem and love than the physician, who has the cure of bodies.' This is because of the nature of Hebrew and Christian teaching on the subject of the soul: 'joined in some mysterious way to the body at birth, and condemned for a long period to travel through this life in its company, clogged and confined, by its ignoble associate', the soul resumes at death 'its own privileges as spirit, infinite, eternal and unchangeable', while its companion is 'consigned to the darkness of the grave, and to disgusting decay, from which the ignorant mind' shrinks 'with abhorrence'.[20] The consequence of this doctrine is that:[21]

bodily health, the proof of a virtuous physical life, is not proposed as a chief end of our endeavours, nor regarded as an honour to its possessor. It is rather thought of as a blessing bestowed by prudence, or inherited from our parents, with the attainment of which the individual's self has comparatively little to do. The laws of health are as little reverenced as understood. While the infringement of a moral law involves the deepest guilt, and is considered worthy of infinite punishment, to break a physical one, and thereby incur disease, is not deemed an offence at all but only a misfortune.

The chief purpose of Drysdale's book, accordingly, was to redress this balance, to persuade its readers to make it their religious goal:[22]

that every one of us, man, woman, and child, should possess a large, powerful, vigorous frame, whose blooming health shall set consumption and the other diseases of debility at defiance. Each man and woman should take exactly as much pride in the cultivation of the bodily, as of the mental virtues, feeling deeply the grand truth, that the interests of our race are just as much bound up in the promotion of the one as of the other .... We should cultivate all those sports and manly exercises, which promote bodily health and vigour, just as sedulously as we cultivate the moral virtues, and should have an equal honour for physical, as for mental excellence, wherever we see it. We should learn to take an equal pleasure and to have an equal reverence for the sensual as the intellectual enjoyments, for the physical as the mental sciences, and in everything to attain to an impartial and well-balanced sense of the equal grandeur of the material and the moral universe of a true Physical and Spiritual Religion.

In this context of a muscular anti-Christianity, the solution of the social problem, expanded in the third edition from a section of Part III (Natural Religion) to a long, new Part IV (Social Science), consisted of the attempt to demonstrate the truth of the Malthusian 'Law of Population' as revealing the 'real cause of the great social evils of old countries' and to

propose 'preventive sexual intercourse' as their 'only remedy'.[23]
Whole chapters of Malthus's 'Essay' were reproduced in the book
in order to make self-evident:[24]

the *necessary* existence of the preventive and positive check
to population; of poverty and early death on the one hand,
and of sexual abstinence or abuse, and prostitution, on the
other. Our choice at this hour is exactly the same, as was
that of our forefathers; namely, between moral restraint, vice
and misery, not independent of them; and whichever of them
we seek to mitigate, we must necessarily by so doing
aggravate the others. Thus if we wish to avoid premature
death, and to raise the average of life, it cannot *possibly*
be done (while food is increasing at its usual ratio) except
by increasing sexual abstinence, or a sexual intercourse
which hinders, like prostitution, the birth of children. A
decrease in any one of the three immediate checks, moral
restraint, vice, or misery, is *necessarily* attended with an
increase in the others. In this way we see that premature
death in former times obviated the necessity of sexual
abstinence or prostitution; while the longer average of life
at present has *necessitated* a great increase of these two
evils.

In brief, although Malthus's 'Essay' provided Drysdale with
a satisfactory explanation for the social evils of his time,[25]

the solution proposed by Mr. Malthus, although guided by a
profound knowledge of the true cause of the evils, (and
therefore the only one which had the slightest chance of
being right), was in fact no solution at all; it merely recom-
mends, as a remedy for the difficulties, the very thing,
namely, sexual abstinence, which itself constitutes the
difficulty.

How could this be? Drysdale's answer was what he called 'the
Malthusian dilemma', the choice[26]

between two modes of death; by poverty, or by sexual
misery; by want of food and leisure; or by want of love ....
Poverty, taken in its widest sense, means the want of *love*
as well as of food; and the ignorance or disregard of this
truth is the greatest of all errors in reasoning upon social
matters.

There was, however,[27]

a way, and but one possible way, of surmounting these evils,
and of securing for each individual among us a fair share of
food, love and leisure; without which human society is a
chaotic scene of selfishness, injustice, and misery .... The
means I speak of, the only means by which the virtue and
the progress of mankind are rendered possible, is PREVEN-
TIVE SEXUAL INTERCOURSE. By this is meant sexual intercourse, where precautions are used to prevent impregnation.
In this way love would be obtained, without entailing upon
us the want of food and leisure, by overcrowding the
population.

Many people, Drysdale admitted, objected to preventive
sexual intercourse:[28]
because, they say, it is *unnatural*. But sexual abstinence
is infinitely more unnatural; in fact it is so unnatural, and
therefore sinful, that it is totally incompatible with health
and happiness, and produces the most wide-spread and deso-
lating diseases. It is granted that preventive intercourse is
unnatural, but the circumstances of our life leave us no
alternative. If we were to obey all the natural impulses, and
follow our sexual desires like the inferior animals, which live
a natural life, we would be forced to prey upon and check
the growth of each other, just as they do. We must of an
absolute necessity act unnaturally; and the only choice left
us is to take the course from which the smallest amount of
physical and moral evil will result. It is not with nature that
preventive intercourse is to be compared, but with the other
necessary checks to population, sexual abstinence, prostitution, and poverty. We have to choose *between* these checks,
not independent of them.
But, say others, preventive intercourse is a sort of murder, a
form of infanticide. We must admit, replied Drysdale, that:[29]
the moment a human embryo is produced by the union of the
spermatozoid with the egg, its life is as sacred as that of the
adult, and to take it away is murder; but to prevent impregnation is a totally different matter. We do prevent impregnation every day, when we refrain from sexual intercourse;
and we do waste seminal fluid and eggs every day, and the
only alternative left us is not whether or not they shall be
wasted, but whether or not we ourselves, shall be wasted
and destroyed along with them.
This, then, despite Drysdale's rejection of the term, was the
secularist case for birth control, a case which was both a protest against the specific, speculative errors of supernatural
religion in so far as the population question was concerned and
an advocacy for a specific moral truth to be tested by the
experiences of life. Drysdale, for these reasons, filled many
chapters of his book with dreadful warnings of the physical
and mental consequences of the conventional response to the
Malthusian dilemma within the framework of Christian orthodoxy. Much of his Part II (Sexual Religion) was devoted to
diseases of the male and female generative organs, as they had
been identified by the medicine of his day - balanitis, gonorrhoea, syphilis, spermatorrhoea, dysmenorrhoea, menorrhagia,
leucorrhoea, ovaritis, metritis, and so on - with details of their
treatment, but with far greater emphasis on the assertion that
prevention was always better than cure. But, in his attempts
to avoid 'morbid delicacy, to the inevitable ruin of mankind'[30]
and to raise the level of popular understanding of these and
associated subjects so that all men and women might become
'more or less physicists [sic!], as all have become more or less
moralists',[31] he did not apparently consider the extent to which

such frank discussion of questions, usually not talked about
in public at all, might repel rather than attract them.

As one reviewer put it, 'The Elements of Social Science' laid
'bare to the public ... the sores of society, caused by anoma-
lies in the relation of the sexes'. In the process it went into
'all the minutiae of the treatment of diseases thence arising.
For these reasons this book may be extensively read; it is not
likely to be spoken of except *sotto voce*, nor to be reviewed
in the proper organs of general science and literature',[32] a
prediction which turned out to be quite accurate in spite of
what Himes called its 'warm reception', thirty-five editions up
to 1904, the year of Drysdale's death, and translation into
'at least ten European languages'.[33] The advocacy of birth control in the 1850s required a courage which not many of the
convinced possessed. 'The task is a heavy one, and from my
experience there is scarcely a person to be found who would
take an interest in such a subject, for fear of what the orthodox party might say of them. I myself have had a goodly share
of abuse for this subject.'[34] Christians held that the notion
of the passions being gratified, without the 'inevitable' consequences being permitted to follow, ought not to be talked
about, amongst Christians themselves at any rate. Even 'a
formal refutation of doctrines so revolting would be an insult
to morality'.[35] Certainly there was no formal refutation of the
secularist case as set out in 'The Elements'; whenever the
book was referred to in the press generally, which was not
often, what received attention were the more extreme of Drysdale's doctrines, usually interpreted as unregulated licence,
free love, and 'artificial expedients to frustrate fecundity'.[36]
Outside the ranks of the readers of the free-thought newspapers and journals, where the book was given rather more
serious attention, the secularist case for birth control through
contraception was learned in secret, if at all.

This raises the question of the likely effect on the spread of
family limitation amongst the upper and upper-middle classes
which might have been brought about by this secularist propaganda in favour of what later, in deference to Malthus's
own views on the subject, came to be called neo-Malthusianism.[37]
Even if the secularists themselves did not read 'The Elements'
or any one of the handful of pamphlets which it seems to have
inspired after 1855 to join those still surviving from the 1830s,[38]
they could scarcely have not seen the articles by G.R. which
appeared in the 'National Reformer' from 1860.[39] The secularists,
it is true, were divided amongst themselves over the issue,
and the immediate editorial policy of the 'Reformer' came to
grief over what one of the first pair of joint editors called the
'Unbounded Licence Party' of the neo-Malthusians.[40] As Bradlaugh put it in 1862, apparently in the context of this editorial
wrangling, 'we honestly affirm that we have had opposition
more severe and unkind offered to our approval of the opinion
of Malthus than to our most extreme heterodoxy in theology.'[41]

Yet even had all the secularists been wholeheartedly in favour
of limiting their own families through the use of some kind of
contraception, it is hardly likely that they would have made
quite that impact on the statistics, published by the Registrar-
General after the 1911 Census, which first made plain beyond
question that it was amongst the more prosperous, and more
respectable, sections of the population that family limitation
was most practised and had been practised longest.

The difficulty is not so much that the secularist movement
never had probably more than 100,000 supporters at its peak,
since their influence may have made itself felt on friends,
relatives and passers-by who listened to the message without
bothering to join the movement. Rather is it that its members,
and therefore their most likely audiences, were recruited
for the most part from amongst artisans, followers of those
trades 'which offered regular employment and a degree of
social security'. From Edward Royle's careful analysis of the
evidence of secularist support it would seem reasonably
clear that very few indeed of those people who were actually
practising family limitation consistently and successfully during
this period were supporters of the secularist movement. The
family planners were gentlemen of independent means, and
professional and semi-professional gentlemen. The secularists
were members of the upper working class and lower middle
class, most prevalent in those areas of the country where
Owenism had been strongest.[43] The one case where the
possibility of a direct link between a belief in secularist doctrines and the practice of family limitation might be supported
is amongst the textile weavers of the north west; for some of
these - the weavers - have been claimed by Royle to have
been an 'influential group' amongst Victorian unbelievers,[44]
while it was the wives of cotton weavers whose fertility was
claimed to be lower even than other textile workers, the
group as a whole being the first occupational group amongst
the working class to be described statistically as effective
family planners.[45]

The question is, of course, complicated by the fact that
the area generally was noted for its low church attendance in
1851,[46] so that there was probably even more unconscious
than conscious secularism at work. It is also complicated by
the fact that a much larger proportion of the wives of cotton
weavers than of the wives of cotton spinners continued to
work in the mills after marriage, and the employment of mothers,
then[47] as now,[48] is associated statistically with smaller families.
Thus, even if the claims 'that barren women went to work and
that women with large families quitted their work'[49] is dismissed
as a simplistic interpretation of the statistics, the issue of
whether the Lancashire weavers practised family limitation
because they were convinced neo-Malthusian secularists, or
because they were accustomed to the wives going out to work
and to that degree were obliged to accept some emancipation

on their part from complete economic dependence on their
husbands and therefore also some sexual independence, still
remains to be considered. This raises the question of whether
these two issues were linked through part of the secularist
case for birth control consisting of a case for equality between
the sexes. What, in brief, was the relationship between
secularism, neo-Malthusianism and the emancipation of women?

4   THE EMANCIPATION OF WOMEN

For the most part the Owenites and later co-operators expressed
themselves as especially favourable to the claims of women for
equal civil rights with men. As Holyoake described it, in their
discussions 'the subject is never obtruded and is never long
absent. It continually occurs as though women were an equal
part of the human family and were naturally included in Co-
operation.'[1] Indeed, quite regularly the claim was made that
a particular virtue of the community 'arrangements for mutual
co-operation' was that they established a 'just equality of
rights and duties' between the two sexes.[2] Full membership
rights and equal participation in the self-government of these
communities, just as in the management of co-operative societies more generally, was open to all adult persons, irrespective
of sex.[3] Hence Owenites saw this attempt of theirs to remove
the barriers to equal participation by women in the common
affairs of the community as leading inevitably to an ideal
situation in this respect, described by one of the missionaries
in unconsciously patronizing terms as a circumstance where:[4]

the females were equally as intellectual and accomplished,
equally as noble-minded and beneficent as the males. Instead
of being able to converse upon simple, frivolous, or commonplace subjects, as is generally the case with females in the
present state of society, they conversed upon the most intellectual and philosophical subjects with an ease, elegance and
propriety that was truly delightful; though with that modesty
and diffidence peculiar to intelligent and virtuous females,
and which renders their conversation so highly pleasing and
attractive.

This notion of equality between the sexes, in spite of their
'natural' differences, is what some of the Owenites regarded
as their particular contribution to social progress, since it was
not necessarily shared by other reformers. As William Thompson
put it in 1824,[5]

however equal men may have been proposed to be made to
each other, the relative inferiority of all women to all men,
has been ever insisted on: old association and the brute right
of superior strength, have everywhere prevailed, amongst
religious fanatics as well as amongst republican institutors.
The weaker sex, as the weaker men, have been universally
the prey of the stronger.

This conviction led Thompson to make a spirited attack on the
utilitarian, James Mill, whose article on government, published

as a supplement to the 'Encyclopaedia Britannica' in 1820, had asserted that all those individuals whose interests were indisputedly included in those of other individuals might be struck off from political rights without inconvenience. This applied obviously to children and to 'almost all' women. In an 'Appeal to one Half of the Human Race, Women, Against the Pretensions of the Other Half, Men, to Retain them in Political, and Thence in Civil and Domestic Slavery', Thompson not only attacked Mill's arguments, but presented a careful examination of the way in which every social, political and legal influence on women combined to create in them a slave-like mentality which, by implication, Co-operative Communities would abolish.

In this respect one of the major problems facing women, argued Thompson, was that the bearing and rearing of children placed them inevitably in an inferior position vis-à-vis men who always had 'therefore superior opportunities of influence, of attaining their ends, of protecting themselves by indirect means without the protection which the direct check of political rights gives them'.[6] He thereupon advocated that in the Co-operative Communities children should be reared apart from their mothers by a 'superintendent':[7]

man or woman as may be most convenient, intelligent in the theory and practice of physical and mental culture, or if necessary both, surrounded with favourable circumstances merely, and thus giving an impulse to the development of minds of hundreds indiscriminately of both sexes; or as children have been aptly termed, all of them of the *neutral* sex.

In his 'Appeal' Thompson did not raise the issue of family limitation but, as had already been noted above, he was conscious of the Malthusian argument against the possible success of the Owenite experiments and thought birth control to be the answer. For his part, on the other hand, Robert Dale Owen made the question quite explicit: one of women's rights was that of making birth-control decisions. 'No man,' he wrote,[8]

ought even to *desire* that a woman should become the mother of his children, unless it was her express wish, and unless he knew it to be for her welfare, that he should. Her feelings, her interests, should be for him in this matter *an imperative law*. She it is who bears the burden: and therefore with her also should the decision rest.

Within the context of their Malthusianism, however, those secularists who advocated birth control regarded this otherwise completely emancipatory attitude to women as necessarily tempered by considerations to which women were just as subject as men. Couples could not be left to breed up to the limit of their fecundity, just as they thought fit or the woman desired. 'The sexual life of women,' claimed Drysdale,[9]

lasts from its maturity at fifteen, to its decline at about forty five years of age: that is, during a period of about thirty years. Thus if we allow two years for the production and

nurture of each child, which is amply sufficient if the woman
live a healthy life, she could produce in all about fifteen
children. This is a moderate average of the reproductive
powers of women, when these powers have their full scope,
and are not checked by difficult circumstances.
In sum, the Malthusian dilemma was held always to be operative,
and a satisfactory limit must be set to the capacity of women to
breed. So, concluded Drysdale, although[10]

impregnation and child birth are certainly of the very greatest
importance to the health and happiness of woman, and hence
every woman should produce her fair share of offspring ...
it is probable that two or three children during life would be
quite sufficient to secure these advantages.

The Malthusian secularists, in brief, could not escape the
implication of their generally pessimistic attitude towards the
growth of population. Large families spelt poverty, if not
immediately for themselves, for posterity. The secularist case
for birth control, accordingly, emphasized the benefits for
both parents and for society in general, which were conferred
by the smaller, deliberately restricted family.

What is not so clear is whether this particular secularist
point of view also contained the notion that the emancipated
woman of the future should not have to be obliged to choose
between getting married in order to have a family, albeit a small
one, and following a career. Beyond Thompson's reference to
the possibility in co-operative communities of rearing children
by specialists of both sexes there seems to have been no discussion by secularists of what to do about child-rearing,
especially in the homes of emancipated women outside such
communities. Amongst the secularist activists themselves, to
be sure, the women seem to have been 'nearly all wives or
daughters of Freethinkers',[11] and this may have reflected a
form of enlightenment on the part of their menfolk that they
were prepared to undertake, or at least to participate equally
in undertaking, the duties of raising their offspring in order
to make it possible for their wives and daughters to play as
full a part as they in the propagation of the secularist ethic.
The better known women secularists, however, seem to have
been spinsters, like Harriet Martineau,[12] or wives separated
from their husbands, like Anna Wheeler[13] and Annie Besant,[14]
who were committed to accompanying motherhood with earning
a living because their husbands refused to support them. The
exceptional nature of secularist women must be constantly kept
in mind when attempting to understand the circumstances of
typical nineteenth-century wives and mothers.

This reference to the obligation to combine motherhood with
paid employment, or other forms of income earning, is very
relevant to the position of working wives in the textile industry.
Some of these, at the end of the Victorian period, were certainly recorded as 'women deserted by their husbands',[15] as
no doubt others of them were so deserted throughout the whole

period. Yet others, at its beginning, were the wives of handloom weavers, 'forced by bitter necessity to leave their homes',
since without their earnings their families would have been
faced by 'utter starvation'.[16] In so far as such obligation to
find paid employment on the part of married women, who were
still living with their husbands, has been regarded by one
social historian as responsible for leading women to see themselves 'increasingly independent of parental and husbandly
authority, masters of their own emotions and, ultimately, of
their own fertility', the relevant so-called 'structural shift in
the economy' which converted their necessity into the consciousness of the possibility of 'personal autonomy'[17] would
seem to have been the opening up of employment for unmarried
girls and married women and widows away from their homes.
Whereas domestic production had been carried on inside the
house or its adjacent outbuildings by parents and children
together, alongside the performance of routine household
domestic chores, including setting the younger children to work
and training them in their daily tasks,[18] factory and similar
workplace employments required the mother to leave her personal care of children, as well as of household, until after her
day's work was finished, or to complete then what she had
started before it began. The important question, therefore,
is the extent to which the separation of income-earning occupation from income-spending and unpaid home duties forced
working-class women to become economically independent of
their husbands, irrespective of what either of them thought
about it, as opposed to the women consciously choosing factory
employment because they found it in some sense more personally
satisfying than the care of house, husband and children alone,
since this latter concept is what following a career usually
implies.

In the context of family limitation this question may be
reformulated in terms of whether textile women came eventually
to restrict the number of their conceptions in order to go out
to work as an alternative to housework - or in addition to
being housewives - because they needed to supplement their
husbands' earnings and could no longer find childminders
cheap enough to make this economically worthwhile without birth
control; or whether they conceived fewer children because
they had become 'emancipated' to the degree that, while still
unmarried, they had come to value their occupations in the
factories and the wages that employers paid them directly for
their work, and were not prepared to give up these personal
advantages to become completely dependent on the allowances,
household and personal, made to them by their husbands. The
evidence of the period from which the secularist literature on
feminism, referred to above, was taken bears witness to the
extent to which married women in textile towns, like Preston,
were able to continue to work in the factories in spite of having
perhaps quite large families, because there was an elderly

relative living in their homes who had no alternative source
of livelihood and who could, in a sense, 'substantially *increase
the family income* ... by caring for the children at home while
the mother worked in the factory'.[19]

Although sparse, the evidence also bears witness to expres-
sions of a state of mind which automatically related the unemployment of men to the competition from women, married and unmarried alike, for scarce jobs and which implied that the separation of the workplace from the home had resulted in two distinct fields of activity requiring characteristically contrary
types of behaviour - income earning by husbands, income
spending by their wives. 'Home, its cares and its employments,
is woman's true sphere', asserted a deputation from the West
Riding of Yorkshire to Robert Peel and William Gladstone. The
employment of women in the factories was thus 'an inversion
of the order of nature and of Providence - a return to a state
of barbarism, in which the woman does the work, while the
man looks idly on'.[20] As a crippled ex-factory worker, on tour
through the factory towns of northern England on behalf of
Anthony Cooper, Lord Ashley, reported in 1841, 'it is quite
pitiable to see these poor men taking care of the house and
children, and busily engaged in washing, baking, nursing,
and preparing the humble repast for the wife, who is wearing
her life away by toiling in the factory'.[21] From such a point
of view the working-class family now appeared to be standing
on its head. 'One can imagine,' Friedrich Engels wrote to
his German readers in 1845, 'what righteous indignation this
virtual castration [tatsächliche kastration] calls forth amongst
the workers and what reversal of all family relations results
from it, while all other social relationships remain unchanged.'[22]

Engels, of course, thought that this reversal of occupational
roles happened 'very frequently indeed' but it is nevertheless
unlikely that the unemployment of working-class men at the
same time as the employment of their wives was anything but a
very temporary and localized phenomenon. In the industrializing towns of this period, it has been claimed, 'there were
always plenty of jobs for men only in the skilled trades, or
general labouring, in warehousing and so on'.[23] The handloom
weavers, whose plight has so often been taken as typical of
the impact of the industrial revolution on the manual worker,
were a very special case - if only because they apparently
preferred to let their wives leave their homes for paid employment rather than to enter the weaving sheds themselves, even
when employment was available for them there. Most of them,
in any case, eventually adapted to their new situation and
found themselves 'more promising occupations'.[24]

In so far as all these attitudes are to be interpreted as
relevant to understanding the position of the wives of textile
workers at this time, what appears to have happened was that
by the middle of the century the nature of the labour market
had resulted in the workplace becoming defined as the man's

true sphere and the home as the proper place for his wife; and there is no evidence that the secularists, no matter how radical they might be in other respects, rejected this sex-linked division of labour in their propaganda for the emancipation of women and no evidence, therefore, that it was the teaching of the secularists which inspired the textile women to seek emancipation in this respect, if it can be assumed that this is what they sought. Nor is there evidence that the feminists as such, and especially that little band of ladies from Langham Place who were in the vanguard of the agitation for women's rights at this time, had any objection to such a division of duties between husband and wife, except in so far as it was sometimes not carried on harmoniously. For the most part, that is to say, the feminists were concerned with the married woman and mother only when she became widowed or penalized by a husband who was 'invalided or not forthcoming'.[25] They were more agitated by the economic hardships and necessity of 'surplus' women whom monogamy rendered unmarriageable and whose numbers in Great Britain increased by 16.8 per cent between 1851 and 1871, resulting at the end of this period in an imbalance of women over men amounting to 463,700 individuals, aged fifteen and over,[26] whose fate would not have seemed so desperate had not the separation of workplace from home, and the consequential conversion of the latter into an income-spending rather than income-earning sphere, turned the unmarried daughters and sisters of the employed into economic liabilities for their menfolk.

It is true that the Society for the Employment of Women, established in 1859, and the Female Middle Class Emigration Society (1862) were later products of that same committee of ladies who had collected signatures for the petition on behalf of the Married Woman's Property Bill of 1855; but this earlier campaign had not been inspired by a desire for women to enjoy property ownership as a satisfaction in its own right which men already enjoyed: rather had it been prompted by the need to protect those married women whose husbands used their legal prerogatives to the disadvantage of their wives, that is, the Bill had been designed to protect women whose marriages had proved to be a disaster. The search for opportunities for the employment of single and widowed women, similarly, was in order to give them economic independence so that, among other things, they would not be obliged to 'barter soul-and-body for money and rank', to give them the opportunity to marry or not to marry as they thought fit.[27] There was no question here, or anywhere else at that time, of the feminists working to make Victorian marriage so much of a partnership that the wife could become a breadwinner while the husband stayed at home to take care of the household chores, or indeed that both would so share in the care of home and children that the wife and husband could pursue separate careers along the lines of, say, the twentieth-century 'dual career' profes-

sional and quasi-professional families.[28] In many respects the
feminists of the 1850s appear to have accepted as quite proper
and correct the Christian conventions of their day that the
husband's career and occupation came first, while the middle-
class and upper-middle-class wife was as much his 'help-meet'
as the working-class wife was 'minister' to the wants of her
man.

Of course, the feminist leaders did not interpret this in
quite the way that was customary amongst Anglican clergymen,
like the minister of Regent's Park Chapel, who inferred the
'mission of woman from a consideration of the wants of man' and
claimed that therefore:[29]

the young woman who wishes to qualify herself for being the
help-meet of man, will not deem it unimportant to give attention to those humbler attainments, as they are sometimes
deemed, which, from their bearing on domestic comfort, are
not a little conducive to the fulfilment of her mission.

Rather were the feminists closer in spirit to many of the women
writers who rejected the case for sex equality outside the home
as merely the opposite side of the coin from their assertion
that inside:

the autocrat should decidedly be the lady, the mistress.
The master, be he father, husband, or brother, has quite
enough to do without doors. He is the bread-winner; the
woman, the bread-keeper, server, and expender. Nature as
well as custom has - save in very exceptional cases - instituted this habit of life, and any alteration of it, making
mamma attend the law-courts and Exchange, or drive about
on a series of medical visits, while papa stays at home to
cook the dinner and nurse the babies, would assuredly be
very bad, if not for himself, for the dinner and the babies.

A man, that is to say, had 'no business to meddle in the management of the house'.[30]

Possibly because they came 'almost exclusively'[31] from
families in which there was a tradition of involvement in phil-
anthropy and reform, the pioneer feminists saw many of their
activities as necessarily taking them outside their homes but,
however exceptional they might be in this and other respects,
they accepted this clear division of functions - work for the
husband, home-making for the wife - and they apparently
never associated their campaigns to improve the lot of women
with the more radical advocacy of the secularists. Although
Holyoake claimed to have discussed his notion of women as a
Fifth Estate with Bessie Parkes and Barbara Smith in 1847,
as well as with Harriet Martineau,[32] there is no clear indication
in their lives' work that either of these young ladies was very
much impressed by his secularism or even by Harriet's brand
of freethinking. Barbara Smith, it is true, once called herself
a freethinker but took care to add, 'I am also profoundly
religious',[33] so that it is more than possible that what weighed
most with her were the principles of her Unitarian background,

working for the salvation of this world as a means for personal
salvation in the next.[34] Bessie Parkes, with a similar background in Christianity as primarily a way of life rather than as
a system of doctrine,[35] might have been an agnostic at this
time, but by 1864 she did not find it particularly difficult to
join the Catholic church.[36] Other feminists were, quite openly,
practising Christians. In so far as their social nonconformity
had roots in non-Anglican beliefs these were Nonconformist
not secularist. As with the religious objections to Malthus - a
continuing theological controversy inside the Christian church
of his day - so this later controversy about the place of women
in the social order was a controversy amongst Christians.

The dominant view of the day towards what Mrs Sarah Ellis
had earlier called 'the minor morals of domestic life' was that
no woman could neglect these 'without serious injury to the
Christian character'.[37] For the Christian woman, whether she
espoused the feminist cause or not, domestic virtues were
exercised in the name of love, 'woman's all - her wealth, her
power, her very being. Man, let him love as he may, has ever
an existence distinct from that of his affections. He has his
worldly interests, his public character, his ambition, his
competition with other men - but woman centres all in that one
feeling, and "In that *she* lives, or else *she* has no life".[38]
Thus, the issue of the relationship between the emancipation
of women and family planning turns on the emergence of these
relatively 'modern'[39] notions in a society where the older values
of women's domestic virtues vis-à-vis their ministering lov-
ingly to the wants of men were commonly propagated. How did
it come about that middle-class and upper-middle-class housewives at about this time - and working-class housewives in
the textile districts some little time later - uninfluenced by
secularism, unaffected by the birth-control propaganda
associated with secularism, disregarded by feminists with other
objectives in mind, nevertheless became so emancipated that
their 'role in the decision to limit the number of children' they
conceived 'was indeed crucial',[40] if indeed it was?

Clearly, this question cannot be satisfactorily tackled without a consideration of what 'emancipation' meant to such
housewives at this time, and this requires a systematic attempt
to ascertain which housewives in fact became 'emancipated' or
'modern' in the sense of using contraceptives. In so far as
family limitation as such is concerned, the only detailed source
of information about the families born to women throughout the
whole of their child-bearing years during the relevant period
is the 1911 Census volumes on the fertility of marriage. In
particular, Table 35 in part II of the fertility report[41] provides
information on marriages contracted before 1851, between
1851 and 1861, between 1861 and 1871, and so on, where both
couples were still alive in 1911 and where therefore the husband's source of livelihood was still ascertainable from him.
Inevitably in these circumstances, the proportion of couples

who had been married in these years and who were still alive
in 1911 was likely to have been small and one estimate reckons
these at 32.3 per cent of those married between 1861 and 1865
and 43.9 per cent between 1866 and 1870,[42] so that the number
of children born to these couples was undoubtedly greater than
the average for marriages contracted during these dates,
since those husbands and/or wives who had died before 1911
included a number who had died before they reached the wife's
menopause. What the survivors represent are couples with
the maximum exposure to the risk of conception and provided
that comparisons are made largely or wholly between those of
more or less the same social position it is not unreasonable
to regard those with the smaller number of children born to
them as the 'pioneers', so to speak, of family limitation at
this time. Inevitably, also, the number of surviving couples
who had been married for over 60 years by 1911 was rather
small; and for present purposes these have been added to the
marriages of 50 to 60 years' duration to give two categories
for the relevant period, namely couples married before 1861
and those married between 1861 and 1871.

The 1911 Census was unique, of course, not only for this
first attempt of the Registrar-General to make such a detailed
study of fertility, but also for his more general grouping
of occupations into 'classes', intended to be indicative of the
different social grades in the community in 1911. As the
Report emphasized, Class I in this grading scheme turned out
to have the lowest fertility both for marriages contracted
before 1871 and consistently throughout the remainder of the
century, and Class I included 'all occupational groups of
which the majority of the members', as tabulated at the Census,
could be assumed by the Registrar-General as belonging to
the upper and middle classes of the community. It included
such occupations as commercial and railway clerks and insurance
agents and excluded the artisan 'even though his wage may
be higher than the clerk's. While including the clerk, who is
always distinguishable, it frequently excludes his employer,
who is not'.[43] This reference to the clerk is particularly
illuminating in the present context, because in the figures of
married couples in Class I commercial and business clerks
accounted for only about 5.8 per cent of the total of those
married before 1861 but as many as 12.1 per cent of those
married between 1861 and 1871. The average number of children
born to those clerks, married during the former period, was
7.05 when the mean for all Class I was 6.41. In the latter period
the comparable means were 6.09 and 5.90 births respectively.

Thus, although on this occasion the mean number of children
born was closer to that for Class I as a whole, and even for
Class I when the clerks themselves were omitted from the totals,
the consistently above-average births to the wives of men in
these occupations suggest that clerks were not amongst the
'pioneers' of family limitation in the strict sense; and it is

perhaps reasonable for present purposes to leave them out
of the account, indeed along with all those other occupations
where the mean number of children born was consistently
above the Class I average for marriages contracted before 1872.
In the following list of occupations, therefore, only those have
been included whose couples had a mean number of children
below the means for Class I for both marriage cohorts. However they achieved this, through the deliberate use of mechanical forms of contraception or in some other way, the
'occupations' in Table 4.1 were the 'pioneers' of family limitation at this time.

Table 4.1   'Pioneers' of the smaller family: married before 1871

| | Mean number of children born | |
Occupation of the father	Marriages before 1861	Marriages 1861-71
Officers of the navy and marines (effective and retired)	5.11	4.57
Authors, editors, journalists, reporters	5.33	5.61
Accountants	5.61	5.71
Physicians, surgeons, registered practitioners	5.64	5.54
Civil, mining engineers	5.68	5.87
Painters, sculptors, artists	5.81	5.50
Army officers (effective and retired)	6.01	5.07
Gentlemen of private means	6.04	4.48
Solicitors	6.11	5.78
Ministers, priests, of bodies other than the established church	6.15	5.78
All Class I	6.41	5.90
Number of couples in Class I	2,555	16,667

To maintain logical consistency two occupations from the
Registrar-General's Class II should, no doubt, be added to
this list. Class II, of course, was 'intermediate between the
middle and working class because it consists of occupations,
such as the shopkeeping trades, including many members of
both classes'.[44] The relevant occupations are in Table 4.2.[45]
    The tobacconists - 'Tobacconists', Fancy Goods Importers;
Tobacconists' Sundries: dealers, shopkeepers, shop assistants;
Tobacco Pipe importers, dealers' - form a particularly striking
addition to the list of pioneering family limitationists, not only
because they were apparently so much in the vanguard of the
smaller family movement before 1871, but also because they
appear to have been the only occupational group in that vanguard which had amongst its numbers cases where the couple's
income came from the conduct of a family business in which the
wife could play as great a part as her husband in its affairs.[46]

Obviously, in the case of authors, etc. and painters, etc.
the husband's work need not necessarily have been separated
from his home life and in this respect the families of such men
could have been organized as an income-earning, as well as
an income-spending, unit in much the same fashion as the family
organization of a tobacconist's shop, although there is little
evidence about how far this occurred. In all the other occupations in the list this could hardly have been possible.

Table 4.2   *'Pioneers' of the smaller family from Class II: married before 1871*

	Mean number of children born	
	Marriages	Marriages
Occupation of the father	before 1861	1861-71
Tobacconists	5.07	5.34
Hospital, institutions (not Poor Law) and benevolent society servants	5.20	5.26
All Class II	7.37	6.64
Number of couples in Class II	4,334	33,368

This should not be misinterpreted to imply that the mother
of these other pioneering smaller families made no contribution
to the family incomes. In Class I marriages contracted before
1861, for example, 42.8 per cent of the husbands were recorded
as being gentlemen of private means in 1911, and if this figure
contrasts sharply with the respective figure of 19.0 per cent
for marriages contracted between 1861 and 1871, this is no
doubt because the older patresfamilias, especially those who
were gentlemen of private means from the time of their marriage, had enjoyed better life expectancies than other men,
even of their own social standing. The wives of such gentlemen, it seems reasonable to assume, for the most part brought
some income of their own to the partnership in the form of a
dowry or other settlement from their fathers. Under the common law, it is true, most forms of property held by a wife were
assigned to her husband and the whole of her income, no
matter what its source, belonged to him. Under equity, however, 'a long course of juridical legislation had at last given
to a woman, over property settled for her separate use, nearly
all the rights, and a good deal more than the protection,
possessed in respect of any property by a man or a *feme sole*'.[47]
In this regard, even before the Married Women's Property Act
of 1870, some of the inequities of the married woman's position,
at least amongst the propertied classes, had been overcome
in the sense that the legal rights of the husband were not
exercised by him to the disadvantage of his wife. To this

degree women of such marriages were 'emancipated' because
their fathers had prevailed upon their husbands to forgo their
common law rights, although whether they were emancipated in
other senses remains to be considered.

The gentlemen of private means, it might be claimed, were
to some extent also exceptional because for the most part they
were gentlemen of leisure and as such able to participate fully
with their wives, if they wished, in the care of the household
and the upbringing of their offspring. This could hardly have
been true of army and navy officers on active service or of
accountants employed in City houses, civil engineers and
solicitors and doctors with busy practices. Here the separation
of work from home meant that the husband and father spent
many hours of his day away from the household and in so far
as his earnings were the sole, or the major, source of family
income, his wife's task as income-spender was no different
from that of the working-class housewife, already referred to
above in the context of this separation of tasks. Unlike the
working-class woman, to be sure, she normally had domestic
assistance provided for her, and it is important to emphasize
that for Class I families such as these this assistance was of a
rather different kind from that of the working agricultural or
the prosperous pre-industrial family for whom, it has been
pointed out, possibly more servant labour 'was spent on
agricultural, industrial, productive tasks ... than was spent
on housekeeping'.[48] The domestic servants of the 1850s and
1860s were income-spenders rather than income-earners for
the families who employed them, and the middle- and upper-
middle-class housewife's task in organizing them was to ensure
that they were occupied efficiently so that they did not become
in fact income-wasters. Household management for such a wife
was mainly servant management, even if she also spent some
part of her day in household chores herself.

Of course, even in the pre-industrial age where the assistance of the wife had been necessary for the more efficient
pursuit of her husband's affairs, she often engaged servants
to free her from 'household drudgery' when her own income-
earning capacity was greater than the cost of a servant's
wages.[49] So now, in the 1850s, women who could earn money
at home, by writing novels for instance, could afford to employ
domestic servants to relieve them of such drudgery. The point
to emphasize, however, is that the majority of married women
in the class to which this discussion applies sat for most of the
day in drawing rooms, as one feminist put it, 'eating the
bread of idleness' despite the fact that 'an educated woman, of
active, methodological habits, blessed with good servants, as
good mistresses generally are, finds an hour a day amply
sufficient for her housekeeping'.[50] The emancipation which these
women experienced, by contrast with their working-class
contemporaries, or even by comparison with their lower middle-
class 'sisters', was emancipation from an average day, 'filled

with housework, washing, cooking, crying children, quarrels
with the maid, shopping, and never-ending financial problems'.[51]
   Such 'emancipated' women, it must be emphasized, were for
the most part the wives of army and navy officers, authors,
editors, journalists, accountants, physicians, surveyors,
registered practitioners, civil mining engineers, painters,
sculptors, artists, barristers, solicitors - in brief, members
of what Harold Perkin has called 'a class curiously neglected
in the social theories of the age'[52] - the wives of men who had
themselves by this time become emancipated from dependence
on a few, rich patrons because their services were now
demanded by 'the many comfortable clients of their own social
standing'. Such men were, in Harold Perkin's sense, comparatively aloof from the struggle for income between capitalists and wage workers, since their 'professional' returns
were apparently only indirectly influenced by the ebb and flow
of market forces. Once established in their careers, such men
'could generally rely on a steady income, not subject to the
same mutual competition as rent, profit and wages',[53] and their
wives, accordingly, could also rely on a similarly steady housekeeping allowance. Indeed, to the degree that the twenty years
before 1871 witnessed an increased demand for the services
of their husbands, as indicated by a disproportionate growth
in the numbers employed in most of these occupations as compared with the increase in the total population,[54] not only
could these women look forward to the future with a sense of
being economically secure, they could even expect to receive
ever-increasing sums for their domestic arrangements as their
husbands' incomes rose with the demand for their services.[55]
There can hardly be any doubt that the growth in the numbers
of housekeepers, cooks, housemaids and nursemaids employed
between 1851 and 1871, especially when compared with the
smaller, although still disproportionally great, increase in the
employment of general servants,[56] is an indication of the manner
in which these couples laid out their newly acquired affluence.
This, together with what Hilda Hookham appropriately called
'the paraphernalia of gentility'[57] of this section of the population is what constituted the level of living of the 'pioneers' of
English family planning.
   The relationship between this level of living and the standard of life which such couples regarded as appropriate for a
civilized existence must be re-emphasized here. Clearly, without such a regular and rising income it would not have been
possible for them to realize whatever aspirations they had. In
this respect the independent career opportunities of these
professional and quasi-professional husbands was a necessary
pre-requisite for the type of emancipation which they - and
in this respect also their wives - experienced; but these
opportunities do not of themselves explain sufficiently why they
spent their incomes as they did, on more, and more expensive,
domestic servants, on keeping horses and a conveyance, on

expensively entertaining their relations, friends and acquaintances, on clothing themselves more elaborately, on taking
holidays abroad, etc.[58] In particular, these opportunities do
not explain how it came about that, when these housewives were
able to employ more domestic labour, they did not do so in order
to be able themselves to follow one or other of the activities so
much worked for by the feminists, but rather set themselves
up socially in such a way as to arouse feminist hostility. By
the 1870s, that is to say, the mothers who were giving birth
to fewer children even than the Class I average were - except
no doubt for the wives of tobacconists - women who aspired
to, and in fact achieved, the standards of the 'perfect lady'
of the day, leisured, elegant and obviously expensive. As
Leonore Davidoff has pointed out, the especially striking feature of Victorian society was the way in which what were
'essentially middle-class patterns of behaviour were grafted
on to the honorific code of the aristocracy or gentry to produce
the widened concept of "gentility"'.[59] Their husbands, to be
sure, were perforce obliged to pursue their daily vocations in
order that the wherewithal would continue to flow into the
household; but these wives could - and did - follow the
etiquette of the 'best circles', behaving rather like the wives
of the gentlemen of private means, the ladies of leisure.
  In this sense the 'emancipation' from household chores for
these women was achieved only because they became even more
economically dependent on their menfolk than women of their
social standing had traditionally been, and this was a depen-
dency which did not tie them to the confines of the home in the
manner in which their more economically independent pre-
decessors had been tied. Morning calls on one another, tea
and whist parties, visits to and longer periods of sojourn with
friends, took these upper-middle-class housewives out of
their homes. They thus had much more freedom of movement
than that 'silent sisterhood' in the lower ranks of middle-class
society who, in spite of the employment of a domestic servant,
were much more personally involved in the domestic routine,
possibly because of 'the restrictions of a narrow income in a
society of rising costs and constant innovation'.[60] On the face
of it, if these upper-middle-class women became 'pioneers' of
family limitation in their own, rather than in their husbands'
interests, it was in order to give them more freedom of movement of this sort, 'emancipation' from the confines of the home,
freedom to follow the etiquette of the leisured classes; yet
there is no evidence of any revolt on their part against the
authority of their husbands over sexual intercourse, no
evidence of what has been called 'domestic feminism' by such
'emancipated' women which is supposed to have 'manifested
itself in the desire to avoid needless pregnancies',[61] if by this
is understood pregnancies which would interfere with the
lady's freedom of movement and which her husband did not
regard as needless at all.

Indeed, for so long as there were plenty of domestic servants available, especially nannies, nurses and governesses, it is difficult to appreciate how, beyond the last few months of pregnancy and the period of confinement itself, such upper-class and upper-middle-class mothers could have been much incommoded by even quite large families, since these domestics 'cushioned' them, not only from housework but from 'the unpleasantness of dealing with their own children at times'.[62] This made it possible for them, if they wished, to devote themselves to playing with their infants, teaching them desired skills, caring for them in any way that the mother found pleasurable, simply because the unpleasant tasks could be handed over to paid labour. Of course, it cannot be denied that such wives, whether they conceived frequently or not at all, were expensive luxuries and some bachelors might well have decided not to marry because the economic burden involved would interfere with their pleasures. In a letter to 'The Times' in 1861 one complained that:[63]

years ago, when contemplating a certain important step, I sounded my then 'soul's idol' as to her expectations of the style in which we were to live. She intimated blandly enough that her aspirations were of the humblest order - 'Just a brougham and pair, a saddle-horse (necessarily implying two), a house in a quiet part of Belgravia, a cottage in the Isle of Wight, an occasional box at the opera.' Her fortune was under 2,000 l., my income being at the time 500 l.! On testing subsequently the views of other damsels, I found that the discrepancy between them was slight. What wonder, then, that I, for one, should bid adieu to all hopes of matrimony.

Yet at this time 88 per cent of the total population were married by the time they were 54 and this figure seems to have been fairly stable,[64] so that if the expense of both wife and children was seen by upper-class and upper-middle-class men as prohibitive, it might well have been they, rather than their wives, who had come to desire the end to needless pregnancies. If child-rearing had become an economic burden to them might they not have provided the impetus towards the smaller family?

5   HOSTAGES TO FORTUNE

The Anglican ideal of the prudent marriage, especially as this had been expressed by Malthus, had not been so exclusively linked with avoiding poverty and misery as the neo-Malthusian secularists tended to imply when they applied his arguments to support their own doctrines on sexual questions. Although it is true that even during his lifetime some of Malthus's orthodox followers had taken a very gloomy view of his position, assuming - as Nassau Senior put it in 1829 - that poverty was a necessary consequence of additional numbers in the population,[1] others had taken a much more optimistic stand by concentrating on the circumstances facing each individual family. These claimed that the sexual instinct was 'in civilized communities, controlled in a greater or lesser degree by prudential considerations' which took into account the possible destiny of parents and children when sexual restraint was exercised for financial reasons.[2] To such writers on the population question it was 'abundantly certain' that sexual self-control was commonly practised by 'the greater number of persons in the more elevated stations of life, as well as those who are peculiarly ambitious of rising in the world, and those of all ranks who have learned to look at the consequences of their actions'.[3] Such people postponed marriage until they could afford it. Some, indeed, were claimed to 'find it expedient to pass their lives in a state of celibacy. And it is fortunate that such is the case, and that the good sense of the people, and their laudable desire to preserve their place in society, have made them control the violence of their passions'.[4] The desire of bettering one's condition was 'as natural a wish as the desire for marriage'.[5]

By contrast to the argument in 'Prosperity and Parenthood',[6] it may now be asserted that there was nothing especially novel about this phenomenon of postponement. As John Hajnal has claimed, albeit from rather meagre statistics, from at least the beginning of the eighteenth century a marriage 'pattern' had been typical of Europe, except in its eastern and southeastern part, which was 'unique or almost unique in the world'. This European marriage pattern had two distinctive features: couples married at relatively late ages when compared with the rest of the world, and a relatively high proportion of the population never married at all. Possibly this pattern was related to the relatively high level of living enjoyed in this part of the world: 'Europeans, a large proportion of them, not just

the rich, had better housing, better clothing, a greater variety
of food, more furniture and utensils, than people elsewhere.'
Possibly also it was related to the relatively high standard of
living, to the aspirations which Europeans held about the level
of living to which they were entitled. They insisted on the
possession of the necessary resources as a prerequisite for
marriage, varying according to the social position of the individual. The farmer could not 'afford' to marry until he had
acquired land, the apprentice until he had finished his appren-
ticeship.[7] Englishmen, like their counterparts across the
Channel, had taken very seriously Francis Bacon's essay on
marriage and the single life: 'he that hath *Wife* and *Children*
hath given Hostages to Fortune'.

To the degree, therefore, that certain couples, married
before 1861, or between 1861 and 1871, and still living in 1911,
had produced on average a smaller number of children than
was common even for people of their own social and economic
circumstances, to this degree some feature of the third quarter
of the nineteenth century had influenced them, once married,[8]
deliberately to control the production of offspring and this was
exceptional even within the framework of the uniquely European
marriage pattern. Contemporary writers at this time had no
doubt about the essential wisdom of this pattern itself, even
when they were disturbed, as many clearly were, by its side-
effects. They were agreed that there was 'a proper time' to
marry and that, although they might disagree about the details
in any particular instance, this 'proper' time entailed that
the couple should wait until they had what in 1858 the High
Church 'Guardian' called 'a competent support' in the form of
an income sufficient to maintain 'a due social position'.[9] At
that time there was considerable disquiet about the extent to
which prostitution – the great social evil – with 'its fearful
consequences on virtuous unsuspecting wives and innocent
children'[10] was, or was not, related to excessive caution in this
respect. What had been a sufficient competence for their
parents was now claimed to be no longer considered appropriate
for a civilized existence by the young couples of the day,
especially in the middle and upper-middle classes. They
expected, complained 'The Times' on 2 July 1861 'to begin where
their fathers and mothers ended', and this entailed an ever-
increasing expenditure on an ever-rising standard of living –
more expensive furniture and fittings, more luxurious food and
drink, more domestic servants, more of all the external signs
of affluence, the paraphernalia of a style of life which proclaimed the essential 'gentility' of the mid-Victorian paterfamilias and his wife, the perfect lady.[11]

Yet, the very emphasis on the postponement of the wedding
day, and the analysis of the problems of the middle and upper-
middle classes in terms of the effect of late marriages, rested
on the assumption that once a couple were married children
would follow as a matter of course. In part, no doubt, this

assumption was consonant with the awareness that their offspring were not particularly expensive to raise, especially
when considered in the light of their parents' incomes at this
time. Children's food was, if anything, simpler and less expensive than that consumed by the domestic servants to the family.
Their toys cost little to buy. Much of their clothing was made
by servants at home.[12] If their mother was quite 'genteel' or
of poor health, or if the number of children was growing rather
fast, an upper-middle-class family would have been obliged to
employ a nursemaid to cope with all the children; but such a
girl would have cost about £30 a year for keep, plus wages of
£11 a year in 1850, rising to £17 a year in 1870, a percentage
increase much less than an estimated rise in incomes for the
middle classes over this period,[13] and below the cost of a cook,
whose labour was regarded as essential if the household were
to be complete in all its functions and the housewife were to be
a manager of the home rather than a labourer within it.

In so far, then, as certain couples in the upper middle
classes at this time were practising family limitation because
of the economic cost to them of the children which they might
otherwise bring into the world, this cost is most likely to have
been that of educating them, especially the boys amongst them.
As the 'Quarterly Review' put it in 1869, in the context of a
discussion on the desirability of educating girls:[14]

> even wealthy men find the expense of sons at the Universities
> quite as much as they like; but then they 'grin and bear it',
> because they know that such education is a passport to
> employment and independence. Many professions are only
> reached through the Universities. It is the best investment
> of capital. In the upper classes of professional life the demand
> is even increasing. Where men sent one son to Oxford and
> Cambridge, they now much more oftener than a short time
> ago send two or three. The future clergyman, lawyer, or
> civil servant will not take up his father's position in life
> unless he has cost from one to two thousand pounds at school
> and college. The statesman, the squire, and increasingly, the
> merchant and the man of business, must carry the University
> stamp.

One to two thousand pounds per boy, especially when spread
over a period of, say, twenty years from the time the first
entered one of the boarding schools at twelve and the last left
Oxford or Cambridge at twenty-two, meant a considerable
commitment of pecuniary resources by a family in a single direction. In terms of the estimates worked out by the anonymous
author of 'A New System of Practical Domestic Economy' this
would have required in 1824 an income of anything between
£7,500 and £15,000 a year, where the family in this case would
have comprised a gentleman, his lady and three boys, supported
by an establishment of at least 'thirteen male and nine female
servants; in all twenty-seven persons, ten horses, a coach,
a curricle, and a Tilbury chaise or gig'.[15]

The assumption here, of course, was that the boys would
have been sent to one of what were called 'the great schools',
those which had 'always educated principally with a view to
the universities'.[16] Of these schools, Westminster, St Paul's
and Merchant Taylors' would have cost the parents less, relatively speaking, because they were day schools and economies
could be introduced into the boarding and lodging of their
pupils at home, in spite of the greater expense generally of
living in or near London. Parents could also avoid the more
exorbitant charges of Eton or Harrow by sending their offspring to Winchester, Shrewsbury, Rugby or Charterhouse,[17]
or to one of those other schools, soon to be described by the
Schools' Inquiry Commissioners as 'between' those of the
labouring classes and the 'public' schools. These more frugal
parents, according to the Commissioners, were 'identical, or
nearly so, with those whose sons are in the nine schools that
have been already reported on by a previous Commission; men
with considerable incomes independent of their own exertions,
or professional men, or men in business, whose profits put
them on the same level'. Such fathers customarily kept their
boys at school until they could matriculate at eighteen or nineteen, because they were 'very anxious that their sons should
not fall below them', and they were consequently accustomed
to complaining regularly about the expense of all this.[18] Yet,
despite the expense, the striking feature of these years was
the establishment of a large number of such schools to cater
for the demand. Although there are difficulties in ascertaining
just how many genuinely new schools of this kind were established and how many were much older schools simply re-
organized to meet the demand, about thirty seems to have been
most likely,[19] constituting a rate of growth over the years
1840 to 1870 which was much greater than ever before, or
since.

The question at issue, therefore, is whether or not these
schools catered, above all, for the sons of those fathers whose
occupations were listed in Tables 4.1 and 4.2; and this is a
question which it is virtually impossible to answer. Certainly,
between 1800 and 1850 the entrants to eight of the 'great
schools' - omitting Merchant Taylors' - showed only a modest
relationship with the occupational characteristics of the family
limiters. It has been estimated, for example, that some 53 per
cent of the twelve-year-old boys in titled families went to these
schools over this period and 46 per cent of the sons of the
gentry, that is, some 47 per cent of the boys whose parents
had private means, whilst only 18 per cent of the sons of the
clergy, 8 per cent of those with fathers in the services, and
3 per cent of the sons of professional men went to these schools.[20]
Does this mean that the remainder, along with the sons of
tobacco dealers and others, went to the minor proprietory
schools? Lacking detailed information about the families of origin
of the pupils in all these schools, this question must necessarily

remain unanswered, even if some qualitative remarks of the
Victorians themselves suggest that this may have been the
case.[21] In any case, in the light of the quotation above, from
the 'Quarterly Review' of 1869, it is pertinent to ask whether,
and why, so many gentlemen of private means now found it
necessary to provide their sons with education as 'a passport'
to employment and independence when they apparently possessed the resources to provide them with independence without
employment. As a German observer put it, even as late as 1904,
the 'gentleman' farmer was still one who 'rides, hunts and
pursues various kinds of sport, as do his sons, while his wife
enters local society and his daughters learn music and paint-
ing'.[22] It is difficult to understand why education at public
school, followed by university, was in any way necessary for
the pursuit of such activities, in spite of the obvious emphasis
in such places of education on 'the amateur ideal'.[23]

One possible way of dealing with this problem is by making a
contrast with the circumstances of the families of gentlemen of
private means in the previous century. Because child mortality
was high up to the end of that century, it has seemed to at
least one author almost self-evident that it was 'a very risky
speculation to invest capital on a prolonged and expensive
education .... The decline in the mortality rate at the end of
the eighteenth century has therefore been an important factor
in stimulating secondary and higher education in Western
Europe.[24] Certainly, even among ducal families, child mortality
was high in the eighteenth century,[25] and it is true that many
of the sons of peers, baronets, squires and merchants were
educated at home at this time,[26] but it does not follow from the
juxtaposition of these facts that their education was neither
prolonged nor expensive, since it was not uncommon for them
to go on from their homes to one of the universities. For
example, some 51 per cent of British peers, born between 1685
and 1785, went either to Oxford or to Cambridge, while a
further 33 per cent went to other universities. 52 per cent
of baronets, squires and other gentlemen of independent means
also went to Oxford or Cambridge and 33 per cent to other
universities. Some 42 per cent of the remainder of that British
elite born between those dates, whose names have been
recorded in the 'Dictionary of National Biography' accompanied
them to Oxford or Cambridge and 27 per cent elsewhere.[27]

Although the differences between these comparable percentages do not differentiate significantly, statistically speaking,
between those with private means and those who followed an
occupation or profession for their livelihood, they nevertheless
indicate that the fathers of the former were not at all unpre-
pared to spend money on their sons' education. 43 per cent
of the Englishmen and Welshmen amongst them, incidentally,
had been to one of the nine 'great' public schools and only 33.5
per cent had been educated at home, possibly by a private
tutor rather than by their parents and such a tutor would not

necessarily have been cheap.[28] The education of these men had
been relatively prolonged and in that sense constituted, it
would seem, an investment of capital in a risky speculation.
What is open to question, therefore, is whether this money was
spent in order to fit the boys of wealthy parents for some kind
of future employment. An alternative interpretation, which has
rejected the investment argument altogether, has emphasized
that as a matter of fact opportunities for 'lucrative professional
employment' lagged far behind the educational expansion of
the nineteenth century.[29]

> Boys in the mid-nineteenth century Public Schools were not
> for the most part, groomed for well-paid employment but
> handicapped in their search for it by an irrelevant education
> and the outward signs of genteel status .... The new Public
> Schools make sense only because a family was already wealthy
> and because unpaid or ill-paid careers in Parliament, the
> Army, Church, or at the Bar, brought not a livelihood but
> valued status.

Yet what still remains unclear is why this status was valued
at all. Why had gentlemen of private means for so long regarded
either home education or public school education as an essential
preparation for university education? and why, indeed, had
they regarded a university education as necessary for their
sons, just as it had been seen by their fathers as necessary
for them?

The most notable feature of the lives of most of these
gentlemen - and their ladies - was, of course, that it constituted
a leisured, not an occupied existence, even if it was also true,
as the 1871 Census put it, that the greater part of these people
were probably not idle: 'many of them are most usefully engaged
in public and charitable works to which the busy cannot
attend'.[30] Their leisure, together with their prerogative to
decide whether to be idle or useful, was 'inherited as a right
attaching to private property'.[31] For some 200 years or so the
aristocracy and the landed gentry had employed the legal device
of settlement 'to secure the family estate to the head of the
family for the time being'. At twenty-one the eldest son 'normally barred the entail with his father's consent' and thereby
obtained 'a measure of financial independence for he was normally given an annuity charged on the estate'.[32] This meant,
among other things, that eldest sons were more likely to marry,
to marry at younger ages, and to have larger families than
younger sons.[33] Even the younger sons, however, for whom
because of primogeniture, the case for investment in education
might seem much stronger, usually had a 'portion' of the
estate settled on them. Such portions were 'capital sums to be
raised from the land and paid to the younger children to start
them in life. The right to a portion usually became indefeasible
at twenty one or on marriage (so as to facilitate marriage
settlements), payment being made at the death of the life tenant
or earlier with his consent.'[34]

Such a capital sum might be laid out in the purchase of, say,
an ensigncy, a lieutenantcy, or even a captaincy, in an army
regiment, in the expectation that sooner or later the incumbent
would retire on half-pay to wait for a vacancy at a higher rank
open to him to purchase. In such a fashion the sons of the
aristocracy and the gentry, eldest and younger alike, followed
a career as army officers, eventually reaching high rank, since
above that of lieutenant-colonel all promotion was by seniority.
Although, in times of war especially, men from the ranks and
relatively poor members of other classes could achieve promotion through valour and efficiency in situations of crisis,
most army officers could afford such a career only with constant
financial backing from their families. In terms of the evalua-
tions of the day army pay was poor and the price of commissions
high. As Sir Charles Burrell put it in a debate on the Army
Estimates on 15 March 1822, 'if an ensign in the guards were to
sink the purchase-money of his commission in an annuity, he
would get a much higher rate of pay than he received in virtue
of his commission'.[35] Nor was it a matter of alternative prospects
of returns on investments. By 1860 a cornet in the cavalry
paid £450 for his commission. His outfit, dress uniform and
horse, etc. would then cost him a further £220. For this
expenditure of £650 he would receive in pay £146 per annum,
but his expenses were likely to amount to nearly £200, leaving
a deficit of about £50.[36] Thus, it has been argued, 'nobody
supposed that a young officer's pay would take him off his
family's hands'.[37] Nevertheless, his possession of a saleable
commission did mean that when he decided to retire he would
receive a capital sum for investment in, say, an annuity. However, the main feature of this conception of an army career
was obviously very different from that kind of investment
implied by the 'Quarterly Review's reference to 'a passport
to employment and independence'.

What, then, was that 'valued status' of the leisured, propertied class which was not a vocation in the sense of an income-
earning career but for which parents were prepared to spend
often a great deal of money for their sons to possess? The
'Report' of the Commissioners on the public schools in 1864
described these schools as:[38]

> the chief nurseries of our statesmen; in them, and in schools
> modelled after them, men of all various classes that make up
> English society, destined for every profession and career,
> have been brought up on a footing of social equality, and
> have contracted the most enduring friendships, and some of
> the ruling habits, of their lives, and they have had perhaps
> the largest share in moulding the character of an English
> gentleman.

Such gentlemanly statesmen entered the House of Lords as a
peer, if head for the time being of certain of those great, family
estates which had come to be such a striking feature of the
country in the eighteenth century,[39] or as a prelate, if because

as a younger son he had entered the church through a family
living and had risen to the higher ranks of the church through
the patronage of the monarch.[40] Younger sons might enter the
House of Commons, alongside eldest sons who had not yet taken
over the peerage from their fathers. Between 1734 and 1832,
for example, 341 younger sons of English peers and 290 eldest
sons had been elected to parliament,[41] presumably in the
majority of cases from family or proprietary boroughs,[42] some
of which still continued to determine who was elected to parliament after 1832.[43] At this time, of course, Members of Parliament were not paid salaries for the work, and there is some
evidence of rising costs in obtaining seats from the end of the
seventeenth century onwards,[44] so that public service of this
kind, although clearly status conferring, was an amateur, not
a professional, pursuit.

This point needs further elucidation. In 1820, as John Wade
was able to show, amongst the aristocracy there was 'hardly
a single family, some of whose members, in addition to their
private incomes, are not in receipt of a large proportion of
the public money'.[45] The 'valued status' of the gentlemanly
statesman and his relatives in the church, the army and the
law entailed the receipt of money from places, pensions, grants,
sinecures, as Wade listed them,[46] some of them often quite small
sums, others surprisingly large, but all constituting fringe
benefits, so to speak, from public sources to supplement from
elsewhere the incomes which had made it possible for their
possessors to enter public service in the first place; and it was
this essentially amateurish conception of public service which
made relevant the emphasis by such gentlemanly statesmen on
the value of a classical education, the learning of Latin and
Greek grammar rules by heart, the memorizing of prose and
verse passages from Horace, Sallust, Ovid, Cicero, Virgil,
Terence and Aesop, as well as the names and dates of generals
recorded in Greek and Roman histories - a practice which was
carried on well into the second half of the nineteenth century,[47]
so that the Commissioners on the Public Schools could regard
it as an undoubted service that these schools had maintained
'classical literature as the staple of English education, a service which far outweighs the error of having clung to these
studies too exclusively'.[48]

Such accomplishments served very well to divide off those
who had been to public school and perhaps to Oxford or
Cambridge from those who had not, and in this sense they were
the perpetual demonstration of genteel status and gentlemanly
universality and exclusiveness rather than technical specializa-
tion; they might, indeed, for precisely this reason be used as
criteria by which to select between the various candidates for
office in the various professions of the day, although the family
connections of the candidates were much more likely to have
been the deciding factor in such a selection; but they could not
in any sense be regarded as educational achievements of a

directly vocational sort. From this point of view the period of
sojourn at a university, like the grand tour, served as a kind
of progress through a finishing school in which the young man
acquired proficiency in the fine art of conversation, sprinkled
preferably with Greek and Latin tags and literary references,
with the very people with whom he would eventually, perhaps,
share the responsibilities of public service. 'The aspiration of
the English aristocracy,' it was asserted in 1865, 'is to be, not
the best educated, but for practical purposes the most cultivated.'[49] It was for this cultivation that the gentlemen of
private means spent some one to two thousand pounds on each
of their boys and a rather smaller sum on the girls.[50]

The significance of this aspiration is best understood by
reference to that distinction, already referred to on page 8,
between a level and a standard. Gentlemanly exclusiveness,
exemplified not so much by the obvious possession of wealth
but by a ready familiarity with the language, literature and
history of Greece and Rome, was a demonstration that what was
considered appropriate for a civilized existence – a standard
of excellence – had already been achieved by those who had
passed through one of the great public schools and even
perhaps a university on their way to adulthood. What was already a level of actual well-being for them was a standard to
be achieved in the future by those who, without this background themselves, had obtained the opportunity to acquire it,
not for themselves to be sure, but for their sons. A 'cultivation'
of this kind was, that is to say, valued for itself for the most
part and certainly much more for itself than for whatever
economic rewards it might lead its possessor also to acquire as
a result of admission to those social circles where patronage
usually held sway, although such extra advantages would not
be rejected or even despised.

This, incidentally, is why it is correct to regard the standard
of living as having economic consequences, such as the expenditure of resources on education rather than on something else,
without seeing it also as a necessary means to other goals,
especially economic ones. The classical cultivation of the gentlemanly ideal was an end in itself, which not all the members of
the ruling class were able to reach, as is exemplified by the
fact that although 26 per cent of the Members, elected to Parliament between 1734 and 1832 had been educated at either Eton
or Westminster, 66 per cent had not been to any of the seven
great public schools, or that although 43 per cent had been to
either Oxford or Cambridge, 52 per cent had attended no
university at all.[51] The social exclusiveness of the gentlemanly
statesmen and their parliamentary relatives did not prevent
other, less 'cultivated' men from sharing their parliamentary
duties and, no doubt, their parliamentary advantages. Nor were
such 'under-privileged' necessarily prevented from purchasing
their way into landed society, even if – as Gordon Mingay has
intimated – by the middle of the eighteenth century it would

have cost them about £30,000 to obtain an estate worth £1,000
a year.[52] Entry into the ranks of the established by these
means was clearly open to the very few.

What, it might be asked, has all this to do with family limitation in the 1850s and 1860s? The answer seems to lie in a
particular version of the Malthusian principle which had already
been in operation for some time, for all that neither Malthus
nor his contemporaries were clearly aware of it. During the
nineteenth century some new estates may have been formed
'at the expense of the smaller properties', but the noteworthy
fact is that the cost of acquiring that £1,000 per annum estate
had risen to £40,000 or more by the 1860s.[53] The number of
landed families settled on an entailed estate had grown very
slowly indeed over the hundred years, if at all.[54] Given generation reproduction rates of, say, 1.5 for parents born between
1730 and 1829[55] and a mortality rate amongst ladies of, say,
30 per cent by age 40,[56] over one generation the number of
distinct, although interlinked, family lines would have increased
by about 5 per cent, giving a total increase of roughly 16
per cent over a hundred years; and this would have been the
case despite the fact that some wholly male lines would have
become extinct to be replaced by 'new' lines, created by marriage with heiresses.[57] Clearly, the supply of such families
of landed origin outstripped the supply of landed estates on
which to settle them, and some 48 to 64 gentlemanly families
had by the 1860s to be supported otherwise than by capital
derived from the entailed estate. The problem facing the
gentlemen of leisure, that is to say, was not what to do about
their younger sons, but what these younger sons themselves
were going to do about their sons, granted their own inability
to live appropriately on what their portion of the entailed
estate amounted to in capital terms, and granted that they had
come to value the kind of education which the public schools
and the universitites had accustomed them to thinking as essential for the cultivation of a gentleman.

One possible way out of the difficulty, of course, was to find
sources for the investment of capital other than in land purchase; and it is perhaps relevant in this context to notice that
the 'impressive record' of British economic growth in the 1850s
had been attributed by one author to 'an intangible phenomenon,
the spirit of risk (or perhaps even speculation) which prevailed'.[58] So far as the landed gentry were concerned, this
might have been termed a spirit of desperation, were it not for
the fact that there now seems no way of learning just who
invested this capital on such a scale. Landowners certainly
borrowed during this period, in part to improve their estates,
and it would not seem unreasonable to suppose that they could
more easily borrow from relatives with capital to invest than
from strangers.[59] Nor does it seem unreasonable to suppose
also that part of their speculation, borrowing and lending alike,
consisted of a search for alternative sources of unearned

income. Yet, as the Census figures indicate, showing a decline
in the number of male 'Persons of Rank, or Property, not
returned under any office or occupation' - from 31,261 in 1851
to 25,510 in 1871[60] - the most obvious alternative for the sons
of younger sons was to take advantage of the patronage,
possessed by their more fortunate uncles and cousins, to find
them places in government service, in the army, in the church,
or in the law.[61] This indeed is where their educational experience
would prove to be most acceptable, not because they had been
'trained' to occupy such posts, but because it marked them off
from whatever other aspirants for them there might arise from
amongst the sons of professional, commercial and industrial
families who had not this public school and university background. The rise in the number of minor public schools, established at this time, might well be explained by the aspiration
of such families for their sons to be cultivated as gentlemen
and hence become eligible for patronage. As the Member for
Middlesex expressed it in 1868, in the context of a confession
that after ten years at a public school he was still unable to
translate a sentence from the Greek, 'the fact was, public
schools had become mere hotbeds of social exclusiveness and
aristocratic prejudice, where people sent their sons to pick up
what they called gentlemanly connections'.[62]

The striking feature of all the gentlemanly occupations,
favoured by young squires and their less fortunate cousins,
which marked them off from commerce and business, on the one
hand, and from certain professions such as medicine, on the
other, was the growing emphasis in them on service to the
community rather than to the individual. This quality of public
service demanded of the aspirant to office a willingness, nay
eagerness, to accept collective responsibility and to display an
esprit de corps with his colleagues. The equally striking feature of the more famous public schools, especially during the
period 1760-1860, was the emphasis on precisely such an esprit
de corps amongst the boys, and it was apparently this social
characteristic of the schools which upper-class parents valued
more highly than what was formerly taught by the masters.
The team-games of these schools, their dormitory and refectory
living and discipline, and above all, the prefect-fag system
which the boys themselves developed during this period and
which was only later taken over as a tool by the masters,
emphasized the essentially military nature of the gentlemanly
ideal and its conception of collective action by social equals,
organized into a hierarchy of ranks, informed by the group
loyalty of both leaders and their subordinates.[63] Such a gentlemanly ideal found expression also, obviously, in the organization
of the officer grades in the army, in the church, increasingly
in the civil service, and to a lesser extent in the law, from the
barrister upwards. The kinds of career for which the public
schools most fitted the sons of gentlemen, that is to say, were
those in which there could be a fairly steady progression

upwards through the various levels of the hierarchy, from
ensign to field marshal, from curate to archbishop, from clerk
to Under-Secretary of State, from barrister to Lord Chancellor,
even if the number actually moving up decreased at every level.

This hierarchy of ranks was also a hierarchy of economic
rewards, and it was essentially the opportunity for future
advances in income that some students of the population question had regarded as responsible for the postponement of
marriage amongst the middle classes of their time. As the son
of a clergyman had put it in 1832, although 'marriage is a
present good' and 'the difficulties attending the maintenance
of a family are future', for some there was 'a motive for pro-
crastination' in

the assured prospect of an advance in circumstances with
the advance in age: a curate, who is without hopes of further
advancement, settles his mind to this condition, and marries
at once upon his curacy. But, if he has reasonable expectation of preferment, he is apt to feed himself with hope, and,
raising his ideas of comfort, and of the rank in society which
he would wish his wife and family to hold, to the standard of
his future prospects, to postpone his marriage until these
prospects can be realized.

This author, incidentally, assumed that such a motive for
choosing between immediate marriage on the one hand and pro-
crastination on the other operated equally 'throughout all ranks
of society'.[64]

The important point to emphasize here is that, beyond the
immediate effect on the wedding date produced by economic
boom or slump conditions and their repercussions on income or
employment opportunities, there was no longer-term incentive
for men who were not on a clear ladder of advancement to postpone a marriage and the children which, it was believed,
automatically ensued. For those who were on such a ladder at
this time there was an added incentive over the realization of
prospects for themselves, namely that of postponing or curtailing childbirth, not because of its immediate costs which
were reckoned relatively small but because of its ultimate costs,
based on the calculation that some ten years after the birth of
every male child it might well be necessary for its parents to
incur the much greater expense of a public school education,
necessary if sons were to find their places on the same sort of
career ladders as their fathers. The impact of this educational
emphasis, in brief, was to extend the concept of the career
backwards in time, so to speak, to a period some ten years or
so before it could actually be entered; and it may well have
been essentially the hierarchical nature of this type of upper
middle-class life expectation which accustomed its holders to
think in terms of their own and their sons' future prospects as
reasonably predictable. Such a future-time perspective was
rather different from that which informed everyday experience
in the capitalist, business enterprise proper, where the

commercial man and the industrialist gambled on being able to
sell for a satisfying profit in a relatively risky future what he
had sunk his money in today. This is possibly why, with the
exception of some of the tobacconists, none of the occupations,
listed in Tables 4.1 and 4.2 was entrepreneurial in this risk-
taking sense.

Not all of them of course, emphasized the elements of predictability to the same degree as the high status occupations
into which the sons and grandsons of the landed gentry and
aristocracy made their way at this time. Some of them, however,
such as author, painter, sculptor, artist, no doubt relied so
much on personal, even idiosyncratic talents, that men following them might reasonably have assumed that their sons would
be unlikely to be able to pursue them in their turn. Expenditure
on education at public school, even a minor one, and university
might therefore be reckoned as prudent investment on their
part. The main characteristic of the 'pioneers' of family limitation, nevertheless, is that the high status occupations amongst
them were precisely those where the hierarchical career, based
on public school education, became the standard of expectation
during the middle years of the nineteenth century. Hence, in
order to understand how it was that, in these years especially,
sons became important hostages to the fortunes of such parents,
it is necessary to be clear about the manner in which this element of predictability in the life experiences of such parents –
most significantly the fathers – became consolidated to establish
that special sort of future-time perspective which is relevant
to family planning. In terms of the economic issue of the cost
of children this consolidation must necessarily be understood
as a process of change in the organization of such occupations,
leading to education becoming less and less an end in itself
and more and more the criterion of merit for admission to the
career.

6   THE MERITOCRATIC EMPHASIS

The reference in the previous chapter to the purchase of commissions in the army may be taken as illustrative of the essentially entrepreneurial approach taken by the sons of the aristocracy and the gentry, and by the sons of those sons, to the opportunities offered by the offices they aspired to fill up to the third quarter of the nineteenth century and a little beyond. Not only in the army, but in all those other posts of the machinery of state which provided paid posts to be 'officered' by members of the 'cultivated' classes, the incumbent for the time being regarded recruitment and retirement as very much a matter of private negotiation between himself and a likely successor, or some other party with an interest in the post, for all that the duties of the office were public and collective. Thus, although from time to time reigning monarchs and their secretaries of state had made attempts to restrict the scope of private enterprise in the role and purchase of commissions by fixing a regulation price at which they should change hands, the most striking feature of all these attempts from 1719 onwards was their relatively short-lasting success. As the Commissioners, appointed to inquire into over-regulation payments on promotion in the army, reported in 1870, 'experience has shown that the most explicit prohibitions and the most stringent regulations have utterly failed to prevent or even check the practice'.[1]
What these failures demonstrated was that amongst officers themselves tenure in the rank which was open to purchase was thought of as very similar to the freehold possession of land. It belonged to the incumbent in much the same fashion as an entailed estate belonged to the heir who inherited it. Within the limits set by specified restrictions on its use it was his to dispose of as he thought fit, not altogether unlike any other parcel of privately owned but publicly registered property, so that even when for some purely military reason a man was promoted without purchase, the commission was his to sell in due course. This convention, indeed, could be justified at this time on the ground that a poor man who rose from the ranks would be obliged to retire eventually 'on the wretched pittance of half-pay' if he could not sell his commission, whereas 'under the purchase system, he could (after serving his country as long as he was fit) realize a handsome competency, which enabled him to fix his family in the position of life to which his gallantry and his good conduct had conducted him'.[2]
Nor was this all. Up to 1900 the British army was little more

than 'an aggregation of regiments',[3] and each regiment was to
such a degree 'the property of the colonel'[4] that his pay was of
less substance as income than the 'allowances' for clothing
the men and other costs which he might incur and from which
he was entitled to make a profit if he could, at least until the
Crimean War.[5] The relevant interpretation of military commissions of this sort is that a colonel was provided with sums of
money by his sovereign to undertake certain military adventures
on behalf of the Crown. These duties were not paid for in the
usual sense because, although allowance was made for profit
on expenses, it was assumed that the main return to a regiment
for its efforts, and therefore to all who served in it according
to their rank, was the prize money which they could obtain from
plunder, from holding prisoners to ransom, or from the ren-
dering of other services overseas.

In the summer of 1796, for instance, Arthur Wesley, the
future Duke of Wellington, while Colonel of the 33rd Regiment
of Foot, received £4,000 in prize money for restoring order at
Seringapatam in India.[6] This enabled him, for the first time
in his life, to pay off all his outstanding debts with the exception of £6,000 which his oldest brother, Lord Mornington, had
lent him to buy promotions and by now had decided to treat
as a gift. Nine years later when, now Major-General Wellesley,
he returned to England to get married, he possessed a fortune
of at least £42,000 in prize and other money,[7] all of which seems
to have been accumulated as a result of his military campaigns
since, apart from his army pay, all he had when he became an
ensign with the 73rd Highland Regiment at eighteen in 1787 was
a private income of £125 a year.[8]

In the light of such cases it does not seem too fanciful to
conclude with Owen Wheeler that army pay was:

> really a survival of the old days of the merchant adventurers,
> when those subordinately employed in an enterprise were
> given payments, partly by way of a retaining fee, partly for
> purposes of subsistence, pending the happy time when a
> fuller reward should accrue in the shape of loot, or as the
> result of holding rich persons to ransom.

Commissions, from this point of view, were gifts from the
sovereign to those who invested money in the adventure or to
those whom investors nominated for the receipt of commissions.
This is why they became to some extent negotiable.[9]

The navy, similarly, relied on prize money as an inducement
for recruiting officers in the first instance and for retaining
them in the service thereafter. When the twenty-four-year-old
Captain Horatio Nelson dropped anchor off New York in the
autumn of 1782 he was greeted with the remark: 'You are come
to a fine station for making prize-money.' The response, that
where he had come from was 'the station for honour', is more
witness to Nelson's exceptional attitude than to the usual
expectation of sea-captains and the customary evaluation of
their postings in money-making terms. Even for Nelson it was

a matter of degree, since he had taken off from Port Royal two
years before on 'a cruise' which had netted him £800 in prize
money.[10] This, it is true, was a relatively small sum. Many
naval officers, especially during the Napoleonic Wars, realized
quite large fortunes through the capture of prizes, despite a
government measure of 1808 which gave larger shares to lower
ranks.[11] The navy, indeed, offered far wider opportunities for
the distribution of such booty than the army, and Wellington
himself told a Select Committee on Army and Navy Appointments
in 1833 that for the army prize money, 'in most instances has
done no more than afford the means of purchasing promotion'.[12]

There was, to be sure, no comparable system for the purchase
of commissions in the navy, and there never had been, possibly
because the ship on which a man served had always been provided by the Crown. Yet it is not at all unlikely that money
changed hands whenever a 'Young Gentleman' was appointed
to a ship or was promoted to a senior rank. What was usually
referred to as 'interest' - the right of a captain to accept a
man as midshipman and to recommend him for a commission to
the admiral under whom they were both serving, the right of
the commander-in-chief on the spot to collect on his own flag-
ship those officers whose further promotions he wished to
procure, the patronage generally which men of higher rank
could individually dispense to younger officers - undoubtedly
possessed income potentialities, not only for the men in the
service but for certain non-service patrons, such as the
monarch, peers of the realm, and some Members of Parliament.
Often, of course, this cash value of 'interest' was realized
not in a direct monetary return but in the form of a service
elsewhere for a dependent or a friend, or more commonly for a
relative, so that the effect within the navy was not very
different from the overt purchase of commissions in the army.
The 'private enterprise' character of recruitment and promotion
was noticeable in both, with a personal element of cash or
other bargaining: 'you oblige me now and I will oblige you
later'.

Nor was this private enterprise lacking in the church, at
least as far as the initial presentation of a living was concerned.
'Advowsons were property - often very valuable property -
that not only carried a cash value in the market but meant even
more in terms of social standing or family convenience.'[13] The
right of a patron to make this property available was justified
on the ground that the endowments which the Church of
England possessed 'were not given by the nation, as such, at
all, at any point of its history, but were voluntary contribu-
tions of individual benefactors'. Tithes, in particular, 'were
a charge made on their own estates by the landlords of England,
in order to secure the services of a resident minister'.[14] Thus,
although the incumbent was in effect a public servant, his
appointment to a living was a matter of private negotiation
between him and the patron, be the latter a landowner, a bishop,

a university college, or the Crown; and as late as 1898, in so
far as private patronage was concerned, it was held that 'free
sale in advowsons, under present conditions, is as necessary
as free sale in land'.[15]
Other public servants, it should be emphasized, were also
rarely appointed by the Crown in the modern manner until the
Victorian era. For some time Principal Secretaries of State had
found it increasingly convenient to appoint their own Under-
Secretaries, on their own terms, to cope with the pressure of
business. These, in consequence, were paid widely divergent
fees and received such personal gratuities and other per-
quisites for their services as their masters thought fit. Indeed,
because those 'civil' officers of the state were so closely bound
by private 'interest' to the individual Principal Secretaries
who had appointed them and to whom they were accountable,
it has been claimed that it is not possible to recognize the
existence of a public service at all in the modern sense until
after the 1830s.[16] The history of the third quarter of the
nineteenth century may, therefore, be interpreted inter alia
as the history of the conversion of this privately organized
practice of assistance to a Secretary of State into a 'professional' civil service. It is also the history of a similar waning
of private enterprise in the military services and, to a lesser
extent, in the church, with the replacement of private bargaining over the sale and purchase of commissions and advowsons
by a more standardized procedure of appointments to, and
achievement in, a 'career' in which the various grades or ranks
were paid publicly ascertainable and acknowledged incomes -
salaries.
The example of the abolition of the purchase of army commissions in 1871 is illustrative of how this career structure
came to be established in a standardized form, with important
financial consequences for the parents with many sons. When
the Duke of Wellington's Commissioners for Inquiry into Naval
and Military Promotion had reported in 1840, they had made it
plain how difficult most military men found it to conceive of a
more effective way to promote efficient officers and, indeed,
to recruit them in the first place, than by the customary
practice of purchase. Although both the army and navy had
long experience of an alternative method of promotion, namely,
by seniority, the Commissioners were apprehensive of the
likely effect this method would have, if adopted more widely,
arguing that the quality of the service might well be impaired
in times of peace by the necessarily longer time which would
elapse before a man could move up a rank.

Without a reasonable prospect of such promotion ... the
energies may droop, the habits of application essential to
the attainment of eminence may be neglected, and although
the daily routine of service may be carefully performed, the
spirit of emulation will be wanting, the desire of distinction
deadened, and feelings of dissatisfaction and discontent will

be nurtured to the entire destruction of all the qualifications calculated to form a good and efficient officer.
The problem of identifying 'qualifications' was the stumbling block.

We are not insensible to the advantages which would result from the adoption of a ... system of selection, if any test could be discovered of the respective merits of the different candidates for promotion so certain as not only to afford a safe guide to the Master-General, by whom the choice must be made, but also to satisfy the corps and the public that the preference would, in all cases, be given to the person best entitled to it.

These Commissioners, indeed, could see no alternative to the current practice because of the lack of effective criteria of merit.[17]

For nearly a century, the Admiralty endeavoured to maintain the principle of selection in the promotion of captains to the rank of flag officers, and ... the principle and practice having been repeatedly modified, were, after all, found so difficult in execution, that they were totally abandoned, and the advancement to flag officer's rank has since been determined by seniority alone.

In this connection, the history of the next thirty years may be reasonably interpreted as the history of a controversy about what could be accepted as a relevant concept of merit for purposes of selection amongst likely candidates for recruitment to a service and for promotion within it. In 1849 the Duke of Wellington, as field marshal, tried to lay down two principles, the first of which appears to have been operated with some success, in spite of some adverse criticism of its genuine effectiveness.[18] This was 'that no one should receive a commission, unless he should prove on examination to be possessed of good average abilities, and to have received the education of a gentleman'. The second, by contrast, was reported never to have been implemented. This was 'that no ensign or cornet should be promoted to a lieutenancy, nor lieutenant to captaincy, until he had satisfied a competent tribunal of his professional and general acquirements and fitness'.[19] What worried many officers at this time was that selection, whatever the criteria used, must necessarily be made by some higher authority with all the possibilities for abuse that this might entail. 'However bad it might be on principle to look merely to money as a means of promotion, it would be still worse to have to look to the patronage of men in power,' claimed Colonel North, the MP for Oxfordshire, in the House of Commons's 1860 debate on Lieutenant-General Sir De Lacy Evans's motion, praying the Queen progressively to end the system of purchase.[20] 'Before any scheme of promotion by selection is extensively introduced in the British Army,' a Commission had reported some three years before,[21]

there should be general confidence that the power of selection

will not be misused. The military appointments made during
late years, as well in this country as in the Crimea, have
not tended to satisfy the army with the mode in which the
principle of selection has been applied.

The problem facing those army officers, like De Lacy Evans,
who wished to abolish the sale and purchase of commissions,
was to find an alternative which would enable a man to advance
more quickly than he would normally by seniority alone without
at the same time opening up the system to an alternative set
of abuses. The importance of seniority per se should not be
underestimated. Even the system of purchase depended in part
on length of service, in that whenever a vacancy occurred in
the higher ranks of a regiment 'for the retirement of an officer
by sale' every officer had a claim 'according to seniority, to
purchase the next rank in the regiment, provided that no
objection to his promotion is made by the commanding officer
of the regiment or by the Commander-in-Chief'.[22] There was,
it is true, some disagreement about the extent to which commanding officers ever in fact exercised their power of objection.
Lord Sandhurst, the Commander of the Forces in Ireland,
alleged on 29 April 1875 that the promotion of a man who was
prepared to pay the demanded price was never interfered with
in the past. 'I commanded a regiment under the old *regime*,
under which it did not matter how incompetent or how incapable an officer was (he might have been a madman, or he might
have been an idiot), you were not allowed to get rid of him.'
Understandably, Sandhurst's field marshal, the Duke of
Cambridge, strenuously denied the extremity of this conclusion.
'I cannot conceive such a thing happening, because whenever
a man is reported as being unfit for promotion the matter is
gone into most carefully, and anyone who was a madman or an
idiot would certainly not have been promoted.' Under the old
system? 'Quite so, the case would have been investigated.[23]

It was, indeed, the possibility that such a process of investigation might be more widely applied, not only within the regiments but to the extent of reducing their autonomy vis-à-vis
the army as a whole, which worried some of those officers who
wished in 1871 to keep the purchase system as it was. Thus,
Colonel C.W. White wanted to know what the government had
in mind in this respect: 'is it to be an exaggeration of that
most pernicious and unpopular and un-English system of secret
reporting, than which I know nothing so malevolent and so
disliked among officers of all grades?' The only alternatives to
purchase, another officer added, were 'seniority and selection -
seniority means stagnation, selection means favouritism (or
fancied favouritism, almost as pernicious), discontent, and
stagnation, unless some forced retirement is adopted which
means injustice and expense.[24]

In the event, once the government persuaded parliament to
put an end to private enterprise in the purchase and sale of
commissions by permitting it to buy up such commissions

compulsorily whenever they came on the market, at the market price,[25] it ended up with a system of promotion which was simply

> seniority tempered by rejection ... the lieutenant-colonel in each regiment makes what is called a confidential report at stated intervals upon the conduct, abilities, and military qualifications of the officers under him, and this report is submitted to the inspecting general for his approval and remarks, and forwarded to the Commander-in-Chief. If on these reports, carefully preserved and collated, any particular officer is shown to be unfit for promotion he is not promoted.

Already within five years of the Bill becoming law, it was reasonably clear that the effect of the new system was to slow down the rate of promotion somewhat, especially for captains and majors. In the infantry of the line - 'by far the largest portion of the Army', taken by the Royal Commissioners on Army Promotion as indicative of the 'average rapidity of promotion which obtained in the Army under the Purchase System' - an officer could now reckon on becoming a subaltern at twenty, a captain at twenty-eight, a major at thirty-four, a lieutenant-colonel at forty-three.[26]

In the context of its possible effect on the postponement of marriage, however, too much should not be made of this slowing down of the rate of promotion because the length of service before promotion of all officers in the infantry of the line, at various dates between 1840 and 1870, who had not purchased their commissions, indicates that at their most rapid advance, just after the Crimean War, captains had taken nearly eight years in service to reach this rank, majors nine years as captains, and lieutenant-colonels just under five as majors, while the purchasing officers had moved up into these ranks after about eighteen months' less service in each case, or four and a half years less on average to reach the highest of these ranks, which therefore would generally not be until they were thirty-seven on average.[27]

This account of the controversy about the purchase of commissions has been gone into in some detail in order to make clear the relevant features of these years, which made it increasingly imperative for the 'pioneers' of family limitation to purchase public school education for their sons. If this chronological expansion of the provision of such education is to be accounted for in these terms, it is important to emphasize that although it has been customary for historians to identify the experience of the British army in the Crimean War as crucial in the onset of arguments about army reform, already as far back as 1840, and even earlier, concern had been expressed by army officers themselves about the system of officer self-selection as a mode of recruitment and retirement in these ranks of the service. In this respect it is surely quite clearly the case that 'the much-publicized Crimean disasters

did not begin a debate upon military administration: rather,
they made it imperative to end a debate which had already been
unduly prolonged',[28] even if it still took sixteen years for a
government, backed by a minority of senior army officers, to
persuade parliament to vote it the money for the purpose.

Such a debate was carried on alongside a parallel controversy
on the non-military services about the need for a meritocracy[29]
in departments of state, the heads of which, it had been
claimed in 1854, regarded the selection of junior clerks 'as a
matter of small moment'. Such men, the Northcote-Trevelyan
Report had added,[30]

> will probably bestow the office upon the son or dependant
> of someone having personal or political claims upon him, or
> perhaps upon the son of some meritorious public servant,
> without instituting any very minute inquiry into the merits
> of the young man himself. It is true that in many offices
> some kind of examination is prescribed, and that in almost
> all the person appointed is in the first instance nominated
> on probation, but ... neither of these tests are at present
> very efficacious.

Competition and public examinations for civil servants had been
advocated as a substitute for patronage as far back as 1813,[31]
and throughout the 1840s and the 1850s a series of inquiries
had been made on the working of a number of departments,
although it was not until an Order in Council of 4 June 1870
that 'open' competition was made compulsory throughout the
civil service[32] and the final blow was given to the old style,
private-enterprise patronage system in the civil as well as in
the military services.

The meritocratic alternative which was eventually introduced
in the army - seniority tempered by rejection - was one which
rested on the assumption that, provided reasonable care had
been taken by senior officers in the recruitment of ensigns,
cornets, second lieutenants and sub-lieutenants in the first
place, length of service in an office was sufficient to ensure
competence in all but a very few cases. 'We do not think,'
confirmed the Royal Commissioners on Army Promotion in 1876,[33]

> that any amount of acquired knowledge, tested by any form
> of examination, is a guarantee for the possession of those
> numerous and varied qualities which go to form the character
> of military excellence. Nor are we aware that there is any
> other method but that of experience by which the possession
> of those qualities can surely be known.

Thus, although there was some discussion about competition
and even 'open' competition by 'competitive examination', the
principle which came eventually to replace the sale and purchase
of commissions in the army was the judgment of superior
officers about the merits and demerits of those officers under
them whom they commanded daily and whose command of others
they were aware of daily. In this respect promotion in the
army came to resemble that in the navy, where by 1823 it had

been described as 'a system of seniority, qualified by rejection', operated by the First Lord of the Admiralty on the basis
of half-yearly reports on every officer from the time that he
had entered the service.[34]

No doubt in former times when rank was given for political
motives or political influence, the exercise of this principle
was open to constant and great abuses. But that has now
been modified and according to the now existing practice
nothing could be fairer than the way in which the system is
at present worked.

This reliance, mainly on seniority as equivalent to the
evidence of the capacity to learn the necessary skills on the
job, rested on the further assumption that admission to the
service initially had been limited to those men only who had
already shown, at school and university, that they possessed
the relevant capacity. The basis of such an assumption was
Wellington's principle of 1849, namely, that admitting officers
had satisfied themselves that a candidate for admission to their
'profession' was possessed of good average abilities and had
received the education of a gentleman. The government was
convinced that the great public schools provided the best background for the commissioned ranks of the army, the Under-
Secretary for War told the House of Commons in 1857, 'not
only in an intellectual point of view, but also in the habits of
discipline and subordination, in the healthy and manly tone
of feeling, which it encouraged - the best preparation for a
military career', and a past Secretary of War, who at a later
date was destined to become Secretary for War again, added,[35]

there is no officer in the world like the English gentleman -
I do not mean in the sense in which that term is sometimes
used, applying only to the landed gentry, but a man of
liberal education, who possesses the advantages which result
from such an education. In this sense, looking to the constitution of the English army, I think gentlemen will always
make the best officers.

When, then, Lord Cardwell said of his 1871 Bill that what
the government wanted to secure was 'that there should be an
open career for young men' so that 'any parent may send his
son into the Army with the clear prospect that if he deserves
it he will rise in rank, entirely apart from any reference to the
pecuniary means of his parent',[36] it seems reasonably clear
that the career he had in mind was 'open' only to those young
men whose 'parent' possessed the pecuniary means to make
gentlemen of them in the first place and to send them to a
university, an Arts degree from which would qualify them for
a commission without having to sit the army's own entrance
examination, or to a 'crammer' or a private educational institution which would supplement their public school education with
intensive preparation for army admission.[37]

No doubt there were, as James Fitzjames Stephen had put it,
'scores of men in our great manufacturing towns who, having

pushed their way to great wealth and influence by mere force
of character, would willingly buy the refinement of mind and
manner which early education would have given them at the
price of half their fortunes',[38] but the careers of the upper
middle classes, of which that of the army officer has been taken
here as the exemplar, could be entered only by those who had
already had purchased for them that necessary 'refinement
of mind and manner' of the cultivated classes. These were,
for the most part, not the sons of capitalist merchants and
industrialists, pushing their way forward by private enterprise
in the markets for labour and commodities, but the sons of
what the Secretary of War in 1860 called 'the middle classes,
by which I mean the professional classes',[39] who had made
their way forward, not through the accumulation and reinvest-
ment of capital in a business which they themselves had made
viable in the face of competition from other capitalists, but
through persuading the senior members of their profession,
by their conduct at one level, that there was no reason to keep
them there when a vacancy occurred on the grade above for
which they were the first in the line of seniority. The Victorian
'Gospel of Success' - or, 'How to get on in Victorian England'
- was less a matter of knowledge as power for such men,[40] than
that of education as opportunity.

Technological and organizational requirements, of course,
sometimes necessitated their attendance at purely vocational
courses of instruction. The navy, for example, had found it
necessary to establish an academy for seamanship as early as
1729 and the army created a Staff College in 1854. In this
sense it is true that the first schools of engineering and
technology were military, not civil: 'staff colleges preceded
business schools'.[41] The most striking feature of these upper-
middle-class vocations, however, was that whenever it was
admitted that some kind of vocational education was necessary
- so that, for example, army officers might 'understand the
fundamental principles of the operations in which they were
engaged, so that they might be enabled to avoid mistakes, and
prevent unnecessary sacrifice of life' - there was still no
relaxation of the principle that this was best built upon a
public school background,[42] and indeed the Regulations for
examinations at the Royal Military Academy at Woolwich and at
the Royal Military College at Sandhurst, which were both 'a
somewhat unsatisfactory mixture of a public school and a
military college' and for which the age of entry was not raised
to eighteen until 1858,[43] were drawn up by the Council of
Military Education, after discussions with the headmasters of
'some of the chief public schools of the country, with the view
of ascertaining the amount of knowledge which might fairly
be expected of young men of 17', even if these Regulations
had subsequently to be modified because of the high failure
rate.[44]

What this all added up to, in brief, was the concept of a

career ladder for boys of much the same upper-class and
upper-middle-class backgrounds, up which they climbed step
by step in very much the same fashion as they had moved from
being first-form fags to becoming sixth-form prefects. A few
fell out at each level and a few moved on more quickly than
their fellows – one, indeed, rising eventually to the very top,
as field marshal, First Lord of the Admiralty, Archbishop of
Canterbury or Lord Chancellor – just as one alone at a time
became School Captain. The distinction between this top man
and all the others from the ranks through which he in his time
had moved was simply that of a leader among social equals,
primus inter parcs, just as the faster moving among them
generally were seen as no more than an elite within the single
class of gentlemen, an elite of that politically significant,
politically ruling class, whose members were very much linked
together by birth, intermarriage and other family connections,
and increasingly at this time by the tie of the old school.

Historians of the nineteenth century have been somewhat
divided over the nature of a so-called 'revolution' in British
government during the mid-Victorian years, occasioned
apparently by the onset of industrialization and urbanization,
and exemplified by a series of 'false-starts' in the creation
of a welfare state along twentieth-century lines. Explanations
for what happened have been debated in terms of whether
these modifications in the machinery of government and administration were a consequence of philosophical ideas about the
nature of the good, or a better society, mainly propagated by
the Utilitarians, or whether they constituted merely the self-
generating process of administrative growth by an 'empire-
building' elite of civil servants –- or alternatively, whether
they were the outcome of a successful struggle by a rising,
capitalist and chiefly industrial 'middle' class against the
entrenched authority of the landed aristocracy and its dependants, or were the inevitable result of a search for cheaper
and more efficient ways of coping with the growing class
consciousness and militancy of the industrial proletariat. Most
of the arguments in such debates among historians have focused
on what can be discovered to have occurred in those departments of state most directly concerned with 'the problems' of
'the people' – police and prisons, the Poor Laws, the Factory
Acts, and public health.[45] Rarely have the controversialists
paid much attention to the history of military administration
where most aspects of this 'revolution' may also be recognized.

Yet, the plethora of parliamentary debates, Select Committees
and Royal Commissions both before, and more frequently, after
the Crimean War, indicate the extent to which governments of
different political persuasions and a parliament always to some
degree hostile to the existence of a standing army in peace-
time were troubled by public expenditure on the forces of the
Crown and the efficiency of the state's military services. Just
as the Northcote-Trevelyan Report on the civil service had

emphasized 'the great and increasing accumulation of public
business' as requiring 'an efficient body of permanent officers'
to carry it out,[46] so army reformers might have referred explicitly to the great and growing accumulation of military commitments which similarly required an 'efficient' body of officers
to deploy the men under their command. The purely demographic facts of the government's responsibilities, for all that
they did not determine the direction in which administrative
reforms 'must' move, clearly made some sort of reform inevitable. Between 1851 and 1871, whereas the total male population
of England and Wales grew by 26 per cent, the number recorded
as 'effectives' in the army, the navy and the marines, at home
and abroad, increased by as much as 39 per cent and the army
alone was not much behind the other services, increasing by
35.5 per cent.[47] Although the number of such 'effectives'
obviously fluctuated quite unlike the relatively steady growth
in the population because of a public policy which was influenced
by what Brigadier-General Sir Robert Biddulph called the 'hot
and cold fits of the British public, alternating between panic
and parsimony',[48] the general impression of the overseas
commitments of these years in India, China, Abyssinia and New
Zealand,[49] quite apart from involvement in the Crimean War,
entailed a fluctuating, but in the long run ever-increasing,
expenditure on a military service employing ever more men and
their officers, financed out of general taxation.

Between these two Census years the number of army officers
alone increased from 6,593 to 9,838, while officers in the Royal
Navy and the marines increased from 3,939 to only 4,423; yet
for present purposes the army officer increase of 49 per cent
compared with that of 12 per cent for the fellow officers in the
other two armed services, is of much less significance than
the fact that such an increase in absolute numbers would
necessarily intensify the difficulties of those senior officers in
the army, the field marshal and the full generals, who had to
recruit the kind of men they wanted as junior officers and had
to rely on purely personal contacts for advice on such recruitment. Similar considerations, no doubt, applied to the civil
service which grew from 34,000 to 54,000 (+ 38 per cent) in
these years.[50] From time to time throughout the middle years
of the century some ministers and Secretaries of State had
complained that patronage placed a great burden on them; it
'had probably become a nuisance rather than a privilege'[51] to
them to have to cope with requests and become 'involved in
often a lengthy correspondence'[52] with, and about, people
whom they hardly knew. The Duke of Wellington, indeed, as
early as 1842, had gone to the length of having special slips
printed 'positively and distinctly' declining to solicit favours
'most particularly for a Gentleman of whom he knows Nothing,
not even whether or not he is trustworthy'.[53] The public
school cachet was an appropriate alternative to them for this
lack of reliable personal knowledge when there were so many

vacancies to fill, so many candidates to fill them.

Thus what is sometimes described as the abolition of patronage was in effect its convérsion into a new form of patronage, whereby the individual with the post to offer entrusted the responsibility for reliable recommendation to the headmasters and housemasters of the public schools and to the tutors of Oxford and Cambridge Colleges, who, by the middle decades of the century, formed 'a veritable network of personal contacts within the public schools community' which was 'often a factor in determining staff appointments and transfers'.[54] What in no way occurred at this time was the abandonment of patronage altogether and its replacement by some kind of genuinely open competition in which the sons of other sections of the community - and in particular the sons of that part of the 'middle class' to which industrial and economic historians have paid most attention - were accorded roughly equal opportunities, alongside the sons of their more traditionally recruited political masters, for obtaining a place on the lowest ranks of the hierarchy of established command.[55] For example, over three-quarters of the boys born between 1850 and 1860 who were sent to Winchester, and about whom the relevant information is available, had fathers who were gentlemen of leisure, bishops and other clergymen, barristers and solicitors, officers in the army and navy as compared with 1.2 per cent in manufacturing industry. In their turn some three-fifths of these boys entered the same 'occupations' as their fathers, while only 2.8 per cent of them became manufacturers.[56] Those men who first showed evidence of deliberately restricting the size of their families in a statistically significant fashion, that is to say, contained amongst their numbers a strikingly large proportion in these hierarchically organized career structures, financed largely out of public taxation. What they had to offer their prospective brides was a secure income, not the relative insecurity of the entrepreneurial exploitation of capital.[57]

The particular emphasis here on a meritocracy and the implications of this and the previous chapters should not be misunderstood. If these men, as fathers, had an interest in keeping their hostages to fortune within manageable proportions so that they could commit resources to a period of lengthy education for their sons, their wives - as mothers - had an interest in family limitations also. Quite apart from the obvious likelihood that they would be concerned for their sons to acquire the valued status of membership of the same ruling class as themselves and their husbands, there can hardly be any doubt about the advantages to these women personally, as to women generally, of fewer conceptions. Nevertheless, the important point to notice is that there was nothing especially new in this respect in the circumstances of the mothers who had smaller families at this time. When this question is looked at from the point of view of the Victorian women who were, in the arguments of these pages, 'the pioneers' of family limitation,

it is difficult to appreciate why their part in the decision to
limit the number of their conceptions has been called 'indeed
crucial',[58] since this implies either that wives made this decision
themselves in the light of the apathy of their husbands, who
presumably are thought not to have cared much about it either
way since the care of the children was their wife's responsibility,
or that previously wives of a similar social position had actually
wanted larger families.

The alternative argument, that previously women were fatalistic but now simply became 'modern' in their 'outlook toward
life and death' and hence 'demanded better health for themselves and, relatedly, for their children',[59] cannot be regarded
as at all relevant in this respect – even were the evidence
about the 'demands' of these 'silent' women less ambiguous
than it is – because the outcome of their hypothesized changed
attitude does not seem to have led to any better health on their
part than that which was also the experience of their husbands.
Possibly it was the case that the medical profession, then as
later, was 'slow to recognize the real needs of women',[60] as
no doubt were the husbands of all those who continued to have
many conceptions, but what is clear is that such 'real needs'
in this respect were met only when the requirements of the
wives coincided with the desire of their husbands for a smaller
number of boys to put through school and university into
meritocratic careers; and this was when their standard of
living which previously had contained the ideal of the appropriate education for a gentleman who was not obliged to earn a
living had now become associated with the process whereby
gentlemen, who were so obliged, were selected for advancement to the most prestigious and well-paid offices of state.

In so far as frequency of conceptions may be interpreted as
an indication that the requirements of the wives of such gentlemen were *not* the 'crucial' factor in family limitation at this
time, some evidence may be obtained from Charles Ansell's
1871 study of what he called the Upper and Professional
classes.[61] Some 52.3 per cent of the wives of his respondents,
who had been spinsters when they married and who had children, bore a child within the first year after the marriage and
88.2 per cent within the first two years. 12.3 per cent of them,
who had ten or more children, bore a second child within two
years of the marriage, 47.1 per cent within three years, and
67.3 per cent within four years. Most first children, that is,
were born in the first year, most second in the third year,
and most third children in the fourth year, most fifth children
in the eighth year, most eighth children in the thirteenth
year,[62] although such cases were much more exceptional because
where the couple had reached the end of the wife's child-
bearing period[63] by the time of the survey, the average size
of their families was 5.17 children, born alive.[64] Thus it is
reasonably clear that Ansell's 'sample', coming from roughly
the same period as the marriages included in the left-hand

column of Table 4.1 (p.40), were very similar kinds of people
to the 'pioneers' of family limitation whose attitudes have been
the concern of these pages. 50 per cent of them had their
first birth in 0.96 years after the wedding. This contrasts with
the median of 1.34 years in the case of a number of Swedish
women in three large parishes between 1841 and 1890 where
family limitation is 'unlikely to have been practised'.[65] The
median interval for successive births to these Swedish women
was 2.50 years. Ansell's figures are not comparable; nevertheless, the median for all his subsequent births is 4.78 years
from the marriage, which might be read to imply that more use
of birth control occurred after the birth of the first child.

Much more striking, however, is the relative frequency of
the births, the average number of years to the first birth
being 1.32, to the second 3.02, to the third 4.84, to the fourth
6.69, to the fifth 8.53, to the sixth 10.28, etc., that is, rising roughly from 1.3 to 1.5 to 1.6 to 1.7 years between births
over the reproductive cycle.[66] What these figures might be
read to imply, were other information not available, is that
these Victorian couples were not practising birth control at all;
yet the average size of their completed families indicates that
a large proportion of them must necessarily have done so. Thus,
the figures can only mean that they were practising a particular
form of family limitation, namely, allowing what Louis Henry
has called their 'natural fertility'[67] to operate up to the point at
which the number of children in their families had reached a
maximum which they did not want to exceed - what demographers refer to as 'parity-dependent fertility'[68] - or, more
likely, when they had as many boys as they believed they
could afford to educate, regardless of whatever views they may
or may not have had about the ideal size of a family. Thereafter they avoided conception.

Support for this conclusion comes from the further fact from
Ansell's survey that in families of only one child the mean age
of the mother was 31.08 when it was born, in families of 2 or 3
children her mean age was 34.21 when the last child was born,
in families to 4 or 5 children 37.04, and so on, down to 16
or more children when the mother's mean age was 44.32. All
these figures are, of course, for families in which both the
parents had survived the child-bearing age of the mother.[69]
Such a form of family limitation is compatible with the idea that
these couples were concerned that the mother should not have
too great a burden of child rearing, just as it is with the idea
that too many boy children were expensive to educate. What it
is not compatible with is the notion that these parents were
alarmed by the mother's burden of child-bearing, at least in
the sense of the frequency of her conceptions. Some degree
of awareness of 'the real needs of women' may have motivated
the paterfamilias at this time but the actual practice of family
limitation would seem to have followed more readily from his
recognition of his own - economic - requirements in this matter

than of her hygienic ones. The 'modern'[70] conception of family
planning in the sense of the spacing of births cannot be inferred from the behaviour of these upper-middle-class families.

For this reason it seems more sensible to regard the attitude
of the wives and mothers in these families as still largely
'fatalistic' at this time rather than 'modern', provided that it
is recognized that this fatalism, like Queen Victoria's, was
probably tempered by some desire for relief from frequent *and*
successive child-bearing. When her uncle congratulated her
on her own pregnancy within the first year of the Royal marriage and wished her many more of the same, she replied,[71]

> I think, dearest uncle, you cannot *really* wish me to be the
> 'Mama d'une *nombreuse* famille', for I think you will see with
> me the great inconvenience a *large* family would be to us all,
> and particularly to the country, independent of the hard-
> ships and inconvenience to myself; men never think, at least
> seldom think, what a hard task it is for us women to go
> through this *very often*. God's will be done, and if He decrees
> that we are to have a great number of children, why we must
> try to bring them up as useful and exemplary members of
> society.

So long as traditional Anglican morality continued to dominate
the lives of these women it is difficult to appreciate how they
could have rejected the Malthusian view of the population
question, as set out in chapter 2. 'Moral restraint' within marriage rather than conception is likely to have been the means
they would have favoured to prevent conceptions, to terminate
their families when they were 31 or 34 or 37. The question of
significance, therefore, is whether their husbands also practised moral restraint, or whether they revolted in some way
against the Pauline teachings of the church.

7 THE APOSTASY OF THE PATERFAMILIAS

The emphasis in the last two chapters on the significance of a
public school and university education for the sons of at least
the high status 'pioneers' of family limitation adds further
weight to the implications of the third chapter above, namely,
that the secularist advocates of neo-Malthusianism can hardly
be regarded as having been responsible for the onset of such
family limitation amongst this section of the population, or
indeed in the population generally. For all that the secularists
themselves might reasonably be assumed to have practised
contraception of some kind, their effectiveness in keeping the
size of their own families small could not have influenced significantly the 1911 fertility statistics of couples in the upper
working and lower middle classes, in which categories most of
the secularists would have been classified, because their numbers were proportionately too small. Nor do these statistics
suggest much beyond the rather obvious conclusion that the
neo-Malthusian message does not seem to have got across very
well to the parents in these sections of the population, and even
less to those much nearer the poverty line, to whom it was
mainly directed. Thus, the notion that secularism as such was
an important factor in the advent of the small family can be
upheld only if it is assumed that the upper and upper middle
classes of the 1850s and 1860s practised birth control because
they had come to accept as valid for themselves the teachings
of a muscular anti-Christian moral code, propagated by members of what they regarded as the 'lower orders' and by a
few unorthodox 'radicals' from their own ranks; and this does
not seem very plausible.

By contrast, what may now be provisionally concluded is
that because of their ideal of what a civilized 'calling' to a
vocation entailed for their male members of the ruling class -
that is, public service, collective responsibility and esprit de
corps amongst meritocratic equals, led by the primus inter
pares - and because of the way in which recruitment to such a
meritocracy had come to be based on a new form of patronage -
collective patronage resting upon the influential support of
the public school teacher and the college tutor of their boys -
upper-class and upper-middle-class parents had a clear
economic interest in restricting the number of male children
born to, and reared by, them. To the degree that the kind of
future-time perspective which such restriction entailed was not
at all incompatible with the Anglican conception of prudence,

there was no special reason why these parents had necessarily
to embrace secularism before they could take steps to limit the
size of their families; but in so far as it is possible that they
went further in this respect than the principle of moral restraint, interpreted by Malthus and Archbishop Sumner as the
relevant characteristic of Pauline Christianity, to practise
forms of birth control which Anglican leaders could not con-
done because those practices made marriage 'unholy',[1] some
attempt must now be made to decide how far the 'pioneers' of
family limitation regarded these as nevertheless quite compatible with church attendance, no matter what their leaders
thought. Alternatively, what still remains to consider is to
what extent they gradually came to find themselves more and
more out of sympathy with the church rather than, as was the
case with the secularists, in direct confrontation with it on
this issue.

The problem is clearly that of arriving at some idea of their
depth of commitment to the ideals of the Anglican church, and,
in particular, to the ideal of sexual behaviour which it propagated, during the relevant period. This is complicated by
the evidence that, from at least the time of the early evangelicals, the members of these classes had been regularly
castigated, albeit in very general terms, for their shallowness
in this respect. In 1797, for example, William Wilberforce had
complained that the opinions of the middle and higher classes
about standards of right and wrong were carried out independently of Christianity, as he understood it. These standards
were not formed[2]

> from the perusal of the word of God. The Bible lies on the
> shelf unopened; and they would be wholly ignorant of its
> contents, except for what they heard occasionally at church,
> or for the faint traces which their memories may still retain
> of the lessons of their earliest infancy.

Some fifty years later the editor of the 'Nonconformist' was
still complaining about the same classes' lack of study of the
Bible. The aristocracy, he claimed, were only nominally
Christians.

> Their ordinary habits are well known. Their social customs,
> their favourite pursuits, their amusements, their indul-
> gences, the general tenor of their life, the pervading tone
> of their conversation, are such as must lead the most charit-
> able to the conclusion that as a class, presenting, however
> some notable exceptions, their religion is anything rather
> than sympathy with God, as expressed in the purport and
> provisions of the gospel.

Other sections of the upper and middle classes 'within the
pale of the Establishment' were not much better in this respect.
Although 'their morals are usually decent - the duties of their
domestic relationships are fairly attended to', the large majority
of them[3]

> know scarcely anything of religion but a decent observance

of outward forms .... The suspicion seldom or never worries
their minds, that they are not, in the main, what Christianity
meant them to be. They live in unconcern, and they die in
hope - and they do both without having caught a glimpse
even of the grand moral purport of God's message to their
souls.

How are such complaints from a militant minority to be interpreted in the light of the conviction of many mid-Victorians,
as of many twentieth-century historians, that the clergy of
the 1860s were, in Owen Chadwick's words, 'more zealous than
the clergy of 1830, conducted worship more reverently, knew
their people better, understood a little more theology, said
more prayers, celebrated sacraments more frequently, studied
more Bible, preached shorter sermons'?[4] How can the complaints
of militants, like the evangelicals, be reconciled with the view
that they had had so much influence on those they wrote about
that, by the mid-Victorian period, Bible-reading at home and
family prayers had become much more common amongst members
of the Anglican church, even amongst those in the upper
classes for whom morning prayers, with the family on one side
of the breakfast table and the servants on the other, have
been seen as symptomatic of the 'fundamentally religious'
character of the English at this time?[5] How far does the continuing criticism about the shallowness of the upper classes
conflict with the twentieth-century opinion that by this time
many preachers had become so popular with churchgoers that
the question Victorians of the privileged classes asked each
other on Sunday was not 'will you, or won't you go to church?'
but 'where will you go to church?'.[6]

Part of the difficulty in answering such questions lies in the
very nature of the 'samples' of privileged Victorians who are
used to support the arguments of one side or the other in this
analysis. Kitson Clark was surely correct to claim that 'from
the record of a good many personal histories', it would certainly appear 'increasingly more unlikely that a highly educated
man would be a Christian' from the late 1860s onwards.[7] Yet
it is equally correct to emphasize that, unfortunately, very few
indeed of the 19,222 men in the Registrar-General's Class I,
who had married before 1871 and were still alive with their
wives forty years later, or of the 6,887 'pioneers' of family
limitation amongst them, have left behind personal histories of
any kind, let alone biographies of sufficiently accurate detail
to indicate whether or not they had been either highly educated
or ever committed Christians. Hence the problem is one of
inferring from very inconclusive and often contradictory
evidence just how many of them by the late 1860s might be said
to have been subjected to a Christian upbringing which they
had by this time renounced.

The public schoolboys amongst them, of course, may be
assumed almost certainly to have experienced chapel preaching
by their clergymen teachers and headmasters who, long before

Thomas Arnold, had agreed on the paramount significance of
the chapel for their schools, even if few of these clergymen
themselves preached with such fervour as the headmaster of
Rugby with his conviction that it was necessary to inculcate
godliness, as well as an understanding of the literature of
Greece and Rome, in his pupils.[8] It is also very likely that, at
least as adults, they would have been aware that the Anglican
church of their day was much embattled, its leaders embroiled
in religious controversy after religious controversy, its
theological doctrines under regular critical assessment, not
only by men outside 'the Establishment', but by many within,
although it is very possible that this largely theological furore
was unintelligible to the uninitiated amongst the laity, despite
what the 'Spectator' of 25 May 1861, called a certain 'taste for
discussing half-understood theology' on the part of middle-
class churchgoers,[9] which was surely shared by members of
other classes. In particular, ex-public schoolboys were almost
certain to have come across many newspaper accounts and
articles in journals about whether or not Bible criticism had
made it possible to determine whether the teachings of the Bible
could be understood quite literally. The intensification of both
devotion and doubt, of what, in 1840, James Martineau had
called 'a simultaneous increase, in the very same class of minds,
of theological doubt and of devotional affection', so that 'there
is far less *belief*, yet far more *faith*, than there was twenty
years ago'[10] could hardly have not been obvious also to the
'pioneers' of family limitation in the 1860s.

Yet, it should not be assumed from all this that these
'pioneers' necessarily applied the arguments from these controversies to their own lives in such a way as to make them
change their sexual habits. If they had not really been much
influenced by what was in the Bible, or what was pronounced
from the pulpit before they came to learn about these intellectual and moral controversies, it does not seem plausible to
conclude that they changed their customary practices in
response to the furore. No doubt some of them experienced
extreme anxiety in a crisis of faith, 'a tragedy of unbelief',
not very different from the fictional accounts of soul-searching
by those who came intellectually and emotionally to reject their
earlier Christian orthodoxy in so many novels of the period;[11]
but the immediate point at issue is just how many Victorians
went through psychological periods of despair of this kind and
how many of them were in fact more like Leslie Stephen who,
on resigning his tutorship in 1862 and leaving Cambridge for
a career in journalism in 1864, wrote in a note-book on 26
January 1865:[12]

> my faith in anything like religion has been gradually growing
> dimmer. I can scarcely believe that two and a half years ago
> I was still reading prayers as a parson, and that little more
> than a year ago I was preaching. I now believe in nothing,
> to put it shortly; but I do not the less believe in morality,

etc. etc.. I mean to live and die like a gentleman if possible.
While his biographer can hardly be disputed for alleging that
Stephen 'suffered acutely while his doubts were taking shape
and urging him to action', this suffering was occasioned not by
intellectual and moral uncertainty but by his sense of aliena-
tion[13] from his Trinity Hall colleagues, and other Cambridge
friends, and by the grief he was convinced 'his determination
would cause to some of his family who were nearest and dearest
to him'.[14] Leslie Stephen, of course, had been educated at Eton,
not at Rugby, and he is said to have been fond of recalling
that there was none of the 'cant' about Christian behaviour
and Christian gentlemanliness at Eton;[15] but this, if more
generally true, only makes it more difficult to decide whether
commitment to Anglican doctrine and Anglican teaching on
morality on the part of upper-class and upper-middle-class
males was sufficiently profound as to imply that the description
of 'the age' as witnessing 'a crisis of faith' or even a crisis of
'plausibility'[16] also meant that they, too, personally experienced
this crisis in their own lives, or whether such crises left them
more or less unmoved because their regular church attendance,
and even their family prayers, were little more than a conces-
sion to social convention, disguising that lack of religious
fervour which, their Christian critics sometimes claimed,
marked them off as more alienated from Christianity than the
people of 'the choicest society in several of the capitals of
Europe'.[17]

One fact which is of direct relevance to the present theme
seems reasonably certain. Although the number of Church of
England churches and chapels increased from 14,077 in 1851
to 15,522 in 1871 and although the number of Anglican clergymen rose from 16,194 to 19,411 over the same period,[18] there
is evidence that relatively fewer of the new entrants, ordained
as deacons, came from ruling-class families at this time. For
example, whereas in the 1850s just over 70 per cent of the men
who became deacons had been educated at Oxford or Cambridge,
in the 1860s the proportion had fallen nearer to 60 per cent
and the proportions entering without having been to university
at all increased correspondingly steadily over the ten-year
period.[19] Similarly, to take once again the Wykehamites as an
example of public schoolboys at this time, whereas 121 of those
who had been born in 1820-9 entered the church (34 per cent
of the total), only 97 (26.2 per cent) of those born in 1830-9
and 82 (20.2 per cent) of those born in 1840-9 followed in their
footsteps. Of this last cohort of Winchester boys the church
still took the largest single category, but the decline over
twenty years is quite marked, especially when it is noted that
school teaching for the last two generations of boys increased
from 8 (2.1 per cent) to 31 (7.6 per cent), at a time when the
public schools had begun to recruit teachers from outside the
ranks of the church.[20]

The significance of this decline in recruitment to the

Anglican church from the ranks of the upper and upper-middle
classes should be interpreted in terms of the relationship between the other members of such families and the clergyman or
clergymen amongst their numbers. No doubt there had always
been some clergymen earlier who had taken orders for the
same kind of reason that had motivated Leslie Stephen when he
became a deacon in 1855: 'my real motive was that I was very
anxious to relieve my father of the burthen of supporting
me .... By taking the tutorship I became independent, and
after my degree I never cost my father anything';[21] but whatever doubts clergymen may have had, whatever crisis of faith
and plausibility they may have gone through, it is hardly
likely that many of them would have remained in the church,
eventually to become bishops[22] or even to reach more exalted
clerical stations, had their commitment to the teachings of
their superiors been as lukewarm as Stephen's. This means
that where their relationship with the other male members of
their family was close, open expression of doubt or lack of
belief, open behaviour in conflict with church teaching, was
likely to have been inhibited by the very desire not to cause
distress to another member of the family for whom they had
strong affection; and what seems probable for clergymen seems
equally probable for other members of families with clergymen
brothers, or even more remote relatives in the church.

Of course, there are examples of brothers, like John and
Francis Newman, whose lives, religious and secular, ran in
separate and even hostile channels, but there are at least as
many where it is clear that no such abrupt and open break of
family affection took place, so that it may reasonably be argued
that church attendance and family prayers in those cases where
there was a clergyman in the family, especially in this period
of much greater Christian zeal on the part of the Anglican
clergy, indicated more than a purely nominal adherence to
religious beliefs on the side of that family generally. Hence,
when such a family ceased to have this kind of intimate church
linkage because of the unwillingness of any of its younger
males to take Holy Orders, commitment to Anglican ideals may,
equally reasonably, be interpreted to have waned within that
family as compared with its previous dedication. For some
upper-class and upper-middle-class boys, who were at school
and university during this period of the crisis of faith, it
may have been the case, as the 'Quarterly Review' put it in
1862, that[23]

> the shock which all religious faith has received from the
> strifes, the extravagancies, the treacheries, the disappoint-
> ments, the oscillations of religious controversy, and, most
> of all, from the poisonous scepticism now disseminated even
> by teachers and authorities within the church itself - all
> this has so disturbed, and perplexed, and disheartened the
> most earnest and acute young minds, that they dare not
> devote themselves to the Ministry,

and consequently sought careers elsewhere; but it may also
have been the case that even more of these earnest and acute
young minds at this time had never considered the ministry in
career terms at all, preferring rather to enter one of the other
professions, civil or military, which the meritocratic emphases
within the public schools themselves and the universities promoted. As David Newsome has pointed out, in the context of
the nature of the evidence about the hypothesized 'loss of
faith' and its impact on the willingness of young men to become
deacons, 'it is easier to find general assertions that more men
found it difficult during the second half of the reign of Queen
Victoria than to find instances of men who found it difficult
and told men why';[24] and this is also true of the twenty years
or so up to 1869.

All that the evidence suggests is that in those families which
had never had this kind of church connection the possibility
that one of the sons might become a clergyman was probably
never raised at this time, and in those families which had by
now ceased to have such a connection the question was probably
no longer raised. On the face of it this suggests that the upper
and upper middle classes simply 'drifted' into a kind of 'unconscious secularism', similar to that which Mann had ascribed
to the urban working classes in 1851, because in the 1850s
and 1860s they too were so very much 'engrossed by the
demands, the trials or the pleasures of the passing hour',
even if they were far less ignorant of their futures.[25] Yet, as
this reference to the future indicates, such a drifting into an
abandonment of a religious faith, once held, might in part
have been a consequence of the impact made on the families
of such classes by the ruling-class meritocratic emphasis on
the career ascent up gentlemanly hierarchies, since it presupposed a future-time orientation over a man's working life,
derived also from his educational experiences, which was
essentially this-worldly rather than other-worldly in the traditional Christian sense. Although it would be altogether too
fanciful to suggest that such an experience of earning a living
in a career was responsible for turning the thoughts of committed Christians towards their realizable destinies in this life
and away from the unknowable destinies speculated to be
definite in the next, it is to be noted that the question of how
to ascertain merit for advancement in a career was very much
a matter of public concern at the very same time as Christians,
and churchmen especially, were debating the question of
whether or not human beings could be said to 'deserve' eternal
punishment for sins of which they were hardly aware, as
contrasted with an alternative religious view, frequently
expressed at this time by Christians outside the Anglican
church, that the condition of human beings in this respect was
hopeful because 'the law of God's moral universe, as known to
us, is that of Progress'.[26]

On the whole, that is to say, most churchmen and the

Anglican church officially continued to support the doctrine of
the Prayer Book and the Creeds, partly it would seem because
the terror of damnation was believed to be the main motive force
impelling believers to follow Christian morality. 'People risk too
much now,' wrote Edward Pusey to John Keble on 14 February
1864. 'They would risk everything if they did not dread an
eternity of suffering.'[27] This, no doubt, was why he had
recently been mainly instrumental in the drafting of a Declaration, eventually signed by some 11,000 clergymen of the Church
of England, which they presented to the Archbishop of
Canterbury on 12 July of that year and in which it was maintained 'without reserve or qualification' that 'the "punishment"
of the "cursed" equally with the "life" of the "righteous" is
"everlasting"'.[28]

The occasion for this Declaration was a decision by the
Judicial Committee of the Privy Council that Henry Wilson,
Vicar of Great Stoughton, had not contravened the doctrine of
the Church of England in expressing the hope that there was
an intermediate state after death which would enable all to
escape eternal condemnation,[29] although the Dean of the Court
of Arches had censured him for asserting this in apparent
contradiction to the doctrine of the Prayer Book and the Creeds.
What Wilson had argued, in his contribution to 'Essays and
Reviews', published four years earlier, was that[30]

if we look abroad in the world and regard the neutral
character of the multitude, we are at a loss to apply to them,
either the promises, or the denunciations of revelation.....
The Roman Church has imagined a *limbus infantium*; we must
rather entertain a hope that there shall be found, after the
great adjudication, receptacles suitable for those who shall
be infants, not as to years of terrestial life, but as to spiritual development – nurseries as it were and seed-grounds,
where the under-developed may grow up under new conditions, the stunted may become strong, and the perverted be
restored. And when the Christian Church, in all its branches,
shall have fulfilled its sublimary office, and its Founder shall
have surrounded His Kingdom to the Great Father – all, both
small and great, shall find a refuge in the bosom of the Universal Parent, to repose, or be quickened into higher life, in
the ages to come, according to his Will.

Reviewing the book in the 'Quarterly Review', the bishop of
Oxford had claimed that Wilson was here describing 'the poor
Buddhist dream of re-absorption into the Infinite' and that in
his contribution, as in that by Professor Jowett, 'there is an
absolute lack of all perception of what sin is, and so of what
atonement is – a dreaming vagueness of pantheistic pietism,
which is but the shallow water leading on to a profounder and
darker atheism'.[31] Samuel Wilberforce was not alone in this
condemnation of 'Essays and Reviews'; and the bishops, meeting
in London on 1 February 1861, came to the almost unanimous
conclusion that they should do something about the book because

of the very many complaints which individually they had
received, even if by the time the Lower House of Convocation
had decided that there was sufficient ground for a synodical
condemnation, proceedings in the Court of Arches had already
been taken against one of the clerical authors of the 'Essays'
and a few months later proceedings were taken against Wilson.[32]
The particular details of these events are of no special concern
here. The important point is that there was considerable support among Anglican churchmen at this time for the opinion that
Wilson's view of the Canonical Scriptures was not truly consistent with his remaining a clergyman of the Church of England.
In particular, his assertion that 'the word of God is contained
in the Scripture, whence it does not follow that it is co-
extensive with it',[33] they felt sure, must be condemned, and
the Bible once more pronounced to be wholly the word of God.
In this respect they probably agreed with Wilberforce, who in
his review had linked this remark by Wilson, which he found
'painful to quote', with the opinion of all the other Essayists,
and especially Jowett who had told his readers to 'interpret
the Scripture like any other book'.[34] Conscience and private
judgment, exclaimed Wilberforce, 'that is to say, every man's
own private conviction of what befits God and what befits himself, is for every man to override the Bible'. The 'great'
principle of the Essayists was that 'Holy Scripture is like any
other good book'.[35] This the churchmen were emphatic to deny,
and quietly overlooked the fact that Jowett himself, for example,
had confessed that 'no one who has a Christian feeling would
place classical on a level with sacred literature'.[36]

This reference to classical literature raises an issue which
was little more than referred to obliquely by the churchmen
in this debate, yet which might well have been of some importance for the teachings of the Anglican church on the question
of sin as the natural state of unregenerate man. As the headmaster of Rugby had put it in his opening contribution to the
'Essays',

> there were many points, undoubtedly, in which the early
> morality of the Greeks and Romans would well bear a com-
> parison with that of the Hebrews. In simplicity of life, in
> gentleness of character, in warmth of sympathy, in kind-
> ness to the poor, in justice to all men, the Hebrews could
> not have rivalled the best days of Greece. In reverence for
> law, in reality of obedience, in calmness under trouble, in
> dignity of self respect, they could not have rivalled the
> best days of Rome .... It is in the history of Rome rather
> than in the Bible that we find our models and precepts of
> political duty, and especially of the duty of patriotism ....
> To the Greeks we owe the corrective which conscience needs
> to borrow from nature. Conscience, startled at the awful
> truths which she has to reveal, too often threatens to with-
> draw the soul into gloomy and perverse asceticism: there is
> needed the beauty which Greece taught us to admire, to

show us another aspect of the Divine Attributes.
The classical authors, he continued, 'possess a charm quite
independent of genius. It is not their genius only which makes
them attractive. It is the classical life, the life of the people
of their day. It is the image, there only to be seen, of our
highest natural powers in their freshest vigour. It is the per-
vading sense of youthful beauty.'[137]

If, then, these authors, this way of life, were now regularly
used by the teachers of the young as models on which gentlemen should base their lives, how were they to reconcile such
excellence with that official view of the Scriptures which took
for granted, as Wilson put it in adverse criticism, 'that to know
and believe in Jesus Christ is in some sense necessary to
salvation'?[38] The signers of the Oxford Declaration were giving
a categorical affirmation to the view that the writers of the
classics were condemned to eternal damnation. This surely
meant that those Christians who took the Declaration seriously
were faced by at least a paradox, if not a clear contradiction,
between the 'truth' of the Scriptures and the 'morality' implied
in the teaching of the history and literature of pre-Christian
Greece and Rome. Some doubtless followed the lead of Wilberforce who refused to take seriously the position of the public
school educators: 'we trust earnestly, and we believe, that
the Head Master of Rugby is above the theories of the essayist
Dr. Temple, or we should tremble, not only for the faith, but
the morals of his pupils, who, if he were consistent with his
own principles, would be taught to substitute at will for the
letter of Divine Command so shifting and uncertain an arbiter',
as conscience.[39] Others, however, clearly regarded their conscience as a significant arbiter in their casuistical interpretation of the Bible, and for those of them who had been educated
in the major public schools, the arbiter they used had been
developed, at least to some degree, through the admiration
they had been taught to cultivate for the way of life of 'the
noblest' Greeks and Romans of them all, whom their classical
teachers had held up to them as exemplars of dutiful and
beautiful men of honour.

This aspect of the controversy over 'Essays and Reviews' has
been given prominence here because of the emphasis in it on
this conscience and this nobility of conduct. The controversy
more generally, of course, may be interpreted as a critical
stage in the intellectual history of the transition towards a
largely secularist conception of the universe, equally important
as, if not indeed more weighty than, the impact on the church
of the controversy over Darwin's 'Origin of Species' which
Wilberforce had precipitated a year earlier. Within the priest-
hood itself, at any rate, the issues which had been raised by
Temple and his collaborators over the interpretation of Scripture were much more central to their daily concerns than
arguments about the relationship between natural science and
theology, even if such 'outbreaks of anger' by Anglican

clergymen against both books might reasonably be said to be
'symptomatic of the disquiet within'.[40] The point of significance
here is that in the public school classrooms and chapels what
was taught as correct moral behaviour constituted an amalgam
of Christian precepts and classical exemplars, without reference
to any possible theological contradictions and paradoxes which
this amalgam implied.

It can hardly be correct, therefore, to think of the apostasy
of the paterfamilias in terms of a purely intellectual crisis of
doubt about the literal 'truth' of the Bible and 'therefore' of
its moral exhortations. To interpret the change in sexual
morality on the part of the 'pioneers' of family limitation by
reference to such 'crises' ignores the extent to which the validity and relevance of the church's exegesis of the purely Biblical
lessons on sexual intercourse, masturbation, prostitution and
kindred matters were not contradicted by the classical teacher's
interpretation of the domestic morality of the Greeks and Romans.
If, as Clark has put it, it is 'necessary to think of the years
which followed 1859 not as years of acute crisis of the mind but
rather as the years of the great religious revivals among people
who were probably little troubled by Darwinism and had certainly never read "Essays and Reviews"',[41] it is equally neces
sary to think of these years as those of a fundamental change
in the family-building practices of people who were just as
similarly placed with respect to these two questions. The important question, in brief, is how the Victorian paterfamilias,
postponing marriage and concerned about fitting his sons into
a gentlemanly career, came to regard the teaching of the
Anglican church as more or less irrelevant to everyday morality
in so far as the relationship between the sexes is concerned,
and what, therefore, he substituted for it in those years.

The most obvious characteristic of the Victorian period, in
so far as the conventional male conscience on this question was
concerned, was the way in which different standards of conduct
were applied according to whether the behaviour under consideration was deemed appropriate for a gentleman, as compared
with a lady, although it should be emphasized that there was
nothing especially novel, or Victorian, about this double standard of sexual morality. That 'public opinion', as Thompson
had called it, 'which men club together to form' had existed for
a long time, even if the Benthamites now had their characteristic way of describing it, namely, 'in almost all cases where
all the evil of a vice or a crime can be made to fall on the woman,
and the enjoyment can be reserved for the man, such an
arrangement of pain and pleasure is made'.[42] In the present
context the point to be emphasized is that in such cases one of
the main evils which the woman had to endure was the loss of
social status if she had been born and reared as a lady. Sexual
malpractice on her part resulted in her being thereafter referred to as a 'fallen woman' because there were no fallen ladies.
There were, it is true, no fallen gentlemen either, but this was

because there were no fallen men. Like Wolsey, as the 'Quarterly Review' put it, 'woman falls ... never to rise again'.
She suffers '*without hope*, without a chance of repentance, without the means of escape'.
A man was never in this position.[43]
Let us take one of the opposite sex who yields to the identical sin. Even in the midst of his career he keeps his place at home; there he has a pure atmosphere around him; he breathes sweet air; he does not fall into one unbroken course of dissoluteness - he is not without the pale of amendment; even his deeds of darkness are often times unknown, or perhaps there are rumours that he is somewhat wild - and by lips that no one dares to call impure the hope is expressed that he will soon have 'sown his wild oats'. And oftentimes this hope is fulfilled, he breaks off - he can break off - from folly; his blood cools; he steadies down, wonders at his former self, and lives in usefulness and repute.

Marriage for such a gentleman was regarded as the crucial step in settling down. Marriage cancelled out whatever follies had been accumulated on his record; but marriage could only work in this way, according to this form of public opinion, if the bride were innocent in this respect and, if not a virgin, a widow of unimpeachable past.

Some Victorian commentators, to be sure, looked upon their era as rather more respectable in this regard than that of their fathers or grandfathers. Grantley Berkeley, for example, accounted for the illegitimacy of his older brothers and the subsequent marriage of their father, the fifth Earl of Berkeley, to his former mistress, their mother, in terms of 'a youth and early manhood passed within the influence of several of the wildest rakes who figured most prominently in that licentious period',[44] that is, in the 1780s, just as no doubt some Georgians in his father's youth looked back to their youth at the time of the licentious period of the Restoration rakes. Most Victorians who wrote on this theme in the 1850s and 1860s, however, seem to have regarded their era as particularly difficult for the sexually respectable. 'Of the young men who are ruined by prostitution,' deplored 'Meliora' in its very first issue, 'a large number would have escaped the sin altogether, had they not been exposed to the incessant temptations thrown in their way by the women who infest the streets.'[45] In London, reasoned another author at this time, there were 650,000 women between 15 and 40; two-thirds of these were unmarried, and 'it is certain that at least one-sixth do prostitute themselves'. London has about one-fifth of all the 'abandoned' women in the United Kingdom, hence 'supposing the number of men who are personally involved in this sin to be in excess of the women as ten to one, and one cannot imagine it to be less than that, it would show that at least five-sevenths of the entire adult population of the United Kingdom are guilty of consorting with the prostitute'.[46]

These figures are not quoted here as in any sense being
evidence of the extent to which prostitution flourished at this
time in London, or in the United Kingdom.[47] Rather should they
be read to indicate how some Victorians had come to see the
London of their day as exhibiting all the features of a society
which was permissive in its sexual licentiousness. Prostitution,
they were convinced, was on the increase and it was therefore
important to sound an alarm to the respectable. 'Men, whose
labours on behalf of the needy, the ignorant, and the oppressed, are beyond praise,' complained 'Meliora', 'nevertheless
refuse to take an active part in applying a remedy to a social
disease, infinitely more dangerous and fatal to the well-being
of the body politic than many of the various evils which it is
their business and their glory to hunt out, and to endeavour
to cure.'[48] By this time it was undoubtedly the case, as Oliver
McGregor has asserted, that 'when Victorians spoke and wrote
to the "Great Social Evil" they referred, not to working class
housing, or the sanitary condition of manufacturing towns, or
the working lives of agricultural labourers, but to prostitution'.
Yet, as even he seems to have implied, concern about prostitution appears to have postdated the attempt to deal with the
physical environment and the economic and moral plight of
the labouring classes.[49]

The problem for such social reformers, especially for those
in the upper and upper middle classes, was that they were
only too conscious of the possibility that it was not only the
economic and moral circumstances of working-class girls which
contributed to some of them becoming prostitutes; an equally
important factor was the economic and moral circumstances of
their clients, some of them gentlemen in the same station of
life as those who were most appalled at the extent of the
'great social evil'. For example, in his attempt to account for
the existence of a three per cent 'redundancy' of females
William Rathbone Greg claimed that

so many women are single because so many men are pro-
fligate ... as matters are managed now, thousands of men
find it perfectly feasible to combine all the freedom, luxury,
and self-indulgence of a bachelor's career with the pleasure
of female society and the enjoyments they seek for there. As
long as this is so, so long, we fear, a vast proportion of the
best women in the educated classes - women especially who
have no dowry beyond their goodness and their beauty - will
be doomed to remain involuntarily single.

This occurred because the men who might have married them
were[50]

loth to resign the easy independence, the exceptional luxuries, the habitual indulgencies of a bachelor's career, for
the fetters of a wife, the burden and responsibility of children, and the decent monotony of the domestic hearth. They
dread family ties more than they yearn for family joys.

Some of these bachelors, it would appear, preferred the

expense of a mistress to that of a wife, possibly because she
would look after her patron more cheaply and, indeed, better
from his point of view than a wife since she would have no
false expectations about their relationship.[51] The point of significance here is that very few indeed of such mistresses, even
the 'seclusives' or 'prima donnas', as Bracebridge Hemyng
called them, had their origins in the more privileged sections
of society.[52]

These women are rarely possessed of education, although
they undeniably have ability. If they appear accomplished
you may rely that it is entirely superficial .... Their ranks
too are recruited from a class where education is not much
in vogue. The fallacies about clergymen's daughters and
girls from the middle classes forming the majority of such
women are long ago exploded; there may be some amongst
them, but they are few and far between.

The author of 'My Secret Life', who can hardly be regarded
as reticent about these matters on paper, no matter how
difficult Englishmen were to be persuaded to talk about their
illicit amours at this time,[53] soon learned that the ladies of his
own social standing were untouchable so far as his sexual
desires were concerned, especially because once 'fallen' the
penalties they had to face were considerable: a cousin, Mary-
Ann, who had been married to a cavalry officer in India and
who, having been parted from her husband for nearly a year,
had been caught in the act with a drummer boy, was sent home
to England where she drank herself to death. 'All about her
was kept quiet' in the family, although not so quiet among the
menfolk that Walter could not find out what had happened. In
any case, the inaccessibility of his lady acquaintances was of
minor significance to Walter because by the time he was thirteen
or fourteen he had already 'found out that servants were fair
game'.[54]

This easy accessibility of domestic servants, 'flattered by the
attention of the eldest son, or some friend of his staying in the
house',[55] and the more general 'sport' of seducing pretty young
girls in the lower orders of society appear to have been accepted as a deplorable aspect of the double standard of morality
by both clergymen and doctors writing about prostitution, however much they might otherwise have disagreed about remedies.
Not a few prostitutes, Logan wrote that he was sorry to say,
'who were excellent servants in respectable families, have been
seduced by sons, yea, sometimes by vile masters. These furnish some of the most lamentable cases.'[56] William Acton, similarly,
thought that it could not be denied[57]

by anyone acquainted with rural life, that seduction of girls
is a sport and a habit with vast numbers of men, married ...
and single, placed above the ranks of labour .... Many such
rustics of the middle class, and men of parellel grades in
country towns, employ a portion of their spare time in the
coarse, deliberate villany of making prostitutes .... Men who

themselves employ female labour, or direct it for others,
have always ample opportunities of choice, compulsion, sec-
recy and subsequent intimidation, should exposure be probable and disagreeable .... With these, and with the gentlemen whose *délassement* is the contamination of town servants
and *ouvrières*, the first grand engine is, of course, vanity
- the little more money that will get the poor girl a little more
dress, admiration, and envy than her equals enjoy.

Of course, it should not be assumed that working-class girls
became prostitutes solely because they were seduced by their
masters or the sons of their masters. Most of them, no doubt,
were seduced by members of their own class. Nevertheless,
the emphasis on seduction is important, not merely because
the writers on prostitution at this time stressed it so much, but
also because they related it to another theme about sexuality
which is of significance in the present context. This concerns
the assumption that women of all classes were not sexually
stimulated, except in rare cases, until they were aroused by
men. For example, in an article on prostitution Greg wrote:[58]

in men, in general, the sexual desire is inherent and spontaneous, and belongs to the condition of puberty. In the
other sex, the desire is dormant, if non-existent, till excited;
always till excited by undue familiarities; almost always till
excited by actual intercourse. Those feelings which coarse
and licentious minds are so ready to attribute to girls, are
almost invariably *consequences*. Women whose position and
education have protected them from exciting causes, constantly
pass through life without ever being cognizant of the prompt-
ings of the senses. Happy for them that it is so! We do not
mean to say that uneasiness may not be felt - that health may
not sometimes suffer; but there is no consciousness of the
cause. Among all the higher and middle classes, and, to a
greater extent than would commonly be believed, among the
lower classes also, where they either come of virtuous parents, or have been carefully brought up, this may be offer-
red as a general fact.

The overcrowded state of working-class homes and the 'commerce of the sexes' in the crowded state of working-class city
neighbourhoods were regularly regarded by writers of this
persuasion as contributing causes for the arousal of sexual
feelings in girls whose parents were unable therefore to keep
them innocent. Thus, the 'milliner-girl', Louise Baker, one of
his noble working-class Amazons, was described by Arthur
Mumby in terms of this kind. She, 'though a virtuous respectable girl, has not - nor can any such girl have - that *ignorance*
of vice which one desires in a lady'.[59]

It is not difficult to show that medical opinion on the question
of the sexual innocence of femina sensualis was never unanimous.[60] Acton expressed himself in 1857 in words almost identical to those of Greg in 1850 and added 'as a general rule, a
modest woman seldom desires any sexual gratification for herself.

She submits to her husband, but only to please him; and, but
for the desire for maternity, would far rather be relieved of
his attentions'.[61] Drysdale, on the other hand, argued that what
was sexually true of man was equally true of woman.

In her, too, the sexual organs are early developed, and
powerful sexual appetites aroused; she is liable to analogous
states of sexual enfeebleness and derangement, consequent
on the non-exercise of her sexual organs ... the fact is, that
there are few men, who, on calmly considering the subject,
would fail to see that a due amount of sexual intercourse is
one great thing needed to preserve and restore the health in
the youth of both sexes; and it is a common remark among
men on seeing a girl languid and sickly, that what she needs
is venereal gratification.

There was, he continued,[62]

a great deal of erroneous feeling attaching to the subject of
the sexual desires in woman. To have strong sexual passions
is held to be rather a disgrace for a woman, and they are
looked down upon as animal, sensuous, coarse, and deserv-
ing of reprobation. The moral emotions of love are indeed
thought beautiful in her, but the physical ones are rather
held unwomanly and debasing. This is a great error. In
woman, exactly as in man, strong sexual appetites are a very
great virtue; as they are the signs of a vigorous frame,
healthy sexual organs, and a naturally developed sexual
disposition.

Evidence may thus be easily presented to support the late
twentieth-century argument that the opinions of men like Acton
were 'more of an ideology seeking to be established' than a view
which currently prevailed amongst Victorian women themselves,
although it is much more open to doubt whether it contradicted the prevalent 'practice of even middle-class women'.[63]
What Drysdale's treatment of the subject suggests and what
Acton's tends to confirm is that the conventional emphasis on
the disgraceful nature of sexual passion in ladylike women was
sufficiently inhibitive for them to suppress the open mani-
festation of this feeling towards men, even to the point of its
repression into their unconscious and its appearance patho-
logically in the form of what Drysdale referred to as 'some
deep-rooted *sexual* morbidity, which, if we analyse the case
well, we shall find to be the very essence of the disordered
mental state'. This he discussed in the context of an 'extraordinary disease' amongst women of 'very great frequency',
namely, hysteria which, at least in the shape of 'regular
hysterical fits and hysterical counterfeits' was never seen in
man and was not, he thought, found in woman before puberty.
'In the vast majority of cases,' he continued, 'it is in the single,
and in women who are not happily married, or who are without
children, that the aggravated form of the disease is seen.'
Although he admitted that cases of hysteria occurred in all
classes in the community, 'it is most common among the upper

classes'.[64]

Unfortunately, Drysdale made this statement quite baldly, so
that it is not now possible to estimate how far upper-class ladies
suffered from hysteria and hysterical 'counterfeits' with their
origin in sexual repression. Yet, the fact that he associated
these diseases with the peculiar circumstances of ladies, unmarried or unhappily married, suggests that the views of Victorian
gentlemen at this time about the sexual characteristics of an
ideal wife were not only widespread but also sufficiently effective amongst the ladies of their acquaintance to familiarize
medical men with the physiological symptoms of neurotic dis-
turbances of an hysterical kind. At this time, too, there
appears to have been growing medical concern about the 'frightful' consequences of masturbation, especially as a precipitating
factor on the road to the mad-house, as Walter's godfather put
it,[65] even if as early as 1818 John Hunter had claimed the
practice to be too common to cause the diseases people attributed to it.[66] This suggests that 'solitary indulgence' which,
according to Drysdale, was 'often adopted more out of sport or
ignorance of the consequences it may lead to, than from any
more serious purpose', may nevertheless have been adopted
seriously by some, at least before marriage, in the attempt to
cope with their sexual predicament.[67]

This is particularly significant in the present context because
of the possible influence of what has been called the 'powerful
Christian tradition that condemned onanism'[68] and which showed
itself in the stand taken by some doctors, at least, in their
treatment of male sexuality. On 9 December 1843 the 'Lancet'
carried a letter from a Dr Henry Bull, complaining that on 18
November it had printed a report on a lecture by G.N. Dangerfield on 'The Symptoms, Pathology, Causes and Treatment of
Spermatorrhoea' which had argued that sexual intercourse,
and illicit at that, if necessary, was the best preventive of this
disease. 'If it indeed be true that regular sexual intercourse
is necessary for the preservation of health', exclaimed Bull,
'what is to become of religion and morality?'[69] Bull's approach to
sexuality rested on the assumption that 'the laws of physiology
are never at variance with those of morality', and he added
later, in a reply to *his* critics, 'I must be pardoned for making
one brief digression, to condemn strongly the practice of
many medical men of the present day who, when a case of confirmed spermatorrhoea presents itself, at once recommend
sexual intercourse.' He also took the opportunity to reject
'utterly' the implications of a rhetorical question put to the
Lancet on 23 December 1843, when Dr Chatto asked: 'What
medical man is there but daily sees the ill consequence upon
the health of forced celibacy in the numerous ailments it gen-
erates in women?'[70]

What divided these medical men was the extent to which sexual
continence could be regarded as either a cause or a cure of
spermatorrhoea, and by implication, hysteria. Bull claimed it to

act as a cure; others, like Robert Dudgeon, asserted that it
was not, because 'nocturnal emissions and exotic dreams' preceded the onset of the complaint.[71] Yet others, like Morgan,
claimed it could never cure because it was one of the causes.
'I have known several patients, professed religionists, too,
whose continence failed them. In them I know prolonged continence brought on spermatorrhoea.'[72] Another doctor, under
the pseudonym of Amicus Veritas, admitted that 'self restraint
ought to be urged on the patient, and carried out as far as
possible' but this did not always work. Hence the solution had
to be 'meretricious intercourse'. Apart from this 'nearly the
only alternative is masturbation'. What Bull failed to understand, he thought, was that 'to hinder the due employment of
any organ to the extent commensurate with or necessary to
health, is to contravene the law of God and Nature in deference
to the absurd and unnatural prejudices of man'. The laws of
physiology were Creator-given and infallible. The 'morality of
men' was 'wavering and uncertain'.[73]

This discussion of medical attitudes to what a later report in
the 'Lancet' referred to as 'some of the most intractable, and
often, on this account, the most neglected, affections it was
the lot of the surgeon to have presented to his notice'[74] was
terminated by the editor, complaining that although he had
received further letters from several correspondents on the
subject, 'not a few of the writers lose sight of the *medical*
question, and entangle themselves in discussions on religion
and morals'.[75] It is pertinent to consider what this medical
question was. The 'involuntary seminal losses', as the oft-
quoted French physician, who was regarded as the authority on
spermatorrhoea, had called them,[76] were identified as a most
serious disease when patients reported that their nocturnal
emissions had increased in frequency and that they passed semen
during the day, 'whenever any exertion is made; as at stool,
in going into a cold bath, in making water, or even in thinking
on a venereal subject'.[77]

It is likely that recognition of such diurnal symptoms depended
on these patients having read about them in some medical or
quasi-medical literature, or having been asked about them by a
doctor; and it seems equally likely that these and similar symptoms were 'the cause of driving many wretched, nervous and
despairing patients into the hands of some of the most ruthless
and rapacious of the whole tribe of quacks'.[78] At this time,
that is to say, some men were so convinced that nocturnal emissions, other than perhaps very occasional ones,[79] were a source
for alarm that they were prepared to face the expense of medical
advice and the often painful treatment prescribed by quacks
and regular medical practitioners alike as a cure for this condition. Throughout Europe and America spermatorrhoea became
'a familiar, if not a household word, with almost every sexual
hypochondriac diagnosing his real or imagined generative problems in terms of the alarming new disease'. Like the concern

about masturbation, which was sometimes taken to be the
primary cause for the intensification of involuntary emissions,
it is probable that feelings of guilt on the part of patients had
led them to seek medical advice in the first place. In this respect it is not unreasonable to regard the Victorian doctor's
consulting room as having in this sense become a substitute for
the priest's confessional,[80] or its equivalent in the pastoral
advice given by an Anglican clergyman to one of his flock. The
sequence of 'sin', 'confession', 'punishment', or 'penance', and
'redemption' thus took place in a medical rather than a religious
setting,[81] and this made it possible for the gentleman with such
a sexual problem to interpret it as sickness or disease, amenable
to remedy through the correct application of scientific - or, at
least, medical - principles rather than as sin which required
an abandonment of his customary way of life in an attempt at
atonement.

The gentleman's commerce with prostitutes, similarly, could
be judged solely in terms of the physiological risk of catching
venereal disease, whence along with some doctors like Acton
he could support, if only tacitly, parliamentary measures for
the regulation and compulsory medical examination and hospital-
ization of 'fallen women'. This is not the place, of course, to
go into the ramifications for and against the Contagious Diseases
Acts of 1864, 1866 and 1869, although it should be noted that
the first organization which this legislation prompted was the
Association for the Promotion of the Extension of the Contagious
Diseases Act (1866) to the Civil Population of the United Kingdom. This Association issued its first report in 1868, containing
a list of members, including in their numbers 'some bishops,
Church dignitaries, Members of Parliament and others who
subsequently became candidates for Parliament'.[82] Convinced
that the measures introduced in 1864, and extended in 1866,
were succeeding in reducing the incidence of venereal disease
in the garrison towns where they were being applied, these
gentlemen campaigned, albeit unsuccessfully, 'that, for the
reception of prostitutes suffering from venereal disease, hospital accommodation should be provided in all towns where
such persons congregate'.[83] Possibly because the Association's
membership included a fair number of Members of Parliament
and because in 1868 the National Association for the Promotion
of Social Science had presented a petition to both Houses in
favour of such extension,[84] the Medical Officer in the Privy
Council devoted some paragraphs of his Report of 31 March
1869, to presenting the case against it. 'The plan would require
for London alone the creation and maintenance of new hospital
accommodation nearly equal to that which is now given by the
twelve general hospitals of London for all bodily diseases put
together.' This would cost 'at least 100,000l. per annum' to
maintain and almost half a million pounds initially to establish.
'The requirements of the large towns would probably be of like
proportions.' Thus the objection to the proposal was simply

economic: such provisions were unlikely to be met by private contribution and too expensive to meet out of taxation.[85]

There were, of course, a few Members of Parliament, even at this time, who objected to the Contagious Diseases Acts on religiously moral grounds. Thus, the Member for Oxfordshire had referred to the 1866 Bill on 22 March of that year as[86]

a very queer Bill upon a very queer subject. Its object was to preserve the health of Her Majesty's troops, and its endeavour was to remove the penalties which a Higher Power had imposed on sin, and to give the opportunity to sin without punishment. He must appeal to the Chancellor of the Exchequer whether they could expect any blessing upon their legislation if they took these unhappy women, freed them from disease and then turned them loose to follow the same wretched courses, without any attempt to reclaim them.

Subsequent medical evidence to the Select Committee on the Contagious Diseases Act of 1866 was elicited on this very point by the simple device of asking leading questions, which were typically answered by Visiting Surgeons to the Lock Hospitals in terms of the greater success of the Acts in this respect than that achieved by other approaches. 'I think that prostitutes of a large town have never been fairly brought under the advice of clergymen because they have not the opportunity of considering it quietly,' said one, 'but now, during a residence in the hospital, they are amenable to such advice.' Some of them had left the streets in consequence and were now respectably married.[87] Doubtless, there was good ground for the belief that clergymen had not been very successful in their efforts to 'reclaim' fallen women, whereas the legislators could show that only about 90 per cent of those discharged from hospital under the Acts went back to prostitution afterwards![88]

The striking feature of the debate at this time, that is to say, is not so much the relative success of the Acts as the rejection of 'moral' persuasion as an effective measure and therefore the rejection of 'the religious objection' to the Acts, which was seen by many doctors and legislators as belonging 'more to a past than to a present age', as a government spokesman put it. The opinion that venereal disease was inflicted by the Almighty as a punishment for, and therefore as a restraint upon the indulgence of evil passions could be swept aside on such a ground. 'I prefer to remind the House,' this spokesman went on, 'that similar opinions in regard to disease have constantly prevailed from remote antiquity, and have as constantly been refuted by the progress of knowledge ... we are constantly reminded, in the progress of science, that there is far more of mercy than of wrath in Divine arrangements.'[89] The silence of the Archbishops of Canterbury and York and of the bishops in the House of Lords whenever questions about the Acts were on the order paper bears witness to the extent that at this time the purely medical justification for the measures, together with the pragmatic requirement that 'the State is bound

to preserve its combatants from the consequences of an abnormal
practice', that is, enforced celibacy,[90] outweighed references
to religion, morality, justice, and the liberty of those women
suspected of being prostitutes and therefore likely to be infected.

Josephine Butler nursed the suspicion that:[91]

the real reason why men are not here treated in the same way
as women is that Parliament would not endure that men should
be put in prison for solicitation on such slight evidence
before a summary court, as is the case with women, for the
men of the upper classes would be laid hold of by the Bill,
and it would be a terrible thing indeed to the hearts of our
present legislators to think that one of themselves or their
sons might be tackled.

Yet since the suspicion was presumably based on the unwarranted supposition that 'one of themselves or their sons' were
accustomed to make use of the women who were arrested under
the Acts, it is rather more likely that her 'present legislators'
were simply applying the usual double standard of sexual morality to fallen women. The emphasis throughout these debates
and enquiries, that is to say, was on the special problem of
the garrison towns and although it is true that the statistics
of venereal disease in these towns, produced for government
reports at the time, did not indicate the rank of the patients
dealt with by the uniformed medical services, few officers indeed
would have been included in their numbers because gentlemen
of this rank who required medical treatment most probably went
to their own doctors privately. In any case, they are almost
certain not to have been clients of the same prostitutes as the
men under their command.

When, then, an opponent of the Acts complained that 'we
hear a great deal about the "innocent women and children" who
are injured by this disease and by this sin. But if that argument
means anything it means this - that the Chancellor of the
Exchequer is to find money to provide clean women for married
men',[92] it would appear that he had in mind soldiers, sailors
and marines who were married and separated by their postings
from their wives and families. In so far as the gentlemanly
paterfamilias sought to face his sexual dilemmas by keeping
mistresses or becoming a client of the more expensive women of
the town, such legislation was not of his concern. Such clean
women as it attempted to provide were the outcome of a medical
policy promulgated by members of the upper and upper middle
classes for men of the lower orders. Hence its significance lies
in the indication it gives that the religious solution for male
sexual urges had been rejected, as unworkable, in favour of
the medical, and the church leaders themselves who were part
of the legislative body accepted an interpretation of sexuality
which was biological rather than spiritual.

The mid-Victorian preoccupation with masturbation, spermatorrhoea, and venereal disease, in brief, is an indication of

the extent to which young men at this time were believed to
be faced with very special sexual problems. Probably without
exception, all who thought about these problems would have
agreed that the obvious solution was earlier marriage, and in
this sense they continued to hold to the Pauline doctrine that
it was better to marry than to burn. The abandonment of the
notion of redemption through atonement and its replacement by
devices prescribed by doctors made it possible for the respectable member of an upper or upper middle class family to continue to preserve all the other aspects of conventional religious
behaviour. To this degree it was not necessary for him to
become an apostate because the church itself had come to define
these problems in medical terms. Yet both the medical and the
clerical professions continued to be publicly hostile to the
birth controllers right until the end of the century and beyond,
while the 'pioneers' of family limitation continued to be in the
vanguard of the movement towards the smaller family which
became endemic in all sections of the community. Does this mean
that the church leaders themselves were mainly responsible
for whatever apostasy there occurred, because they would not,
or could not, fall in line with their respectable congregations?
Or did they simply define family limitation as moral restraint
rather than birth control? Before such questions can be tackled
it is necessary to examine in greater detail the relevant events
of the next thirty years.

8 THE 1870s AND AFTER

The average annual crude birth-rate per thousand of the
population in England and Wales rose, apparently, from 32.3
in 1841-5 to 35.3 in 1866-70, stayed at this figure until 1876-80,
and then declined rapidly - to 28.2 in 1901-5, 19.9 in 1921-5,
15.9 in 1941-5, before rising slightly thereafter to reach a new
'peak' after the Second World War of 18.1 in 1961-6.[1] There is
clear evidence of the under-registration of births for some years
after the imposition of civil registration in 1836, but estimates
to allow for this have not altered the general picture substantially: the crude birth-rate was high in the first half of
the nineteenth century, reached its maximum in 1861-5 or thereabouts,[2] and certainly in the decade, 1861-70,[3] and declined
steadily thereafter. Although the crude birth-rate is a very
unreliable index because it is based simply on the total population and makes therefore no allowance for variations in the
proportions of people at different times who are incapable of
bearing children, there can hardly be any doubt that 1870,
more or less, marked a turning point in the demographic history
of this country, in so far as such statistics are concerned.
    This has led some demographers and historians to seek for
an explanation of the down-turn of fertility in terms of events
at that time, as though the birth-rate would have remained high
had these events never taken place and as though they had
had an effect once and for all which caused future generations
over the next hundred years to practise family limitation. The
1911 Fertility Census, however, indicated that for the upper
and upper middle classes, at least, the decline in fertility had
already begun before 1861, if not earlier, and there are other
calculations which suggest that reliance on the birth-rate is
quite misplaced.[4] What seems to have happened was that the
'pioneers' of family limitation, identified in chapter 5 above,
were possibly no more than the vanguard of a more general
'movement' towards the smaller family, since the average number
of children born to all parents declined by one fifth between
marriages contracted from 1857 to 1861 and those contracted
for 1881 to 1886,[5] although it should still be emphasized that
the most rapid decline took place amongst the couples in the
Registrar-General's Class I and amongst those of them whom
Innes had classified as 'upper professional'.[6]
    The 'pioneers' of the earlier period, with one exception, con-
tinued to remain in the vanguard in the 1870s and after, as
Table 8.1 shows.

Table 8.1   'Pioneers' of the smaller family: married from before 1861 to 1891

Occupation of the father	Mean number of children born	
	Marriages of 1871-81	Marriages of 1881-91
Gentlemen of private means	3.47	2.18
Army officers (effective and retired)	3.90	2.51
Officers of the navy and marines (effective and retired)	3.78	2.65
Physicians, surgeons, registered practitioners	4.17	2.81
Painters, sculptors, artists	4.23	2.96
Solicitors	4.38	3.02
Civil, mining engineers	4.53	3.06
Accountants	4.54	3.20
Authors, editors, journalists, reporters	4.02	3.26
Ministers, priests of bodies other than the established church	4.62	3.43
All Class I	4.79	3.46
Tobacconists	4.43	3.05
Hospital, institutions, etc., servants, etc.	5.31	5.40
All Class II	5.61	4.15

In this table only those occupations have been included which
were listed in Tables 4.1 and 4.2 as having experienced an
average number of births consistently below the mean for the
Registrar-General's Class I occupations in both marriage
periods. The figures in the present table are for completed
families alone because the inclusion of those couples, married
at these later dates, of whom the wife had not reached her
menopause by 1911, might have made much more complicated
the comparison with couples in the earlier period. As can be
seen by the table, wives whose husbands were servants of
hospitals, institutions (other than the Poor Law) and bene-
volent societies now gave birth to more children than the average for Class I mothers and, indeed, for 1881-91 marriages
for the average Class II mother, while the tobacconists' wives
remained amongst the 'pioneers'. No explanation is attempted
for these differences. What is much more significant for the
discussion of the last three chapters is the fertility practices
of the ladies and gentlemen of private means who had already
moved into first place amongst the 'pioneers' with the smallest
number of children born to marriages contracted between 1861
and 1871, maintained this position over the twenty years and
actually increased their lead for a while. The difference between
the number of their births and those for couples in Class I as
a whole was -0.37 for marriages contracted before 1861, -1.06
for marriages of 1861-71, -1.32 for marriages of 1871-87, and
-1.27 for marriages of 1881-1891 when the mean for Class I as

a whole was only 3.46 as compared with 6.41 for marriages contracted before 1861.[7] Army and navy officers, similarly, maintained their especially clear position, behind the gentlemen of private means, but in the vanguard of the 'pioneers' generally.

These were accompanied in this later period by two new sets of couples with average numbers of births below the mean for Class I. The first of these, listed in Table 8.2, consists of only those whose husbands were in occupations which, in family limitation terms, were intermediate between those in Table 8.1 and those in Table 8.3. This first set of new 'pioneers', that is to say, differed from the old because the average number of their births were above the mean for Class I only for those marriages contracted before 1861. After that date they had moved up to join the original 'pioneers' and they stayed amongst them for at least the next thirty years of marriages.

Table 8.2   Additional 'pioneers' of the smaller family (1861-91)

| Occupation of the father | Mean number of children born | | |
| | Marriages contracted | | |
	1861-71	1871-81	1881-91
Class I			
Barristers	4.48	3.71	2.50
Clergymen (Established Church)	5.54	4.12	3.04
Persons engaged in scientific pursuits	5.66	4.57	3.12
Class II			
Lodging-house keepers	5.08	3.89	2.60

Finally, there were the occupations where married couples became 'pioneers' only after 1871.

The addition of actors and lodging-house keepers from the Registrar-General's Class II set of occupations in these tables and, of course, the implied omission of hospitals, etc., servants from the list of 'pioneers' in the table on p.98 should be noted, although this may in part be explained by the idiosyncracies of the Registrar's classification. Much more important is the striking feature of so many of the occupations in all these tables, namely that some sort of 'professional' or 'quasi-professional' criteria of performance characterized them, suggesting once again that the concept of the 'career', with its meritocratic emphasis, continued to dominate many of the couples whose family limitation practices put them amongst the 'pioneers' after 1870, as much as before; and this raises in a particularly important sense the question of the compatibility of such an emphasis with that usual kind of argument which has continued to associate the fall in British fertility with certain of the events of the last third of the nineteenth century.

Table 8.3   *Latest 'pioneers' of the smaller family (1871-91)*

	Mean number of children born	
	Marriages contracted	
	1871-81	*1881-91*
Class I		
Bankers, bank officials, bank clerks	4.19	2.85
Merchants (commodity unspecified)	4.44	3.32
Dentists (including assistants)	4.49	3.32
Chemists, druggists	4.53	3.30
Architects	4.65	3.17
Schoolmasters, teachers, professional lecturers	4.67	3.27
Law clerks	4.77	3.37
Class II		
Actors	4.17	3.15

In 'Prosperity and Parenthood' attention was directed to the 'Great Depression' of 1873 and afterwards as a possibly 'special jolt' which the Royal Commission on Population claimed had caused the Victorians to lose confidence in the onward march of their civilization and hence set them searching around for alternative ways of coping with the costs of marriage and the raising of a family.[8] There is no necessity here to go again into the question of whether there ever was such a great depression, as opposed to the 'myth' of the time that the country suffered such a one.[9] Nor is it necessary to do more than repeat the point that the real incomes of all those earning more than £150 a year increased throughout the period 1851 to 1911, reaching a peak in the decade, 1871-81, and tailing off thereafter, so that the middle-, upper-middle-, and upper-class levels of living generally can hardly be said to have fallen during this period. What are much more relevant for present purposes are the argument about the standard of living to which the middle classes aspired, irrespective of whether they ever succeeded in reaching it or not, and the conclusion that the operative factor was[10]

the *comparison* members of the middle classes were able to make of their own levels of living at different times with those of their immediate neighbours and acquaintances; and in so far as this had any influence whatever on the strength of their aspirations, it is not unlikely that the period after 1880, by reducing the extent to which men found it possible to scale the income ladder, also resulted in their seeking alternative ways of achieving social mobility or 'social pro-

motion' by cutting down in some departments of expense,
especially those not directly relevant to their appearing
affluent to the eyes of the world.

Of course, as critics have not been unaware,[11] this reference
to incomes of as low as just over £150 per year, like other
references to the servant-keeping classes and to the middle
classes tout court was slipshod, even if the point in the reference was merely to emphasize that[12]

> in comparison with the period 1851-1871, the years of the
> 1870s and onwards were years of some difficulty for those
> in receipt of middle- and upper-range incomes. Prices fell,
> it is true, but incomes suffered something of a set back
> too. Servants' wages rose and their labour became more
> difficult to obtain. Hence, in comparison with the lower-middle
> classes, the better-off sections of society were faced with a
> greater struggle to maintain and extend the differential
> standard. The years of what had promised to be inevitable
> progress had passed away. Some kind of personal planning
> was necessary now if the social hierarchy was to be pre-
> served.

What is now open to challenge is whether this concept of relative deprivation[13] is at all relevant to the question under review.
Far too easily 'Prosperity and Parenthood' fell into the common
practice of its time of assuming that Victorian England was
marked by a rising middle class, challenging the established
order from below; that is, in all the most privileged and exclu-
sive areas of social life individuals and families of traditional
ruling-class origin were effectively replaced by individuals and
families, rising in the social scale from relatively humble origins. The argument of chapters 5 and 6 above, repeated now
for the period of the 'Great Depression', is that the crucial
events of the 1850s and 1860s were associated with the lifestyle
of that establishment itself, concomitant upon its growth in
numbers; and the implication of those chapters is that there
was virtually no challenge from below, or rather, that there
was no marked change in this respect during the relevant
period.

The emphasis at this point is on a curiosity of English ruling-
class ideology from at least the end of the medieval period. As
Alexis de Tocqueville had noted in 1833, although the terms
'gentleman' and 'gentilhomme' were evidently of the same origin,
the former was applied by Englishmen to all well-bred (bien
élevé) men, whatever their birth, whereas the latter meant in
France only the nobly born (noble de naissance).[14] There had
always been such flexibility amongst English landed families,
it seems, which permitted men of education and refinement to
become part of the gentry in a society which has been described as 'less caste-conscious than was the case with the
continental aristocracies'.[15] The reference here, of course, is
to the admission to the gentry through the purchase of a landed
estate, either by men with such refinement already or, more

rarely, by their fathers without it but certain that they would
not be prevented from founding a family line of future gentlemen. The striking feature of the nineteenth century, therefore,
as was emphasized on p.55 above, was the novel Malthusian-
like situation that the number of such family lines fast outran
the provision of landed estates on which to settle them. The
gentry, accordingly, sought to settle their younger sons and
sons of younger sons in those occupations – certain of the
professions – for which their upbringing seemed most appropriate, and such men could be interpreted as having fallen in
the social scale in the light of the assumption that such occupations were no more than simply 'middle class'. However, in so
far as the gentlemen in these occupations might also be deemed
to have risen in significance in Victorian society vis-à-vis the
landed interests, what seems rather to have happened was much
less a movement upwards on the part of the poorly born and
rather more a lateral movement, sideways within more or less
the same family lineages, buttressed of course by the arrival
of some 'new' men.[16] What changed was the relative significance
of estate ownership for political power, not the relative significance of established ruling-class families; and it is of some
significance in this connection to notice that the aristocratic
influence in the Cabinet nevertheless persisted for the remainder of the century, in spite of the industrial eminence of
Britain for much of this later period.[17]

Nor were the 'pioneers' of family limitation much connected
with those sorts of occupations which were for the most part
the province of the more humbly born and which might reasonably be expected to have experienced one of the special jolts
of the 'Great Depression'. Apart from the gentleman of private
means, whose source of income is unfortunately not known,
only seven of the twenty-two occupations with average births
below the mean for Class I in the marriages of 1871 to 1891
might be said to have contained couples who were likely to
have been directly influenced by the crisis of business confidence after 1873 -- lodging-house keepers, bankers, tobacconists, merchants, chemists, civil engineers and accountants --
and only three of these occupations entered the ranks of the
'pioneers' of family limitation after 1871. Moreover, while it is
no doubt true that there was a drive for education on the part
of these new entrants to the ranks of the 'pioneers', as there
was indeed for the lower middle classes generally who aspired
for their sons to obtain 'the appearance, if not the standing
of gentlemen', the education they paid for, although perhaps
not inconsiderable in terms of the size of some of their incomes,
was not that provided in the public schools, which would have
resulted in their sons competing with the sons of the older
'pioneers', but merely sufficient for them to leave school at
fifteen or sixteen and enter a commercial post at £70 or £80 a
year.[18]

For such commercial posts, in spite of the crisis in business

confidence, there was a considerable demand. The number of
clerks in commerce, for example, rose by about two and a
quarter times between 1861 and 1881, as compared with increases of about one-quarter for barristers and solicitors, doctors
and ministers of religion.[19] For the later period, 1881 to 1901,
the comparable growth-rates were not so extreme, being nearly
one and a half times for commercial clerks, about one fifth for
barristers and solicitors and clergymen, and about one half
for doctors.[20] Indeed, in so far as the 'Great Depression' might
be thought to have affected black-coated workers at the bottom
income-ranges of the middle class, it could hardly have been
in terms of a loss of opportunities, for theirs was an expanding
area of employment which might well have been regarded as
favourable to a larger family. Commercial clerks generally were
not, of course, among the 'pioneers' of family limitations, even
if, like civil service officers and clerks, who were also laggardly in this respect, they had reduced the number of children born to them to about one half by the marriage decade,
1881-91.[21]

What seems to have been more important in their case than
the crisis in business confidence associated with the 1873
depression, that is to say, were developments in the clerical
'profession' itself, which, although not so well-documented as
for the upper-middle-class occupations with which this study
has so far been concerned, also seems to have experienced
something of a meritocratic emphasis during the second half of
the nineteenth century. Clerks employed by the Royal Exchange
Assurance, for example, had been paid on a salary scale from
1838 which started them at an annual salary of £70 at age
eighteen and raised them by regular increments to £150 after
twelve years' service. This scale was changed in 1872 to start
at £90 a year and the salaries were thereafter revised trien-
nially, so that by the 1890s, 'the average clerk was earning
£150 in his mid-twenties, and just under £400 at 41, and if he
stayed on to 65 he would receive about £600'.[22] The tradition
of seniority as a principle of promotion, moreover, meant that
only rarely were outsiders introduced into more senior posts
or more rapid promotion given to specially able clerks. Between
1881 and 1901 insurance officials and clerks increased in number
by 404.65 per cent, suggesting a great increase in possibilities,
and as this expansion was accompanied by the amalgamation of
large companies, the impression given by this example of clerical employment is of the emergence of a career structure in a
relatively large organization, not at all unlike that experienced
by the ruling-class occupations referred to above, and including also in some cases a pension at retirement after long service.[23]

The possibility that this inculcated in clerks themselves
employed in such posts, or attracted to such employment men
who already possessed, a future-time perspective, not very
different from that demonstrated by twentieth-century family

planners proper, is strengthened when these similarities are
stressed, although it should nevertheless be emphasized that
insurance clerks, like other clerks, required no special or
systematic training to get their feet on the bottom rung of the
ladder. Young men were recruited to such work after 'a broad
liberal education up to 17 or 18 – from which it was helpful to
derive a good hand writing and arithmetical training, as well
as the more general attributes of a "well-educated" young
man',[24] so that the more laggardly nature of the onset of family
limitation amongst the parents of such young men might perhaps
be accounted for in terms of the shorter time-span over which
they had to provide education for their sons, especially in comparison with those who sent their boys to public school and
university, and increasingly in this later period to the preparatory school.[25] Yet it should not be forgotten that the education
of boys to become clerks, relatively inexpensive although it
was, made considerable inroads into the incomes of parents who
were clerks because counting house salaries were not very large
on the whole.[26]

In terms of the attempt to explain the decline in the birth-
rate what appears to have happened in the 1870s and later was
a marked expansion in that type of meritocratic career,
exemplified here by the case of insurance, which was located
not so much in the professions, which grew at this time at
only about the same rate as the population of England and Wales
generally,[27] as in all kinds of non-manual work where large-
scale organization of labour was rapidly occurring. It is, to be
sure, largely a matter of influence back to that period from
the present rather than hard evidence which suggests that, as
such organizations grew in size, managerial and clerical careers
were established on the civil service and army and navy models,
although not necessarily always as a result of direct copying.
The railways, it is true, adopted a kind of quasi-military structure in the early days of their history to provide the 'officers'
to command a large number of manual workers, employed on a
variety of specialized tasks, sometimes with ex-military men at
the top,[28] and the railways operated a system of superannuation
for their employees, based 'largely on civil service practice'.[29]

The railways, indeed, presented in a striking fashion the
emergence of such a meritocratic career pattern in the relevant
period. Whereas between 1850 and 1869 the 'corporate execu-
tives' who managed the fifteen leading railway companies,
dominating the development of the industry up to 1922, had of
necessity been recruited mainly from outside the industry, from
1870 onwards over 60 per cent of them had followed careers in
it before reaching the top and had on average spent sixteen
to twenty years with the same railway company before being
promoted to this level. After 1870, also, their salaries in this
post were increasingly related to the size and prestige of the
company rather than to their own performance in making profits for it, which had been the guide for salary fixing pre-

viously; and increasingly service in this post was followed by
promotion to the Board of Directors of the company, or of some
other railway company.[30] There were, altogether, 180 railway
companies in the United Kingdom in 1850, rising to 476 by 1867,
but declining thereafter to 250 by 1900 and 220 by 1914,[31] so
that although the practices of the leading fifteen should not be
assumed to be typical of all railway companies, the decline in
the total number in the later period, which resulted from the
amalgamation of small companies to form larger ones, no doubt
extended the meritocratic career pattern to a growing number
of railway officials, as their proportion in the total railway
labour force declined, although it also had the effect probably
of diminishing the chances of any one of them getting right
to the top.[32]

   The railways were, of course, the pioneers in the joint-stock
system of business organization which took much longer to
develop in other industries, possibly because English businessmen generally, it has been argued, were 'especially reluctant
to raise new capital through procedures that might have
weakened their control over their family firms';[33] but as companies grew in size, especially where they were controlled by
boards of directors and run by 'professional' managers, a
hierarchical structure of authority and salaries was created
along very much the same lines as the railways had pioneered
for private enterprise. The point of significance here is that
those whom Roger Clements has dubbed the 'crown princes' of
British industry, that is, 'men whose start, progress and
achievement in business can be largely ascribed to close family
links with the ownership or top management of the firm',[34] for
all that they moved faster and went eventually further than
ordinary commoners, so to speak, nevertheless followed a
career which consisted in their mounting the managerial career,
responsibility and income ladder, if not necessarily from the
very bottom; and this was a practice which gathered momentum
for the most part in the last quarter of the nineteenth century.
In terms of the meritocratic emphasis on future-time expectations, businessmen in their personal careers more frequently
abandoned the entrepreneurial posture for the civil and military
service models. Yet, as the reference above to the reduction
in the number of children born to commercial and business
clerks implies, in spite of the lower costs of education in this
case, such an emphasis on the overriding importance of the
meritocratic career for some people should not be allowed to
obscure the possibility that there were other influences at work
to reduce the fertility of all couples during this last quarter
of the century. Table 8.4, for example, shows that railway
officials and clerks, unfortunately classified together, were
not even 'pioneers' of family limitation amongst railway employees. Many working-class railwaymen, placed severally in Classes III and V by the Registrar-General, were in the vanguard
amongst the employees of this industry.

Table 8.4   *Children born to railway employees: married from before 1861 to 1891*

Father's occupation	R.-G. Class	Marriage dates			
		Before 1861	1861-71	1871-81	1881-91
Signalmen	III	6.65	6.03	4.96	3.46
Porters	V	6.73	5.86	5.11	3.50
Guards	III	7.22	5.92	4.96	3.46
Officials and clerks	I	7.20	6.51	5.16	3.74
Platelayers	V	7.21	6.42	5.52	3.70
Pointsmen	IV	7.41	6.35	5.31	3.94
Engine drivers, etc.	III	9.90*	7.60	6.23	4.81
Labourers	V	7.41	7.20	6.53	5.16

* eleven couples only

Such railway employees, it is true, were aware that the railways had scales of different rates of pay for different grades
of manual work and those rates, it has been claimed, were
'closely related in terms of promotion',[35] so that there was held
open the possibility of transfer from one grade to another,
except perhaps in the cases of enginemen and permanent-way
men who, incidentally, had the largest number of births
throughout the period. But it would surely be an exaggeration
to regard this practice as a meritocratic emphasis in manual
work, sufficient to inculcate the kind of future-time perspective necessary eventually for strict family planning. As Table
8.5 indicates the railwaymen, although in the vanguard, were
only in the vanguard of a more general decline in the number
of births to a marriage amongst manual workers who also
limited their families, although employed in jobs where no such
scales of pay for different grades existed.

Table 8.5   *Labourers: mean number of births by marriage dates, before 1861 to 1881-91*

Father's occupation	Before 1861	1861-71	1871-81	1881-91
Dock labourers	7.44	7.52	7.04	5.67
General labourers	7.85	7.37	6.72	5.32
Agricultural labourers	7.96	7.25	6.64	5.38

The marriages of dock labourers in the decade of 1881-91
thus produced fewer births than even the gentlemen of private
means who had married before 1861 and fewer also than all
the members of the Registrar-General's Class I who had married between 1861 and 1871. By the 1890s the practice of family
limitation was endemic to all classes of the community. This,
of course, is why the average annual crude birth-rate

continued to fall and had done so from 1876-80.[36] The important sociological question, therefore, is what relationship
there was, if any, between the 'pioneers' of family limitation -
and/or the experiences of those 'pioneers' - and the rest of
English society, especially during this later period; and the
immediately obvious answer is that of direct diffusion through,
perhaps, simple copying of family limitation practices, as
desirable, by those sections of the population most closely
associated with the upper and upper middle classes. For example, men in those working-class occupations which caused them
to become familiar with the domestic situations of 'pioneer'
families might be presumed to be the first to demonstrate a
similar desire for, and success in, limiting the number of their
offspring; and, as Table 8.6 indicates, especially by contrast
to that immediately above, there is some indication that this
could have been so.

Table 8.6   Mean number of births by marriage dates: selected occupations

Father's occupation	Before 1861	1861-71	1871-81	1881-91
Soldiers and non-commissioned officers	No cases	4.57	5.00	4.59
Men of the navy	(1 case only)	(7 cases only)		
and marines	6.00	10.00	5.47	4.15
Coachmen, grooms	7.03	6.38	5.39	4.04
Domestic gardeners	6.96	6.42	5.39	4.04
Gamekeepers	7.85	7.22	6.46	5.03
Domestic indoor servants*	7.00	5.40	4.26	2.95

* other than in hotels, lodging houses, and eating houses

The case of the male domestic indoor servants is particularly
striking in this table, because those of them who married as
early as the decade, 1861-71, had moved into the ranks of the
'pioneers', below the average for the Registrar-General's Class
I in terms of the number of children born to them. Of all
working-class males, of course, these men were the most likely
to have been intimately aware of the relationship between their
employer and his wife. It is likely, too, that these men themselves married other indoor servants with similar experiences
of upper- and upper-middle-class homes to their husbands.
Indoor male domestic service, to be sure, was a contracting
field of employment at this time,[37] and it is highly probable
that the husbands whose family-building practices became
immortalized in the tables of the 1911 Fertility Census, were
upper servants in relatively high-status families.
The reference to the wives of these domestics having themselves no doubt been indoor servants, before and after marriage, raises the question of whether the personal, intimate

experience of the way of life of the 'pioneers' of family limitation, and of those who followed rapidly in the same path, may
have become 'diffused' to the working class through such
female domestic servants. At no Census between 1851 and 1901
did the proportion of occupied females employed in domestic
service fall below 40 per cent,[38] and granted that there would
have been movement into and out of the occupation between
Censuses, it is not unreasonable to conclude that a large
proportion of manual workers married girls who had had some
experience of indoor, domestic service. This conclusion, of
course, implies in this context that some of the driving force
behind the extension of family limitation to the working classes
at this time came from these women rather than from their
husbands, although it would obviously not be correct to interpret this as a revolt of women - a kind of aggressive 'domestic
feminism',[39] inciting them to limit the number of their offspring in their own, personal interests. Davidoff's well-argued
thesis that girls in domestic service 'moved from parental
control, in their parents' home, into service and then into
their husband's home', thus experiencing a lifetime of personal
subordination in private homes suggests a marked contrast
in their possible 'aggressiveness' as compared with the growing number of girls who began to find other forms of work
towards the end of the century.[40]
    Nor should the flight from domestic service as such be
interpreted simply as a revolt of working-class women, following on the earlier 'revolt' of the manservant, against being
thus 'mastered for life' and wearing livery. The servant-
employing classes had always recruited the great bulk of their
domestic servants from rural, working-class families, and
between 1831 and 1901 the rural population of England and
Wales fell from 54 per cent to 23 per cent of the total,[41] so that
such employers were faced not so much by a revolt as by a
declining pool of traditional labour from which to draw. There
is, of course, some evidence that those female domestic servants who shifted to factory work at this time were 'enthus-
iastic' about the social life in the factories and the freedom
from restraint which factory hours constituted, by contrast
to domestic service,[42] so that there may have been much
unexpressed desire to become their own 'masters' among such
women who might, therefore, be presumed to have dominated
the working-class men they married; but this does not seem
plausible in the light of the account of the relationship between
working-class couples, derived partly from documentary
evidence of the period and partly from oral history interviews,
used by Standish Meacham in his study of the English working
class at this time.[43] While there can be no doubt about a desire
to be relieved from excessive child-bearing and child-rearing,
there is no evidence of any marked revolt on the part of such
wives over their husband's claimed right to have sexual intercourse as a matter of course, irrespective of the wife's

feelings and fears of yet another pregnancy.

The question of what Angus McLaren has called 'tactics'[44] is important for a consideration of family limitation amongst such couples in the late Victorian period. With 'rubber letters' at 2 shillings to 10 shillings a dozen and quinine pessaries at 2 shilings a dozen, it might have seemed to be prudent, economic policy for working-class couples to invest in contra- ceptive sponges at 1 shilling each or a syringe, ranging in price from 3s.6d. to 5s.6d. each in 1896;[45] but it does not seem very likely that many working-class couples, even amongst the 'aristocrats' of labour whose wages at this time were 45 shillings a week or a little more,[46] would have spent much money on any of these contraceptive devices, especially when one- fourth to one-third of their family income was already com- mandeered by rent.[47] They would perforce have had to rely on long courtships marked by sexual restraint,[48] abstinence even when once married, mutual masturbation, and coitus interruptus mainly, falling back on attempting to induce a miscarriage or, failing this, on a back-street abortionist when all such methods failed.

The question of abortion should not be misinterpreted in this connection. Like contraception generally, and infanticide, abortion had been practised by some women in various societies as far back as the historical record stretches and modern social anthropologists infer.[49] The issue for the last quarter of the nineteenth century, therefore, rests on the extent to which abortion as a form of family limitation became sufficiently widely practised, especially amongst working-class wives, to reduce the number of their offspring to the degree reported in the 1911 Fertility Census. There is no doubt that some Victorians had become worried about abortion at this time, just as there is evidence earlier that stories were 'floating in society, of married ladies, whenever they find themselves pregnant, habitually beginning to take exercise, on foot or on horseback, to an extent unusual at other times, and thus making them- selves abort'.[50] Yet, in his estimate of the incidence of abortion for the Royal Commission on Population, based on pregnancies which terminated before the seventh month, Ernest Lewis- Faning arrived at a figure of 10 per cent of conceptions for the women in his survey who had been married before 1910, and even when allowing for the possibility that such older women may have forgotten many of the details of their earlier pregnancies, the abortion rate measured by such an index was not likely to have been much greater than 16 per cent.[51] The reduction in the number of births to the wives of indoor domestic servants by 42 per cent over thirty years - or to those of railway signalmen by 48 per cent - suggests either a great decline in the number of abortions amongst working- class wives, married at the beginning of the twentieth century, or the use of other methods of fertility reduction by the women who married earlier, so that conception as such did not take

place to the same extent as it had to wives married in the
middle of the century.

All this would seem to imply, indeed, an increasing reliance
on coitus interruptus, an essentially male technique, even if
one acquiesced in by the women who experienced it. The uncer-
tainties of old wives' remedies to induce miscarriages - including unwonted exercise on foot or on horseback - and the
serious danger of lead poisoning from makeshift drugs or the
perforation of the uterus by a partially sterilized crochet hook
or knitting needle, manipulated without benefit of any pain-
killer stronger than an aspirin,[52] no doubt caused most working-
class women to rely on such methods only in circumstances
which were of dire necessity to them, such as a possible birth
outside wedlock, or yet another birth to an already desperately
overburdened mother. While it is true that 'more advanced
medical technology, including anaesthetics and antiseptics'
was available by the end of the century, which could have made
abortions safer or less unpleasant and therefore 'less frighten-
ing to some women with unwanted pregnancies',[53] the fact that
such operations were illegal and could be performed by a
qualified surgeon without legal penalty solely when they were
deemed necessary to save the life of the mother[54] raises very
serious doubts about the extent to which, even for those
women who were prepared to pay relatively large sums for a
safe, illegal abortion, members of the medical profession, as
such, carried out a sufficient number of abortions materially
to influence the number of births recorded in the 1911 Fertility
Census.

The attitude of the medical profession is significant for the
conclusion here that the chief method of family limitation in
all sections of the population was most probably increased
restraint on the part of husbands or, even more likely, coitus
interruptus, save by those who were bold enough to buy
those 'questionable rubber goods' which were sold 'in a
stealthy shamefaced way'.[55] This attitude was clearly expressed
on a number of occasions throughout the last twenty years of
the century. Thus in 1887 Dr Henry Allbut had his name
erased from the Medical Register because in chapter 7 of a
book which he had published under the title 'The Wife's Handbook' he had given details of methods whereby its readers
could effectively prevent conception, including descriptions
of appliances, with prices, among which was his own introducer
for Rendell's soluble pessaries, all apparently in the light of
a conviction, expressed in his Introduction, that 'most wives
are anxious to do their duty as wives and mothers'.[56] Although
there was clearly some objection to Allbut's non-professional
conduct in advertising, what seems most to have worried his
accusers was that he had advertised contraceptives as such.
The terms of the General Medical Council's indictment of the
author of 'The Wife's Handbook' included the specific charge
that the booklet was sold 'at so low a price as to bring such

work within reach of the youth of both sexes, to the detriment
of public morals',[57] a point which had also troubled the editor
of the 'British Medical Journal' in May of that same year when
he had commented on the earlier indictment of Allbut by the
Fellows of the Royal College of Physicians of Edinburgh.[58]
   The 'Journal' had taken the opportunity to decry all birth-
control propaganda on this ground at that time because such
pamphlets could not be commended even when they fell into
the hands of people with sufficient moral and intellectual capacity to deal with them. A few years later it returned to this
question of public morals in an attack on 'the indecent advertisements with which so many managers of newspapers, no
doubt greatly to the grief of their editors, persist in dis-
figuring their pages' and which the 'Journal' took to be mainly
disguised references to abortifacients. These advertisements,
it claimed, were 'a direct incentive, not only to undesirable
practices among the married, but to all sorts of immorality
among the young, by holding out a promise of relief if difficulties should arise'.[59]
   What such doctors were most concerned about, far above
anything else, was that the growing practice of making explicit
that conceptions could be prevented would lead not only to a
decline in the birth-rate but also to an increase in 'illicit intercourse', as the 'British Medical Journal' put it, a consequence
of 'the desire of young people for a life of luxury and display
which is incompatible with early marriage'. While it had no wish,
it emphasized, 'to minimise the offence of medical men who
prostitute their medical knowledge by using it to relieve - for
excessive fees - foolish girls from the consequences of folly',
heavy sentences 'on the few abortionists who have the misfortune to be found out' would achieve less than 'family training' to maintain children in clean, plain and healthy ways,
and 'by giving them such opportunities of forming desirable
acquaintances among the opposite sex as shall make them early
wishful to enter into the honourable state of matrimony'.[60] To
the degree that the official mouthpiece of the British Medical
Association correctly represented the views of the great bulk
of its members, it seems reasonably clear that neither female
methods of contraception nor abortion were spread widely
through the population at the prompting of doctors.
   By 1914, it is true, a medical man was able to admit to the
Dean of St Paul's that advice on the spacing of births was much
more frequently given to parents by doctors than had been the
case thirty or forty years previously, but the context in which
he made this admission was where there had been 'very dangerous confinements' or more generally in order that the mother
should nurse an infant 'for about a year'. The Dean himself
appears to have thought that such advice would be acted on
only by 'people capable of self-restraint' and although his witness did accept from another questioner that 'voluntary artificial restriction' was widely used and that 'medical men them-

selves' were 'the cause of the fall in the birthrate',[61] the most reasonable inference from expressed medical opinion at this time is that doctors advised the spacing of births to be desirable without actually specifying the means to be employed so that parents were left to fall back on self-restraint or to find out about birth-control for themselves.[62]

The public opposition of the doctors in the first three-quarters of the nineteenth century has been attributed to both professional and moral considerations, the former arising out of the advocacy of contraception as a kind of medical self-help by 'quacks' and from the need at that time for the developing profession to establish its social standing in the eyes of respectable society, still influenced by Christian morality.[63] Yet, provided that the term 'moral' is understood to imply a rather confused set of beliefs and exhortations about the desirability for human beings to restrain their sexual impulses, it is clear that even when, by the end of the century, the medical profession had become well established in the eyes of the public, the moral objection to the use of artificial means of contraception was still strongly felt by the great bulk of practitioners and therefore possibly just as strongly expressed in their consultations with patients. They had assumed 'the role of public censor once fulfilled by the priest',[64] interpreting their own concept of the family doctor as more than a merely medical 'expert'.

The Malthusian League itself had been received with hostility by spokesmen from the profession at its resurrection in 1877 and this hostility was sustained until well after the First World War, in spite of the fact that a few medical men - like Henry Allbut! - had always publicly supported it and in spite of the fact that the League itself officially gave no information on contraceptive methods as such until 1913 and then only to people who had filled out and signed a declaration stating their age, marital status, and agreement with the tenets of neo-Malthusianism.[65] The president of the League, Dr Charles Drysdale, the younger brother of the author of 'The Elements of Social Science', confessed in the 1890s that he was bewildered by 'the attitude of reserve maintained by the mass of British medical practitioners in face of the all important problem contained in the Population Question'.[66] Yet this bewilderment ought not to have arisen, because he himself had given evidence on behalf of the defendants at the Bradlaugh-Besant trial on the publication of birth-control literature in 1877, as had his wife, and the League, re-established after the trial by Charles Bradlaugh and Annie Besant with their aid, and that of a few friends,[67] had been far too long too closely associated with the secularist movement, and therefore with the secularist case for birth control, for respectable general practitioners to show anything but hostility when pressed, and indifference when not.

The impact of the League on the attitudes of the Victorians

with respect to family limitation is somewhat difficult to estimate,
even if its third president, on winding the organization up in
1927, was convinced that its work by then was completed since
the birth-rate had been reduced over the fifty years of its
existence from 36 per 1,000 to 18.[68] In addition to its monthly
journal, the 'Malthusian', of which it was selling about 1,200
copies a month at the end of the century, the League apparently
issued some three million pamphlets and leaflets between 1878
and 1922;[69] and it was no doubt their awareness of the extent
of this publicity which convinced its presidents, officers, and
even supporters that the message was being sufficiently relayed,
both widely and effectively, to bring down the number of
conceptions. Nevertheless, it was not only the medical profession and, of course, the clergy who were inhibited by its
secularist connections and who treated it publicly with indifference and occasionally with overt hostility but also the late
nineteenth-century feminist and socialist movements - the former
because, whatever middle-class advocates of the rights of
women may have thought about the desirability of working-
class women to have smaller families, contraception as such
seems to have implied to them yet another example of the subordination of women to men - in this instance the treatment of
wives as nothing more than the instruments of their husbands'
sexual desires[70] - and the latter because the propagation of
doctrines, derived from the writings of Thomas Robert Malthus,
were regarded as providing simply no solution to the problem
of the class subordination of the workers to the owners of land
and capital, and, even more to be deplored, as likely to direct
the attention of those workers away from the 'real' cause of
their misery.[71]

The most that can be claimed for the Malthusian League,
therefore, is that it made available, to those who were already
looking for it, information about the probable extent to which
the people of the day were concerned to limit the size of their
families. Even if more precise details about ways and means
were not provided in the League's literature - and for this
reason many who went to it for such details may well have been
disappointed, or indeed frustrated, by their lack - at least it
made it plain that some quite prominent, and therefore 'respectable', members of society were of the opinion that there was
nothing especially shameful about employing such means;
and by the end of the century many publications, quite
independent of the League, and commercial handbills, catalogues
and sex manuals[72] were fairly obviously available for those who
were sufficiently motivated to seek them out. The question of
motivation, that is to say, is crucial for understanding the
general adoption of some family limitation at this time. In the
case of the three subsequent sets of 'pioneers' identified above,
and of people socially very similar to them, this motivation may
be accounted for in terms of the growing importance of a life
experience which entailed a future-time perspective about the

education for, and advancement in, a possible career hierarchy of increasing responsibility and income. Even the Anglican clergymen, it will have been noticed in Table 8.2 (p.99), had been sufficiently influenced apparently in these regards to have entered the ranks of the 'pioneers' by the 1860s. The question of motivation for working-class parents, however, cannot be so easily explained in these terms, and these 'unconscious secularists', for all that they were probably not much aware of the propaganda of either the secularist or the neo-Malthusian movements, were also not widely subject to traditional Christian sermons, hostile to what the propaganda of these movements enjoined, save perhaps as children at Sunday school,[73] when the message would probably have been so obscure to them in its sexual connotations as to have remained of little influence on their behaviour when they reached adolescence and adult-hood. Nor should it be assumed that the doctrines of the feminists and the socialists led to widespread changes in family behaviour as a direct consequence of this teaching. Hence, working men and women generally may be said to have been neither attracted to, nor repelled from family limitation as a result of some kind of intellectual commitment to any of these doctrines; and the cause of their smaller families must be sought for elsewhere than in these terms.

For his part, McLaren has attempted one such explanation by reference to their alleged economic rationality in adapting to new conditions. Whereas their 'high fertility norm' was 'rational' when 'children raised frugally and put out to work were valuable assets', a new, lower norm was adopted once compulsory schooling and tighter restrictions on factory employ-ment converted children from being less 'potential wage earners' than 'dependants whose well-being was determined in part by the family's budget not being outstripped by the number of mouths to feed'.[74] Yet the evidence of working-class behaviour at this time hardly supports this argument. Thus, from his survey of York Benjamin Rowntree argued that 'the life of a labourer is marked by five alternating periods of want and comparative plenty'. Want began in childhood when each child virtually competed with brothers and sisters for food. Then, when the older children in the family began to go out to work and their earnings, wholly or in part, were taken to supplement the family income, the level of living of the family was raised above the poverty line. As young adults, however, working-class men and women, other than perhaps amongst the 'aristocrats' of labour, experienced a second period of want, once their own children had grown too numerous to be adequately supported on what the father, or more rarely the father and the mother, could earn; and they moved into comparative plenty once again when eventually some of their children started work. The parents then usually ended their lives in poverty because, when they were too old or too infirm to earn themselves, their adult children were burdened with

more of the old people's grandchildren than they could adequately house, clothe and feed.[75]
  It is pertinent to consider how working-class experience of
such a poverty 'cycle' can be made consistent with an explanation in terms of their economic rationality. Some 22.2 per cent
of Rowntree's poverty-stricken respondents were below the
poverty line because they had large families at the time of his
survey; that is, they had more than four children, but an
even larger proportion of those in poverty - 52.0 per cent -
earned insufficient to keep them above his very stringent
poverty line, even with smaller families than this.[76] It seems
quite clear, therefore, from the incidence of poverty at this
time that for a working-class couple to produce babies in the
expectation that once the older of them went out to work there
would be enough for all, implies that they operated according
to a very limited conception of economic rationality, if only
because such parents would surely have been aware, from
their own personal experience, how short-lived this relative
relief from poverty was likely to be, since children who were
earning soon began to take advantage of their economic
independence in order to set up house for themselves away
from their families of origin.[77] As an explanation for the onset
of family limitation within the working-class generally, such a
reference to economic rationality seems as implausible for
Rowntree's and Booth's day as it is for explaining the even
larger families at the time of Malthus, although doubtless there
was always a minority of couples in the working-class whose
fertility behaviour was conditioned by such a concept.
  Even McLaren, it should be added, has expressed the view
that the new working-class norm of the smaller family had its
roots for some sections of the population in considerations other
than economic rationality alone.

  Fertility first fell in the textile areas where there was a good
  deal of female employment, but rates remained high in the
  mining and heavy industry areas where there was little. Out
  of an interest both in protecting their family's economic
  stability and assuring themselves a degree of liberty, women
  who worked outside the home revealed a greater desire than
  those who had not to control family size.

How, in terms of economic rationality, could this be? Surely
those women who were unwilling, or more probably unable, to
find employment for themselves should have had every incentive
to keep the number of their children within the cost limits set
by the wages brought home by their husbands! And when it is
recalled that even in the Lancashire mills only about one quarter of the women employed were married,[78] and if it is assumed
that probably less than one in five of married women were
employed at this time, it does not seem sufficiently plausible
to attribute the general fall in working-class 'fertility norms'
either to the economic rationality of housewives protecting their
family's stability, or to the desire for a degree of liberty on

the part of such a minority of working wives.

This does not mean that working-class couples eschewed economic rationality altogether. The correlation between real wages and the marriages of all males, 20-4 years old, for the second half of the nineteenth century was impressively high -- + 0.87 ± 0.06 for 1856-73, + 0.70 ± 0.12 for 1873-90, falling to + 0.66 ± 0.13 for 1890-1907[79] -- suggesting that the ebb and flow of the trade cycle, in so far as it affected the employment and general prosperity of wage workers, resulted also in an ebb and flow of weddings. Thus, fluctuations in the birth-rate then - as no doubt much earlier - were consequences of fairly short-term responses to periods of difficulty by post-poning the wedding day, and therefore the first birth some nine months later; but, save where such postponements were for a relatively large number of couples moving into longer periods of courtship overall, or where they resulted in a large increase in the number never marrying at all, the direct demographic consequences of this sort of economic rationality are clearly very different from those which are the result of a limitation of fertility over the child-bearing period of the wife, that is, over a much longer time-span than is indicated by the statistics of economic fluctuations. What seems much more important, and McLaren has referred to it as a 'new condition' to which the workers had to adapt, was compulsory schooling for their children and the tighter restrictions on their factory employment; that is, new 'norms' of child care were imposed on them by legislation and by a corps of factory and school attendance officers. To the degree that there might have been certain similarities between these new norms and those which the 'pioneers' had adopted for their children many years before, similar circumstances rather than simple dif-fusion, might suffice to explain why it was that the working classes came to adopt similar family limitation practices. for all that their lifestyles remained different. Such a conclusion, however, depends upon a consideration of the changing evaluation of children during this period and that yet remains to be described.

9 THE REVALUATION OF CHILDREN

The story of the silent social revolution, as George Lowndes called it, that is, the history of the endeavours of successive British governments 'to extend a modicum of schooling to the whole mass of the child population of England and Wales',[1] has been told far too many times to be repeated yet again here. Indeed, for present purposes the changes which Victorian politicians and educational innovators succeeded in establishing through parliamentary legislation and local government by-law were rather less important than the extent to which certain parental attitudes endured despite these pressures on them to accept novelty. As Horace Mann commented to the Registrar-General in 1851, although it was sometimes claimed that working-class parents could not afford the school fees which educational aspirations would impose on them, what lay at the root of the unsatisfactory nature of the schooling received by their children was not want of means, save perhaps in the case of paupers, but 'want of inclination: in short, a low appreciation by the parents of the value of instruction to their children, in comparison with those more sensual enjoyments to themselves for the sake of which it is neglected'. Working-class expenditure on beer rather than on school fees indicated to Mann where their priorities lay.

Moreover, he did not believe that the provision of free education for such children would solve this problem, because it was already apparent that the attendance record of those working-class children who were enrolled in the free schools was poorer than that of those in the fee-charging schools.[2]

It is evident that even the lowest amount of wages which the children of a labouring man will receive (from 1s.6d. to 2s. per week) must be so great a relief to the parents as to render it almost hopeless that they can withstand the inducements, and retain the child at school in the face of such temptation. It is not for the sake of *saving a penny* per week that a child is transferred from the school to the factory or the fields, but for the sake of *gaining a shilling or eighteen-pence* per week.

In this respect Mann took a fairly commonplace point of view about working-class attitudes to education, one indeed which had been enshrined in the Factory Acts since 1833, once they had effectively made the employment of children conditional on their part-time attendance at school and thus obliged not only employers but also parents to accept a certain amount of

compulsory education as a legally imposed condition on the
lives of their children.[3] Mann's analysis, however, went much
further than this. Labouring parents, he surmised, took the
view that 'instruction beyond a certain point can never be of
any practical utility to those of their condition'. Yet, they were
not unique in this. A 'very false philosophy' of education was
prevalent in all ranks of society. 'The length and character of
the education given in this country to the young are regulated
more by a regard to its material advantage, as connected with
their future physical condition, than by any wise appreciation
of the benefits of knowledge itself.'[4]

Amongst illiterate parents and those of little education, that
is to say, the interruption of their children's schooling for any
reason was of no particular consequence because they themselves were unaware of having suffered any appreciable hard-
ship on this score. This is possibly why compulsory education
after 1876 may have changed some attitudes after a while
because, as the Royal Commission on the Working of the Education Acts noted in 1888, parents who had now experienced
compulsory, full-time education themselves had begun to accept
it as inevitable for their children, even if it was still the case
by this time that although some 95 per cent of those children
between the ages of 7 and 11, 'belonging to the class usually
found in elementary schools' now had their names on the school
registers, only 76 per cent of those on such rolls were actually
attending school. 'The indifference of parents to education for
its own sake, must, we fear, be reckoned as an obstacle, which
has perhaps been aggravated by compulsion, and has, possibly,
not yet reached its worst, though we believe that it will tend
to decrease in proportion to the improvement of schools.' This
was not a matter simply of the desire of such parents to put
their children to work for the wages they could bring home to
the family. They had other reasons for curtailing their offspring's schooling. 'Home needs, such as sickness in the family,
the absence of the mother at work and nursing babies, keep
many girls away, sometimes for long periods.'[5]

Working-class hostility to the school attendance officer,
which was concomitant to this desire to keep children away from
school, whatever the motive, declined over the last thirty
years of the century, at least in London, where the attendance
record rose eventually to 88.2 per cent, although London may
have been unique amongst urban areas in these respects
because by 1893 only 693 of its pupils were half-timers, as
compared with Bradford's 9,286.[6] All this, therefore, may be
read as the working-class parents' acceptance of their children's compulsory education rather than as their enthusiasm
for it,[7] although this relative indifference to the value of
education as such should not be interpreted as universal within
that class. For all that historians may be reasonably divided
over deciding whether or not working-class agitators were
responsible for the Education Act of 1870,[8] it seems clear that

while some working-class parents were so ambivalent about
education before 1870 that their children attended school with
what one educationalist called at the time 'strange irregularity',[9]
others were quite prepared to pay regularly for the private
education of their offspring, even if this were provided by
'small, ill-organized, and allegedly indifferent seminaries'[10] and
apparently encouraged their attendance.

At the same time, although it was generally understood that
middle-class parents were prepared to spend money on education, especially for their boys, this again was not universally
a case of enthusiasm but sometimes of reluctance within that
class. 'I was most struck in my enquiries with the general
indifference of parents to the education of their sons,' wrote
C. H. Stanton in his 'Report on the Counties of Devon and
Somerset' to the Schools Inquiry Commission. 'This was
especially the case with the smaller farmers.' The presumed
question of why, beyond an interest in education for its own
sake, any of these parents would want to give their sons a
more expensive education than they themselves had perhaps
received was answered by this particular Assistant Commissioner in terms of what he called 'the only spur', goading these
smaller farmers into 'a languid activity', namely, 'the growing
consciousness that their labourers were being better educated
than their own sons'.[11]

Irrespective of class, even though the proportions may have
differed somewhat within each class throughout the country,
three different types of parent may, therefore, be identified
in the nineteenth century, in so far as they are classified in
terms of their attitudes to the education of their children. The
largest proportion in each class apparently took the view that
children should get very much the same sort of education as
their parents had had, their own children being educated to
roughly the same degree as they themselves had been in their
childhood. Some - and here the proportion of them in the
various classes may have varied much more markedly - believed
that their children should be provided with the same education
as that obtained by the children of parents in different, and
socially superior, circumstances from themselves, or by the
children of parents in different social circumstances from their
own parents when they themselves were at school. Whether
they merely aspired for their children to become socially mobile
through education, or whether they had personally been
socially mobile, that is to say, these were parents whose children received education of a different content from that which
they themselves had experienced.

Finally a few, who would seem to have taken the same view
as the majority of educationalists, believed that all children,
including their own, should be given an education which was of
value both to them personally and to the society in which they
would live when adult, and this few thought of their children's
education in this way, quite regardless of the kind of education

they themselves had received when young. Thus, their children may, as a matter of fact, have been provided with the same
education as they themselves had had or with education of a
very different content. The important characteristic of this
last minority of parents in the present context was that their
motives were quite distinct from those of both the conservative
and the socially aspiring parents with whom, in terms of the
education their children actually received, they might otherwise be confused. The argument here is that because their
motives were different, all three sorts of couples, even before
becoming parents, were likely to have approached the questions
of marrying or postponing marriage, allowing their fertility
to reach its unhampered maximum or limiting the number of
children born to them, from very different angles.

In so far as the simple cost of educating their children might
be interpreted as a possible reason for family limitation, the
majority in all classes, conservative in their conception of what
education their children should get and, therefore, possibly
conservative in other family matters, would have adopted some
kind of birth control for this reason only when pressured into
it by rising real costs of education to them at the relevant
period, that is, by rises in educational charges disproportionately greater than other costs, especially when measured
against real income, or in the case of those working-class
parents who were accustomed to sending their children to the
free schools, by the loss of the income which such children
might otherwise have brought into the family at a time when
real costs to them were rising. This argument, it should be
noted, implies a simple 'rational' reaction to economic change
on the part of parents who are presumed to maintain some kind
of cost consciousness when indulging in sexual intercourse,
and it also implies that the economic change in question was
completely external to their family situation, completely beyond
their control. Indeed, one type of change which has been
suggested as crucial in this context which is not economic as
such, but which has been interpreted as having economic
consequences to which parents have reacted, is the decline in
child mortality since the eighteenth century, which had therefore raised a family's total real costs, simply as a consequence
of the survival of more of its children to the end of their
schooling than had been the case a generation earlier.[12]

The assumption that such a decline in mortality was a most
important factor in family limitation, sometimes referred to as
the 'child survival hypothesis', presupposes some unspecified
comparisons with what are referred to as 'traditional' or 'pre-
modern' societies, in which parents are presumed to have
followed 'a strategy' of high fertility to compensate for the
high mortality of their offspring, that is, children in such
societies are assumed to be regarded by their parents as fairly
immediate economic assets above all else, as well as a sort of
economic insurance for them when, in their old age and in

infirmity, they can no longer support themselves economically. On the basis of such an assumption it has been alleged, for example, that in early industrializing societies 'the possibility of employment for young children encouraged families to continue high fertility strategies even as child mortality fell',[13] so that it was only when this possibility of employment declined that fertility was deliberately reduced.

Evidence to support the claim that such high fertility strategies had been followed, that is, to support the 'child replacement hypothesis', is extremely difficult to obtain about past societies;[14] and studies of extant 'traditional' and 'modernizing' societies, when the relevant questions have been put to parents, do not indicate that many of the people in them have been motivated by purely economic considerations deliberately to attempt a further conception at the death of a child,[15] although there is evidence that male children have been highly valued for other than economic reasons, such as to light their father's funeral pyre or because it was regarded as shameful for property to be inherited by a daughter's husband rather than by a son, since it would pass out of the family line and cease to be referred to by the original family name.[16] For such reasons a son-replacement strategy might have been operated where some form of family limitation through abstention rather than contraception was practised, the evidence for even the use of coitus interruptus in these societies being scanty. Yet it is not likely that pre-industrial Europeans operated an equivalent to the former of these, and evidence for the latter is rather thin on the ground.

Moreover, an argument against the child replacement hypothesis can be formulated by inference from the natural subfertility of some parents in presumably all societies. The Royal Commission on Population, for example, estimated that about 7 per cent of all couples are likely to find themselves involuntarily childless, about $4\frac{1}{2}$ per cent limited to one birth only, and about $5\frac{1}{2}$ per cent to two.[17] Unless it is simply assumed that the high infant and child mortality in 'traditional' societies was a consequence of their high fertility, that is, that it occurred disproportionately more frequently in the larger families,[18] at least one in ten of the couples in such societies were not likely to have had any children surviving to adulthood, so that had they operated a fertility 'insurance' policy for their old age, it is surprising that more adoption from the larger families by about one in ten of couples has not been recorded in the histories of these societies, oral and written.[19] If, that is to say, in the present context, no more than a small proportion of pre-Victorian English couples had been accustomed to following a high fertility strategy as a deliberate policy on such economic grounds it is difficult to appreciate how low or falling child mortality rates could have led to more than an equally small proportion of them to practise a family limitation strategy on the same grounds.

Their experience of such falling mortality, indeed, would imply a rather complicated kind of foresight on their part, were they to have followed such a strategy. While it is true that the death rates per 1,000 boys, aged 0-4 declined in England and Wales from about 70 in the 1840s to just over 60 in the 1890s, and the comparable rates for girls dropped from just over 60 to just over 50, the deaths of infants under one year old per 1,000 live births remained approximately the same throughout the half century. The infant mortality rate in 1899, in fact, was higher than it had been at any time during Victoria's reign, except for the two years, 1846 and 1847, so little had any real change occurred in the incidence of death before the age of one year. The most striking improvement in child mortality occurred for children between the ages of five and fourteen whose rates, initially lower than those for younger children, continued regularly to improve, dropping from 9.17 and 5.13 for boys aged 5-9 and 10-14 respectively in 1841-50 to 4.31 and 2.45 in 1891-1900, and from 8.90 and 5.44 for girls of the same ages respectively in 1841-50 to 4.37 and 2.57 in 1891-1900.[20]

In so far as the child-survival hypothesis rests on the assumption that it is the parents' experience that their children do not die which stimulates them to practise family limitation, such a motivation in the Victorian 'pioneers' could not have been prompted when their children were in their infancy but when the oldest child had reached its fifth or sixth birthday, that is, some six or more years after its parents had married and, granted that they did not space conceptions, by the time they already had three or four children. Yet, as the analysis on p. 73 above has indicated, some couples had already stopped before this point, by the time that the wife was thirty-one or thirty-four. Such a termination of pregnancy could hardly have been the simple response to the survival of even the oldest child because this is inconsistent with the information about the relative frequency of conceptions from the time of the marriage. What the absence of birth replacing amongst these couples suggests, on the contrary, is that the decline in child mortality could have had the effect of increasing the size of the families of those couples who wished for at least four children to reach maturity, by comparison with those of a generation earlier who had wanted four or more children but had been unable to achieve this objective because fewer of them had survived to the year at which the mother had reached her menopause.

The implication of 'Prosperity and Parenthood' on the cost of children to the English 'middle classes' becoming increased by the fall in child mortality can therefore be misinterpreted if it is read as 'hard' evidence of a direct response by such parents to the exigencies of their immediate economic situation. The major research task of that book, it will be recalled, was to test that type of theorizing about family limitation which takes it for granted that couples respond 'rationally' to their economic circumstances by postponing the wedding day at a time of slump, for example, or advancing it at a time of boom, postponing a conception in a period of rising costs, conceiving in a period of prosperity, etc. In that 1954 chapter on the cost of children, therefore, what might otherwise be interpreted as a form of the child survival hypothesis was introduced as merely yet another example of the sort of costs which the 'pioneers' of family limitation certainly had to face, but it was not concluded that this was the sole, or even the main explanation for their smaller families; and the argument now is that such a hypothesis is even less plausible for the case of upper-class and upper-middle-class parents than might have been thought earlier when less demographic and sociological information on these kinds of issues was available.

Of course, although virtually nothing is known about the conception frequencies of working-class mothers during the critical period, the possibility that they followed a 'rational' practice of direct replacement for lost children cannot be ruled out altogether even if it cannot be confirmed. Nevertheless, what is known about infant mortality in 1911 does not lend much evidence to this view. The Registrar-General's identification of a class gradient in such mortality to the effect that, proportionately speaking, babies born to fathers in the largely unskilled occupations (Class V) were twice as likely to die before their first birthday than babies born to those in Class I occupations,[21] suggests that the incentive to prevent a conception because of the cost of children could have been very much less for Class V parents. Unless, moreover, the improvement of child mortality, referred to globally above, was evenly distributed across all classes, it could have been the case that a similar class gradient for child mortality became more marked as the nineteenth century wore on, especially if it is assumed, as the Registrar-General believed, that the 1911 class differential in infant mortality, and therefore also in differential child mortality, was a consequence of the different economic and social circumstances of the parents. A 'rational' strategy of child replacement in the Class V case would thus surely have meant that family limitation on their part would have been postponed for much longer than the 1911 Fertility Census figures indicate; but all this suggests making far too many assumptions for the hypothesis to be relied upon as a likely explanation of even working-class behaviour.

None of this alters the fact that government action through the Factory and Educational Acts did make education more of an economic burden for working-class parents than it had been earlier or, if not a burden, an extra cost which had to be met in some way. Nor does it alter the fact that tuition fees in the English public schools were doubling and other increases in the cost of education were occurring for upper-, upper-middle- and middle-class parents at a time of uncertainty about the

future.[22] Granted that the emphasis here is still on those
parents who were conservative in their attitude to their children's education, it is clear that these changes were beyond the
control of the working class, since the education of their
children rapidly became effectively compulsory at this time;
but it is difficult to appreciate how the majority of other parents
could not have brought down the cost of education simply by
terminating the education of some of their children or sending
them to cheaper schools and therefore reducing the demand.
The answer to this problem would seem to lie in the competition
for places, and for jobs afterwards, which they reacted to,
from those other parents, identified as minorities, who either
wanted their children to have a different education from themselves or from the children of parents in the same social circumstances as themselves, or who took much the same view of
education being valuable to all children as the educationalists
of their day.

The first of these minorities constituted an obvious challenge
if only because it consisted of a socially ambitious category
of parents who wished for their children to get on in the world
by being presented with advantages which they themselves
had lacked as children. 'One of the many great uses of our
public schools,' the founder of Radley told its old boys in
1872, was 'to confer an aristocracy on boys who do not inherit
it.'[23] The assumption was that by sending them to 'good'
schools such boys would be 'fitted' to enter occupations, closed
to their fathers, or - in the case of fathers who had themselves
risen by other means in wealth, influence and social esteem -
that they would be able to consolidate a position won for them.
This emphasis on education for children to become socially
mobile has sometimes been interpreted as so pervasive in modern
society that it has been considered sufficient to explain the fall
in fertility.[24] In the present context, however, the argument
must be considered in the form that conservative parents, like
the smaller farmers castigated by the Schools Inquiry Assistant
Commissioner in 1867, felt themselves obliged to spend more
than they otherwise would have done on education as a guarantee of 'security' to prevent their children falling in the social
scale in competition with that aspiring minority seeking 'social
promotion'[25] through educational means.

This social capillarity thesis, as Arsène Dumont presented it
in 1890,[26] rested on the notion of wives and children as hostages to fortune in very much the same fashion as Francis
Bacon and the other English authors, referred to in chapter 5
above. What has to be considered now, therefore, is the extent
to which parents were, as a matter of fact, realistic in their
assessment of the possibility of mobility in Victorian society
in the sense that it was 'rational' for them to provide opportunity, especially for their boys, to rise in the social scale
according to the degree to which their education was appropriate for the position in society which those parents wanted

them to obtain. It is, obviously, important not to over-
emphasize the apparent openness of the society simply from
the evidence of deliberate attempts by some Victorians to make
it more open than it was, as they saw it. A critic of the abolition of the purchase of army commissions, for example, pointed
out in 1876 that:[27]

> the formers of the first great scheme for open competition -
> that for the Indian Civil Service - fancied that they had
> opened a career to every young Englishman, of whatever
> class in life, the actual result being that competition is
> practically limited to those who are able to pay for an
> extremely expensive education of a very special kind. The
> new system is therefore just as much a monopoly as the old.

What seems to have happened, that is to say, was that conservative parents spent more money on education to prevent
their sons from being ousted from such posts in 'open' competition with the sons of that minority of parents who were
prepared to 'invest' in their sons' education as a means of
social advancement. Their essential conservatism continued to
show itself, indeed, in the desire that their boys should
continue in the same socially prestigeful occupations as their
fathers or be gentlemen of leisure like him where this was
possible.

At the same time, purely statistical estimates of the social
class composition of males over fifteen years of age in England
and Wales between 1881 and 1911 - arrived at through somewhat arbitrary although not at all haphazard manipulation of
Census information about occupations - provide the impression
that over those thirty years at any rate there had occurred
some disproportionate growth in the numbers in the Registrar-
General's Classes I to III at the expense of a disproportionate
decline in Classes IV and V. These suggest that changes in the
demand for socially different sorts of occupation had resulted
in some upward mobility for about six men in every 1,000 into
Class I, from between seven and twenty-three into Class II,
and between two and thirty-three into Class III, depending
on how occcupations are aggregated to form these classes, and
how far Class III is regarded as wholly skilled manual.[28] Some
upward mobility was inevitable, that is, irrespective of attendance at the more expensive schools, irrespective of the
Victorian parents' desire for it; and if it was also the case,
as seems likely, that the differential fertility of the classes
more than compensated for their different infant and child
mortality, increasingly over the period upward movement was
also inevitable for a few because the more privileged classes in
the community, and especially the 'pioneers' of the smaller
family within these classes, were not replacing themselves to
the same degree as the other classes.

Thus, for economic and demographic reasons Victorian society
was a little open, from at least about 1881, resulting in some
upward mobility from lower down in the social scale without

any compensatory movement downwards from those higher up. Studies in the twentieth century, moreover, seem to indicate that only children and the oldest children in small families are more likely to do well academically than others,[29] so that if this were just as true in the nineteenth, those parents who practised family limitation in order to provide their sons with educational advantages were likely to have been more successful than they realized or, indeed, could possibly have known at that time; and just as it is impossible that any could have been motivated by certain knowledge that the children of small families were better able to compete academically, so it is improbable that they were genuinely aware of the inevitability of some upward social movement, especially as roughly nineteen men in every twenty or thereabouts per generation did not move socially at all.

Perhaps, therefore, what was more important than whether or not the Victorians appreciated what they were doing in these respects was the fact that any upward mobility that was deliberately sought through education could only have been possible because the parents of these children took a very different view of them from what was customary. In previous generations the significance of the birth and survival of an heir, especially to inherit the estate, was that he represented a perpetuation of the family line, the family name; and sons were necessary for this, not in the economic sense of the child replacement hypothesis, but simply because daughters lost their names and to this degree their family identity at marriage, which meant that daughters' sons, like other boys recruited to the family line by adoption or some other device, involved legal complications which the existence of a male heir avoided. It has been argued, for instance, that landowners who had no sons to succeed them 'must often have felt disinclined' to make the financial effort to pay off their debts. 'In such a situation it was even more of a certainty that the landowner would charge his estate with a more generous round of legacies and annuities for his other relatives and friends than he would have done if he were being succeeded by his son.' That this was not simply a matter of his personal affection for an offspring and concern for its future can be seen in the condition of inheritance that was sometimes imposed on a nephew, or some such distant relative, that he should adopt the surname of the family from whom he was inheriting. Similar devices were also operated in cases of inheritance through a daughter in order to retain the family estate intact and perpetuate the family name.[30] The significance of this emphasis, that is to say, lay in the nature of that kind of family tradition which regarded the incumbent of the estate for the time being as little more than an agent for perpetuating it within the family line.

Perhaps it could be objected here that this family lineage emphasis could have been maintained by a small section of the population only, those with prosperity to pass on from generation to generation, especially those with property which took the very tangible form of land. Yet, as far as the middle and upper middle classes are concerned, it also seems to have applied to family businesses, so that commercial men, bankers, businessmen generally, lawyers and doctors, and no doubt others were proud to establish a family line in whatever economic activity they were engaged upon to make a living and they expected that their sons, or at least one of their sons, would eventually take their place as head of the original firm.[31] The working-class practice of sons following their father into paid employment on the same farm, in the same factory, or down the same mine, usually in the same work, it should be emphasized, might well not have been a consequence of such an evaluation of the perpetuation of the lineage, but have economic causes deriving from restricted employment opportunities in the area where these sons' parents lived, although there is some evidence that, times of unemployment apart, boys were expected to do this rather than to move elsewhere. The important issue here, however, is not how far down in the social scale the emphasis on the family line was significant to parents and their children, but the extent to which a desire for some kind of occupational mobility, so that the son was positively encouraged to seek a different occupation in a different milieu from that of his father, came to be customary at the relevant time, namely, in the second half of the nineteenth century, since it is precisely the hypothesized widespread extension of this desire which lies at the basis of the social capillarity thesis.

The question of periodicity in this report is crucial. Some writers, for example, have claimed that the emergence of what has been referred to as the 'filiocentric' family came much earlier, far too early indeed for it to have been a directly operative factor in the adoption of family limitation, if this is assumed to have been motivated by the desire to give boys such opportunities. It even preceded the French revolutionaries' demand for liberty, equality and fraternity, having its roots in social and demographic changes which predated the emergence of this ideology.[32] From this point of view, family limitation may be interpreted less as ideological in the strict sense and more as a consequence of another kind of child survival experience. The emphasis in this hypothesis, that is to say, is on the psychological – non-calculative, affective, emotional, sentimental, but certainly not irrational – rather than the economic impact of falling child mortality on the parents of such children at this time, as compared with those of a generation or so earlier who 'helplessly' watched their offspring die.

For example, it has been stressed that at the beginning of the eighteenth century the death of children was 'a source of perpetual woe. To protect themselves from excessive pain, parents appealed to the inscrutable will of God, and they encouraged others to moderate their affection for their children, some of whom must surely die.'[33] There was, of course, nothing essentially new about this at the time and the emphasis here therefore must be on the possibility that these experiences had been so common for all parents for such a long time that the reaction to them had become stereotyped into a state of mind about children which persisted even after the circumstances responsible for it had begun to disappear. Thus another historian has referred to what he has termed 'custom and tradition and the frozen emotionality of ancien-régime life', which so gripped 'with deathly force' the mothers of eighteenth-century children that even when 'the network of medical personnel in Europe' had become sufficiently widespread 'to put interested mothers within earshot of sensible advice' many of them quite obviously failed to hear it. 'That is why their children vanished with the ghastly slaughter of the innocents that was traditional child-rearing.'[34]

When child mortality declined, for whatever reason, the pain of parents may be inferred to have declined also, so that they needed no longer to moderate their affection to the same degree as their grandparents and great grandparents had been obliged to do. Hence, 'declining child mortality rates in the later eighteenth century made children worth taking seriously: when they were more likely to survive to manhood, there was more point in taking pains with their early training and education'.[35] From this point on there was also, it might be supposed, a greater incentive to control fertility since this would have provided extra economic and other resources, such as the mother's personal care and attention, for making their early training and education that much more effective. But was it this decline in child mortality which produced this change in attitude to child care, as the quoted passage implies, or was there a change in child nurture which brought about the fall in mortality?

In so far as the English peerage is concerned there is clear statistical evidence for the fact of such a decline and this has often been attributed to the improvement in the medical services which these people could afford.[36]

> Child mortality among the general population was rather slow to respond to medical discoveries and progress in hygiene. Of the children in the general population of England and Wales born about 1846, 31.94 per cent died before they were 15; of those born about 1896, 23.05 per cent died under 15; by 1946 the proportion had fallen to only 5.31 per cent. The corresponding dates when the nobility had similar rates of child mortality were roughly 1741, 1758 and 1927. The slow progress of the general population in the nineteenth century thus contrasts with the rapid advance the nobility had made in the eighteenth, when in some 17 years the same moderate decline occurred which was to take 50 years later on for the population at large.

Yet, it is not at all certain that the drop in child mortality

amongst noble families was due to medical discoveries and progress in hygiene, as the example of tuberculosis in the twentieth century shows, since the introduction of what is, medically
speaking, satisfactory treatment did not occur until 1947, long
after the mortality from tuberculosis in the middle and upper
classes had declined. This improvement in their case has hence
been accounted for in terms of improvements in the nutrition
of the rest of the population. 'Well-to-do people benefitted
from a secondary effect of improved nutrition, for which they
themselves offered little scope.' Similarly, the decline in
upper-class child mortality in the eighteenth century may be
explained in terms of 'the lower prevalence of many micro-
organisms' - especially those borne on the air, in water and in
food - subsequent upon the great increase in food supplies,
which was achieved between the end of the sixteenth and
the middle of the nineteenth centuries, and which resulted in
better nutrition amongst the population generally and its greater
disease resistance, to infectious as opposed to contagious
diseases.[37]

Medical advance certainly occurred and, possibly, some
improvement in personal hygiene amongst noble families, but
what evidence there is on this point, and it is somewhat
sparse,[38] does not suggest modifications in domestic life on a
sufficiently wide scale to bring about the change in rates over
the seventeen-year span which Thomas Hollingsworth's statistics
indicate. The drop in upper-class child mortality was much
more likely to have been the unintended and unanticipated
consequence of those agricultural advances which ducal and
gentry 'gentleman' farmers had made,[39] not a deliberate result
of their wife's improved child care. Since, moreover, the
fertility of the peers did not decline during this period, it is
not at all unambiguously evident that any changed attitude
toward childbirth and child care was widespread amongst them.
If anything, at this time the wives of the peers conceived more
so that the child survival hypothesis in its psychological version
finds little support in this demographical data because, although
there was some decline in the peers' fertility after 1800, it was
not until the marriages which produced children between 1850
and 1874 that a strongly marked drop in the number of children
born to these families occurred.[40]

There is, nevertheless, evidence of some apparent change
in attitude towards children, if not to infants, in England at
this time, showing itself in what has been described as 'a new
willingness to recognize and consider their unique personal
needs'. At least, 'the novelists and educationalists of late
eighteenth-century England were unanimous that the (middle-
class) child had never been treated with such consideration
and solicitude'.[41] One historian, indeed, has located the origins
of what he has called 'the egalitarian family' in this period
amongst, not so much the middle classes, as the aristocracy
of England whose husbands, wives and children are alleged to

have formed 'a new pattern of household interaction - from which servants were excluded. This was domesticity ... [a] pattern of close and loving association between husband and wife, and of doting care for children.'[42] Others have referred to the very harsh treatment of children before this time, in order presumably to emphasize the change which has occurred. 'A very large percentage of the children born prior to the eighteenth century were what would to-day be termed "battered children".'[43] To knock out sin 'the dominant attitude towards children in the seventeenth century had been autocratic, indeed ferocious'.[44] Yet, if so much had changed in the eighteenth century, why was it that the Victorian public schoolmaster's birch was 'as central to the work of teaching as is the text book or the blackboard of to-day, and was used not just for naughtiness but also for faulty work - a wrong tense or even a false quantity'? and why was it that, in spite of the many exposures of disease, immorality and cruelty in the Victorian public schools,[45] fathers who had themselves been victims of these evils continued (dotingly or ferociously?) to send their sons to the same schools as they had attended?

The problem with all qualitative information of this sort, on which such large generalizations are too often built, is that it usually consists of inference from the writings of a small number of people to the assumed attitude of the many silent thousands who have left behind no record of any attachment either way, whether ferocious or doting, to their young. Thus other evidence can be quoted to demonstrate that a changed attitude to children had already occurred in the Tudor period, while examples can still be found of fathers who beat their boys to discipline them for study in the 1960s.[46] Evidence, similarly, can be deployed to show the use of birth control in the first Elizabethan era and unwillingness to use it in the second.[47] All that such citations prove, as Himes pointed out with respect to the history of contraception, is that the desire to control conception and some knowledge of how to control it has always existed throughout human history. It is 'a universal social phenomenon', as also surely is the desire and knowledge of how to raise children with loving care; but, just as 'stress upon the social and economic desirability of birth control is a characteristic of the nineteenth century, and hardly antedates it',[48] so the emphasis on the social and economic desirability of putting the child's future before that of the parents - the filiocentric emphasis - is a very rare phenomenon.[49]

There is no suggestion here of a categorical denial of the strong possibility that from the Middle Ages, say, there has occurred a process whereby the population generally has been 'civilized', initially by imposition on the part of those of higher rank on their social inferiors and later by bourgeois parents on their own offspring.[50] Nor is it claimed that the birth-control and infant and child welfare 'movements' produced the relevant change in attitudes in the population: indeed, it might well

have been the case that the changed attitudes produced these
'movements'.[51] What is challenged here is the possibility that
there occurred so rapid a change in upper-class attitudes to
their children as the focus of non-calculating, affective,
emotional, sentimental concern that it was this change which
brought down the child mortality of the peers fairly dramatically
in the late eighteenth century and also resulted a hundred
years later not only in the democratization of birth control in
the sense of the widespread adoption of it by a very large
proportion of married couples, but in an even more dramatic
reduction in family size in all classes of the community, so
that even laggards like coal and shale mine faceworkers
recorded a drop in the average number of children born to
them of from 8.79 to 6.68 over a generation, and agricultural
labourers of from 7.96 to 5.38.

The argument which is preferred here, therefore, is that
the relevant changed attitude towards offspring which occurred
was not a revaluation of children as objects of emotional
interest, but an acceptance of the possibility that they might
not perpetuate their family's traditions, might not want to
perpetuate these traditions and ought not to be constrained
to perpetuate these traditions. Superficially, this might seem
to imply that state of mind which is presupposed by the social
capillarity thesis. Parents who were prepared to spend money
on a son's education solely in order that he might become
socially mobile could be assumed to have had precisely such
a break with tradition in mind. Nevertheless, it seems reasonably clear that those purchasers of landed estates, at any rate,
who sent their oldest son to a public school expected him and
his oldest son to maintain the family line at this higher social
level thereafter. Why else did they seek 'the paraphernalia of
acceptability, family arms and crests', had they not 'some
dynastic interest'?[52] It is not a necessary condition of social
aspiration, that is to say, that children must be thought of
as persons in their own right who are entitled to decide for
themselves whether they will break their social bonds with
their family of origin in order to advance socially, whether this
is through their own, unaided efforts or through the opportunities they receive from the educational achievement their
parents have made possible for them.

The likelihood that it was neither the conservative nor the
socially aspiring parents, who were responsible for a revaluation of children in the second half of the nineteenth century,
raises the question of the extent to which the relevant change
in attitudes was in some sense a consequence of the activities
of that even smaller minority of parents, identified above,
who thought of all children, not excluding their own, as being
entitled to the sort of education which would be of value to
them individually when as adults they came to live in the world
they would eventually take over from the previous generation,
irrespective of whether they might or might not also become

socially mobile. Such an intention, it is true, could not be
realized without some non-calculative concern for each child as
an individual, as a focus for teaching in its own right; and for
this reason the attitude of these parents may seem to have been
very similar to that which has already been rejected above as
not very relevant for the onset of family limitation. It is equally
true that theirs was a view of children which had been held
by educationalists for a very long time, so that the novelty of
widespread family limitation at this time cannot be explained
in these terms as such.

Of course, it is the case that this minority of parents included
in their number those who took part in founding the schools
to which people like themselves, as well as the educationally
conservative and socially ambitious parents sent their sons.
Within their ranks also were to be found those who were instrumental in creating the legislative and other means whereby
those parents who could not, or would not, educate their children were assisted, or compelled to do so. Yet it is not claimed
here that this essentially pressure-group activity on their part
turned conservative and socially aspiring parents into ardent
supporters of the cause, valuing education for their children
in much the same fashion as these innovators. Rather, what is
suggested is that what occurred was the widespread acceptance
by all three types of parent that educational achievement was
best determined by some examination or test; and the part
played by this minority 'pressure' group of parents was that
of providing active public support in parliament, on local bodies,
and elsewhere for what has been referred to as 'one of the
greatest discoveries of nineteenth-century Englishmen',[53] the
device of the external examiner, as exemplified in the public
examination.

Briefly summarized, at the beginning of the nineteenth
century examinations were virtually unknown in England. The
universities, it is true, awarded degrees on the basis of what
were called examinations, but in Oxford, it has been alleged,
these were little more than casual conversations between the
candidate and three examiners, chosen 'often' by that candidate
himself. In 1800 the university 'willed and decreed' a more
stringent system for which it appointed six public examiners;[54]
and although this may be correctly interpreted as no more
than the first step in that university's examination reform, from
1820 onwards written examinations became increasingly employed
and the examination procedures increasingly standardized and
formalized. Similar changes were introduced at Cambridge
until the examinations at both universities came to resemble 'a
cockpit in which the best young minds of each generation were
tried out against one another'.[55] Probably more important for
present purposes, however, was the establishment of the
College of Preceptors in 1846 for the purpose of 'promoting
sound learning and of advancing the interests of education,
more especially among the middle classes',[56] since this body

instituted written examinations on the basis of printed question
papers, set and marked by external examiners, an example
followed by the Oxford and Cambridge local examinations, which
were 'instituted in 1858 in hopes that they might do for the
schools, what the examinations for the Bachelor of Arts degree
do for the Colleges in the two Universities'.[57]

Nor was the education of the poor exempt from this process.
Anglican school visitors had been accustomed to test the
children's knowledge of the liturgy and the catechism in order
to assess the efficiency of a school and its teachers, and an
analogous practice was implemented by the government inspectors, appointed in the 1830s and 1840s. Before 1862, however,
such 'examination' was not applied consistently to each child
in the school.

> The Inspector took a school class by class. He seldom heard
> each child in a class read, but he called out a certain number
> to read, picked at random as specimens of the rest; and when
> this was done he questioned the class with freedom, and in
> his own way, on the subjects of their instruction.

After 1862 the inspector no longer tested the class as a whole
but tested each child in reading, writing and arithmetic by
reference to the standards laid down in Clause 48 of the
Revised Code of Minutes and Regulations of the Committee of
the Privy Council on Education, 1862.[58] The future of the
school's maintainance grant depended on the attendance of its
pupils *and* the number of them who were successful in the
inspector's examination of them in one of the six 'standards'.
Hence the important point is not the nature of the subjects
that were examined, but the extent to which in these schools,
as in the great public schools and private schools not so
inspected but nevertheless concerned to prepare their pupils
for university entrance or for the Oxford and Cambridge
local examinations, etc., teachers became increasingly so
examination-conscious that they accustomed their children to
work for examinations and tests.

1850, it has been claimed, 'marked the beginning of a decade
in which examinations became really popular. Competitive
examination, in particular, was held up as the panacea for
many educational or social ills.'[59] 1850, on the basis of this
information therefore, marked the point at which increasingly
afterwards more and more children began to think of themselves in comparison with their peers in the same school, in
roughly the same age-group, in roughly the same social class,
and, after about the age of eight or nine, of the same sex as
themselves. Success in school tests, and more especially in
external examinations, thus became for them the measure of
achievement in conformity with the performance of people in
broadly the same social circumstances as themselves; and
although doubtless there was also an element of competitiveness
in this, it was not at all like the competition of the market
economy in which, beyond the political economists' counter-

factual speculations about the nature of perfect competition
between participants equal in knowledge of market conditions
and equal in the resources used to compete with one another,
success depended on much more than the individual person's
capacity to score over his or her rivals when striking a bar-
gain with an employer or an employee, a supplier or a customer.
In the school 'standards' competition did not depend on
differences in wealth, in family connections, in geographical
location, in social prestige, all of which made market competition far from perfect in the counterfactual sense and all of
which were considerably limited in their effect within each
standard, within each school, for all that they were very
influential indeed on the performance of the children in one
school as compared with another.

Achievement for the children through the 'standards' was
thus achievement in the context of whatever was taught them
collectively as appropriate for children of their circumstances
generally. A few children, it is true, moved through the six
'standards' faster than others, while a few lagged behind,
but the majority moved through the school together. Thus,
that standard of expectation, which was described on p.58
above as being consolidated at this time to establish the
special sort of future-time perspective, relevant for family
planning, was not confined to the children of the upper and
upper middle classes but extended by the popularity of examining to all those sections of the community whose children could
be persuaded or compelled to attend school. Parents who had
themselves been subjected to this meritocratic emphasis in
the schools, that is to say, could expect their children to be
subjected to it also. Even more than their own parents, who
had not, they would come to think of their children's achievement in these terms, although they would not necessarily
continue to think meritocratically about themselves once they
had completed their education, if the lives they lived afterwards were not organized hierarchically and meritocratically.
This is why sons were considered quite different from daughters, not only because in terms of their schooling mothers
had competed solely with other girls, but also because it was
assumed that they were destined to become housewives and
mothers rather than to follow a career or obtain a permanent
full-time occupation.

That this examination emphasis as such was more significant
for present purposes than the content of the courses taken
by the children, who were thus examined, may perhaps be best
exemplified by the example of religious instruction. As late as
1895 there appear to have been only nine School Boards in
England which did not provide religious teaching in their
schools, and this was out of a total of more than 2,000
Boards.[60] In 1890 more candidates for the Higher Certificate
of the Oxford and Cambridge Schools Examination sat the
examination in Scripture than in any subject other than

elementary mathematics; and although this was not the case
in 1901, a very large number of candidates sat the Scripture
paper. In the Oxford Local Examinations religious knowledge
led throughout this period at the senior level, while at the
junior it was a popular examination.[61] Children attended Sunday
schools, and church or chapel more frequently than their
parents in working-class areas.[62] In London as a whole, claimed
Charles Booth, 'it is the young children alone who are in the
mass responsive .... Girls are more amenable than boys, and
throughout London the female sex forms the mainstay of every
religious assembly of whichever class.' Nevertheless, he went
on, 'among the working classes there is less hostility to, and
perhaps even less criticism of the Church than in the past.
The Secularist propaganda, though not suspended, is not a
very powerful influence. Pronounced atheism is rare.'[63] In
this respect, perhaps, the more or less universal teaching of
Christianity in the schools had had some effect; although, as
Charles Masterman pointed out,[64]

> the children are everywhere persuaded to attend the centres
> of religious teaching; everywhere, as they struggle to man-
> hood and womanhood in a world of such doubtful certainties,
> they exhibit a large falling away. The sternness and severity
> and compelling claims of the ancient injunctions to repen-
> tance, and an ordered life become replaced by a general
> sense of vague and misty optimism, in which the former
> beliefs are less definitely denied than put aside as negligible
> and irrelevant to the business of the day.

The Anglican church itself, it is true, had by this time made
concessions to its earlier doctrines about the eternity of tor-
ment in Hell, the literal inspirations of the Bible and many of
the other dogmas which the British atheists had for so long
combatted[65] and which had been so prominent in the controversy over 'Essays and Reviews', a generation earlier. The
first contributor to that volume was, indeed, elevated to
become Archbishop of Canterbury in 1896, after a period of
service as Bishop of London from 1885 and, before that, as
Bishop of Exeter from 1869, having been appointed to that
See despite Pusey's protest at 'the horrible scandal of the
recommendation of the editor of the "Essays and Reviews" to
be a Christian Bishop'.[66] Whatever liberalizing of doctrine
these changes implied, however, they did not result in the
Church of England accepting, much less advocating, anything
other than the Pauline conception of marriage and family life
as expressed by Malthus a hundred years earlier,[67] so that if
the content of all this religious instruction and examining in
the schools had been all that influential in the adult lives of
the children subjected to it, the onset of family limitation at
this time might reasonably be explained in terms of the operation of Malthusian moral restraint rather than neo-Malthusian
contraception, whence it becomes difficult to account for the
incidence of the 'great scourge' or the 'hidden scourge', as

Christabel Pankhurst called 'the sexual diseases' in 1913. It is
true that she provided no source of evidence for her claim
that as many as 75 to 80 per cent of men were infected by
gonorrhoea and 'a considerable percentage, difficult to ascertain precisely' by syphilis,[68] but even the more cautious Royal
Commission on Venereal Diseases estimated in 1916 that 'the
number of persons who have been infected with syphilis,
acquired or congenital, cannot fall below 10 per cent of the
whole population in the large cities, and the percentage
affected with gonorrhoea must greatly exceed this proportion'.[69]
While a medical problem of this magnitude might be assumed to
have been the outcome of sensual men postponing marriage
until they could afford its hostages to fortune, or of husbands
seeking for sexual relief from prostitutes because they were
restraining themselves from intercourse with their wives in
order to limit their families, such behaviour is hardly consistent with the teachings of Christianity.

If, then, the content of the courses taught in the schools is
regarded as irrelevant to the onset of family limitation, the
question must be raised as to how examinations as such,
regardless of content, can reasonably be substituted as the
explanatory factor. In this chapter the focus of attention has
been on the revaluation of children by their parents and other
adults in English society, especially in so far as a silent
revolution occurred in the education of children at the relevant period. What examinations achieved in this respect was
to produce a historically novel state of mind in an ever-
increasing proportion of the population, namely, those who
spent much of their time at school, and in other educational
organizations, being prepared for, and, in the majority of
cases, positively preparing themselves for examinations of
their performance, conducted by their immediate teachers, and
more important for those teachers, by external examiners.
This state of mind entailed the almost daily comparison of their
own, individual efforts with those of their school peers, that
is, their roughly social equals, by contrast to the comparison
made at home, especially in pre-examination eras, between a
child and its brothers and sisters, that is, its superiors and
inferiors in family status. It also entailed the notion that with
more or less equal effort on their individual parts, except for
a few 'high flyers' who would push ahead and a few 'thick
heads' who would fall behind, all the children who were peers
in this sense could, and would, achieve a more or less equal
level in performance.

Their 'career' through the examination system was thus
defined for them, and by themselves, as very much within their
personal capacity to predict and to control. While at school,
at any rate, their world was portrayed to them in this way as
one of 'doubtful certainties', involving 'a general sense of
vague and misty optimism'; and although it might be far too
fanciful to attempt to explain the growing working-class demand

for the recognition of workshop organization and negotiation[70]
in similar terms - that is, as an example of the carrying over
into adult life in this same sense of being able to, and therefore also even more strongly desiring to, control the immediate
peer environment – it is not at all fanciful to postulate that
this particular form of future-time perspective within the realm
they could control as adults, that of their family of procrea-
tion, was such an extension into their post-school, post-
examinations experience of habits of mind they had acquired
in this way. In so far, moreover, as such a perspective, applied
to their own children, entailed the expenditure of resources
of some kind on those children's education, by encouraging
them to stay on at school or move on to more advanced levels
of education, there were economic consequences which followed
from it for the family budget and which made children increasingly economic liabilities, although it must be emphasized here
that such consequences would not have occurred had the state
of mind in question not appeared first. Nor should the concern
for a child's education be interpreted as a simple economic
aim - a 'better' job than he would otherwise obtain. The
examination emphasis entailed that achievement was the indication to the examinee himself and to his parents of what he was
capable. This may well imply, indeed, that the examination
emphasis led eventually to a revaluation of girls, and therefore,
of women as such, for all that while single-sex schools were
customary, they would be deemed destined for different
spheres, in much the same way as the leavers from public,
private and state schools, elementary and secondary, were
deemed destined for different spheres.

All this implies, however, that family limitation was an
unintended and unanticipated consequence of an educational
device which seems to remote from family planning that it is
difficult to appreciate how, if this argument is true, it can ever
be of any use for the fertility policy which was discussed in
the opening pages of this book. It suggests, it is true, the
negative conclusion that there is a good case here for treating
as irrelevant for such policy two elements which are often
stressed because it has been simply assumed that they are
essential. These are the economic costs of children, regarded
as rational calculation by parents unaffected by changes in
their concern for children as such, irrespective of economics,
and the education of the population into the desirability of
restricting its breeding, without consideration for their
evaluation of offspring as such. Can nothing positive be concluded from all this?

10 TOWARDS A FERTILITY POLICY

Before governments can pursue a fertility policy for their people to implement, before individuals and groups of those people can attempt to convince others that such a policy is desirable, they must be convinced themselves that it is practical, that it is possible for any government to influence the course of fertility history. By far the greatest impediment to be overcome for anyone to reach this conclusion is the often widespread assumption that the balance between births, deaths and migration is inherently self-regulating, so that any policy formulation in this area is bound to be either futile, if different from what such self-regulation intrinsically achieves, or illusory, if identical to what is automatically achieved without any effort on a government's part. At the present time the most pervasive of such self-regulating conjectures is that which is sometimes supposed to lie at the basis of what is usually referred to as the 'theory' of the demographic transition.[1] This transition, which marks the period between a society's population balance of high birth-rates, matched by high death-rates, and one in which they are both low, constitutes a phase of 'transitional growth', because over the past two hundred years death-rates have fallen initially faster than birth-rates, so that for a generation or so the total population in countries experiencing the transition has grown considerably. The 'theory', however, rests on the presupposition that, historically speaking, the transition period is inevitably short-term because fertility is deemed always to respond inexorably to mortality. Hence population growth may be prophesied to level off in the longer run to a rate which may be accepted as satisfactory from a policy-maker's point of view, even if it is rarely argued that zero growth, a complete balance between births, deaths and migrations, is what is eventually expected.

The evidence of the occurrence of such demographic transitions, as a general experience of societies where population statistics have been adequately collected, has been much easier to find since the beginning of the nineteenth century than that which might have sustained the converse argument, propounded by Malthus, who was convinced that the nature of plant and animal organisms, not excluding the human, was such that rather than fertility responding automatically to changes in mortality, the reverse relationship prevailed. Malthus, it should be emphasized, never denied that periods of rapid population increase had occurred from time to time, here and there, throughout human history. 'Some of the colonies from Ancient Greece,' he wrote,[2]

in no very long period, more than equalled their parent states in numbers and strength. And not to dwell on remote instances, the European settlements in the new world bear ample testimony to the truth of the remark, which, indeed, has never, that I know of, been doubted. A plenty of rich land, to be had for little or nothing, is so powerful a cause of population as to overcome all other obstacles .... But we should be led into an error if we were thence to suppose that population and food ever really increase in the same ratio, that is, one increases by multiplication and the other by addition. When there are few people, and a great quantity of fertile land, the power of the earth to afford a yearly increase of food may be compared to a great reservoir of water, supplied by a moderate stream. The faster population increases, the more help will be got to draw off the water, and consequently an increasing quantity will be taken every year. But the sooner, undoubtedly, will the reservoir be exhausted, and the streams only remain. When acre has been added to acre, till all the fertile land is occupied, the yearly increase of food will depend upon the amelioration of the land already in possession; and even this moderate stream will be gradually diminishing. But population, could it be supplied with food, would go on with unexhausted vigour, and the increase of one period would furnish the power of a greater increase the next, and this without any limit.

These quotations from the first edition of Malthus's essay have been provided here at some length in order to make it plain that he held what was essentially a cyclical view of population growth, with periods of increase alternating with periods of stagnation or even decline. His reservoir and stream analogy apart, the logic of his reasoning was immaculate, granted his assumptions about the inescapable biology of every living creature. Without food the individual cannot survive. With food it not only survives but usually breeds. The caveat - usually - is necessary here, because what Malthus called 'the preventive check' operated 'to some degree through all the ranks of society in England'. Even 'the labourer who earns eighteenpence a day and lives with some degree of comfort as a single man will hesitate a little before he divides that pittance among four or five, which seems to be but just sufficient for one'; but the main thrust of the Malthusian argument rested on the assumption that 'were every man sure of a comfortable provision for a family, almost every man would have one',[3] which meant that, were the labourer's earnings to rise much above eighteenpence a day, his hesitation could be expected to disappear. There was, in brief, no room in this account for a transition from circumstances of high fertility and high mortality to those of low mortality and low fertility. The great increase in the production of food, which has been referred to above (p.129) as a possible source of disease resistance, supplemented no doubt in this effect by the provision of more adequate clothing, housing, and other domestic resources, in consequence of the industrial revolution, has resulted in very marked rises in the expectation of life at birth since Malthus wrote, and these have been regarded as inconsistent with his conviction that food resources, at any rate, could be increased only on an arithmetical basis,[4] although it is rarely argued today that there would have been enough resources of this kind to go round in the nineteenth century to keep mortality rates falling, if fertility rates had not as a matter of fact declined. The problem facing the genuine theorist of the demographic transition, that is to say, is to account for this latter decline in terms of some kind of effective control over what Malthus regarded as essentially biological urges, in direct response to experience of the increased expectation of life.

As the reference to his preventive check makes plain, Malthus was quite aware that birth prevention as such was not only a characteristic of the England of his own day but recorded as having occurred throughout human history. In chapter 2 above this check was described as implying categorical 'moral restraint' for the convinced Christian. Yet such a moral injunction on his part did not mean that Malthus had failed to recognize the extent to which 'vice' of one kind or another – promiscuity, abortion, and 'artificial and unnatural modes of checking population' – had been employed from time immemorial to produce fewer births than would otherwise have occurred naturally, that is, as a consequence of personal control over the biological instinct. What he did not envisage was either that 'natural' means of this sort could in fact be operated on such a scale as to prevent a return to high mortality rates or that unChristian, artificial means would become sufficiently acceptable morally to have the same result. In a different moralistic setting from his this is precisely the problem with which contemporary fertility policy-makers are still concerned. The debate between Malthus and Godwin, it should also be emphasized, turned on the extent to which 'a foresight of difficulties' could become so widespread through a population that couples would continue to limit the size of their families when government action had changed their social circumstances markedly to make them much better off than ever before. The issue, indeed, consisted of a disagreement about whether the more remote difficulties facing a couple would still be operative once the immediate were alleviated.

The unsatisfactory child replacement and child survival hypotheses, rejected for lack of supporting evidence in the previous chapter, rest on the unwarranted assumption that such long-term future-time perspectives were already widespread at the turn of the eighteenth century, or perhaps even earlier, although the emphasis in this case is on the opposite

effect, namely, to prompt couples to have more children than
they otherwise would have done, because infant and child
mortality rates were high, and because such conceptions might
increase the chance that at least one of their offspring would
survive eventually to help them cope with the economic hardships, which they were alleged to have foreseen would most
likely arise for them in their old age. These hypotheses assume,
that is to say, that such long-term foresight far outweighed
the more immediate perception that a mother's economic efficiency
would almost certainly be impaired by successive or frequent
pregnancies and childbirth, with their accompanying debilities,
and/or that while infant and child mortality rates remained
high many conceptions, almost necessarily, meant that a family
would have to carry the burden of maintaining a relatively large
number of small children who could contribute little to the
household economy but nevertheless had to be fed and cared
for, in sickness and health, to prevent them from dying, if
possible. While there can hardly be any doubt about the extent
to which relatively short-term difficulties were expected, and
acted upon, by large sections of the population, who postponed marriages in time of economic depression, for example,
what is problematic is the incidence and therefore the significance of much longer-term expectations.

The importance of this distinction between types of perspective for policy-makers lies in the fact that relatively short-
term effects are regularly achieved by the implementation of
some aspect of population control which a government sets
out deliberately to introduce. For example, in countries where
certain means have been widely used to control fertility it is
known that the execution of measures to restrict the advertise-
ment, sale or production of contraceptives, or to make abortions illegal, has measurable results quite quickly; but whether
or not these are lasting is very much more uncertain;[5] and
the history of fertility control in many parts of the world
indicates that this difference occurs as much with measures
to restrict fertility as with those intended to promote it. This
means that the demographic use of what may be called
'conventional period rates' is 'very hazardous for either inter-
country or inter-temporal comparisons'.[6] Relatively short-term
fluctuations in birth-rates, in general fertility rates, in age-
specific maternity rates, in gross and net reproduction rates,
should not be confused with the fertility experiences of mothers
over a period of thirty years or more.[7] In the present context
this distinction is crucial, for what is at issue is the decline
in the average number of births per woman since the beginning
of the nineteenth century, or thereabouts; and in so far as
this is sometimes claimed to be the inevitable result of what is
essentially a self-regulating process, the negative feed-back
theorist should provide an explanation for it which specifies
the mechanism whereby this decline follows automatically from
the drop in infant and child mortality.

Of course, it is the case that what Hajnal called the European
marriage pattern – the relatively low incidence of marriage in
populations where marriages were contracted at relatively late
ages – predated this decline in fertility amongst the married
women themselves. Such a pattern, once it is thought of as
more than just a set of descriptive statistics derived from the
record in the marriage registers, may reasonably be interpreted as a particular set of ideals and standards about the
wisdom of providing hostages to fortune, a pattern of moral
judgments which indeed resulted in the kind of information
provided in those registers. This implies that the decisions
taken by a couple about whether or not to marry and if so,
when, and about the likelihood that sexual intercourse on
their part might result in conception and what they ought to
do about it, were made in the context of the constraining
influences exercised on them deliberately by their parents,
their siblings, their other kin, their friends and acquaintances,
their peers, and by the advocates of official doctrines on these
matters, communicating to them on behalf of church and state.
The question thus would seem to be, not to explain the reaction of the individual or the couple to such influences, but
whether the pattern itself can be accounted for in terms of
some sort of self-regulating mechanism without the emphasis
on the strength of biological urges within each individual.

One such possible approach, which has found favour from
time to time and which was an amalgam of Malthusian and
Darwinian ideas, is that which was originally employed by
Alexander Carr-Saunders in the context of the nineteenth-
century principle of the optimum number. For his purpose he
formulated this as that density of population in a given
geographical area which was 'most desirable from the point of
view of the return per head of the population'. Human beings
and groups of human beings, he claimed,

> are naturally selected on account of the customs they prac-
> tise just as they are selected on account of their mental and
> physical characters. Those groups practising the most
> advantageous customs will have an advantage in the constant
> struggle between adjacent groups over those that practise
> less advantageous customs. Few customs can be more advan-
> tageous than those which limit the number of a group to the
> desirable number.

In this way, through natural selection, the relevant ideals in
a society – 'that it was the right thing to bring up a certain
limited number of children' – were the consequence of the
biologically most effective form of group survival. Carr-Saunders
was aware that in more economically developed societies – he
called them 'races' – individual deliberation about whether or
not to have children took place without reference to what was
the optimum advantage of the society, for the 'race', as a
whole; nevertheless, he thought, historically speaking the
evolutionary process operated 'to some extent', in the form of

'automatic adjustment to the needs of the moment'.[8] From this perspective the European marriage pattern might be interpreted as nothing more than a set of customs which had evolved in this way because it had simply happened that they produced the 'best' return per head of the population, that is, they had resulted in an average level of living higher than that obtaining in societies where such customs had never taken root. From this perspective, too, the replacement of this largely Christian emphasis on restraint from sexual intercourse by a set of secular customs, sanctioning birth control through mechanical and biological devices, could be interpreted as merely a further automatic adjustment to maintain the optimum, or indeed to increase the economic advantage of those societies which were already relatively efficient over those which had no such advantageous customs.

The main objection to such speculation, quite apart from its possibly tautological principle that what is most desirable is nothing more than that which occurs, is that it is not at all clear what kind of evidence can be obtained at a society level to support, or refute it. For example, it is widely believed that it was France - Roman Catholic France - which was apparently only partially influenced by the European marriage pattern,[9] and which first experienced the vital revolution.[10] In what ways, then, has France demonstrated that this was the result of a pattern of customs which was most advantageous to its people in the constant struggle with their neighbours, especially England? The 'unbound Prometheus' converted Britain, not France, into the first industrial nation. 'The failure of France to excel economically despite its poor birth rate in the past 100 years is an important vignette in this history', that is, in 'the concurrent explosion in Europe of both population and economic development from 1650 onwards'.[11] The periodic nature of French economic 'stagnation' does not seem to accord at all well with French demographic statistics,[12] which show an almost monotonous regularity in the increase of the proportion of the population aged 20-64,[13] from which the economically active are predominantly drawn, while its rates of economic growth between 1861 and 1900, for example, had dropped to almost half the rates from 1831 to 1871. Nor was France alone in this failure of the demographic and the economic statistics to correspond.[14]

Doubtless, each society's economic growth rates, and its relative economic advantage over its rivals, depend on factors other than population alone, but the failure of the statistics to correspond can only mean that those customs which Carr-Saunders referred to as limiting a population to the 'desirable' number have not been more, but most probably less, advantageous to it in its struggle with its neighbours than those which are more directly related to its output per head, such as customs promoting the invention and diffusion of highly productive skills, techniques and methods, those promoting the

regular and systematic application of effort in the use of
those skills, techniques and methods, and so on. Such standards of excellence, put into effect, may conversely influence
the course of mortality and fertility history, especially in the
short run, through their impact on the level of living, that
is, on family incomes on the one hand and on the cost of the
things a family consumes, on the other. They may also influence
them more directly through the promotion and diffusion of
sanitary and preventive medicine, through improved standards
of infant, child and adult personal care, through more effective
birth-control techniques. In spite of all the attempts to clarify
the statistics and to simplify their interpretation, what the
evidence does not support is the thesis that it was the
economically most effective form of group survival which
'naturally selected' the European marriage pattern initially and
the limitation of the size of the family thereafter to a figure
very much below the fecundity of the average couple. A positive feed-back hypothesis in the form of population as self-
regulating through increasing economic advantage needs much
more conclusive evidence than can at present be obtained,[15]
and this may well be because such evidence can never be
obtained to support the hypothesis.

At this point it might be objected that, although clear
indications of group advantage at the national level may never
exist, the hypothesis might still be valid if the focus of attention is turned instead on to competing groups within each
nation. After all, it was argued on p.126 above that those
parents who practised family limitation in order to provide
their sons with educational advantages were likely to have been
more successful than they realized or could possibly have known
at that time; and what is this argument if it is not a claim for
the relative advantage of the most advantageous family-rearing
customs? The groups in question should not, of course, be
interpreted too loosely in simple class terms, because these
might then be taken to imply that in the second half of the
nineteenth century the upper and upper middle classes in
England obtained their differential advantage over others for
no other reason than that they practised the most advantageous
family customs. While the neo-Malthusians, making crude supply
and demand assumptions, often claimed that birth-control on
the part of the working classes would keep their numbers down
and hence send their wages up,[16] it was not the working classes
who first started to practise family limitation, yet it was their
numbers which shrank, proportionately speaking, between
1881 and 1911, if the percentages reproduced on p. 125
are any guide. At the same time taxable incomes over £150
increased in number at least twice as fast as the number of male
employed persons for 1851 onwards, save for the decades
1881-91 and 1891-1901, when they nevertheless still possessed
a growth advantage.[17] Structural changes in the economy, it
would seem, are more important for those effects than

structural changes in the family.

In any case, the kind of differential advantage in question entailed not only the limitation of births by the 'pioneers' in the more privileged occupations but their purchase of expensive education for their sons. Economically speaking, their families were thus both better off and worse off at the same time, when compared with those who did not practise family limitation or tie up their money in this kind of 'investment'. The advantages the former sought to obtain were 'futures' so to speak, delivered not to them but to the next generation, and in that generation to the next, and so on. This is a very far cry from the reference by Carr-Saunders to 'automatic adjustment to the needs of the moment', since the relevant future-time perspective required for such behaviour accords priority over the present and immediate future needs of the family to those which the male children in it may be anticipated to require satisfied over some twenty years or so. It is difficult, therefore, to envisage how such a perspective could have spread through a population to replace earlier customary perspectives by any process of natural selection, even if it is reasonably clear that, given this perspective, a drop in the infant and child mortality rates would necessarily increase the possibility that any given offspring of a union would live to have such needs satisfied.

The term 'natural selection', as Charles Darwin himself soon realized,[18] comes perilously close to replacing phylogenetic investigation by teleological speculation, if only because of the implied suggestion that a process of purposeful or quasi-purposeful picking and choosing operates in 'nature', similar to that undertaken 'artificially' by plant and animal breeders when they decide which seedlings to keep and which to throw away, which members of a litter to raise and which let die. What is at issue in Darwinian 'natural selection' is the recognition that, while variability within the offspring of a species is commonplace, new species are formed only when certain forms of variation survive in the form of inheritance. Many forms of variability are not reproduced through further breeding, that is to say, largely because the individuals with these characteristics do not survive to maturity or are sterile when they do. Other forms of variability, however, are so reproduced, and some, but only very few of these, are sufficiently distinctive for the naturalist eventually to assert that a new species has emerged.[19] If such a conception of natural selection may legitimately be applied to, say, the replacement of the European marriage pattern by the custom of contraceptively controlled fertility, this issue turns on the nature of the circumstances in which certain ideas about what is right and proper and possible in the relationship between the sexes, and certain of such ideas only, came to be so dominant in a society that an historian or a historical sociologist may validly claim that a new era has arrived: in this case the era of what Himes called

'the democratisation of birth control'. The origin of an idea in
itself, it should be emphasized, is of little importance. Like
biological variability, relatively novel ideas regularly occur
and recur throughout human history, even if they seem to
those who express them never to have been thought of before.
What is relevant to the present question is the transmission
of an idea from one generation to another, and its increasing
expression in the form of behaviour - family limitation - by an
ever-growing number of people.

Thus, in chapter 3 above the attempt was made to describe
the more or less coherent set of explicit 'secularist' ideas about
the nature of human society and the desirability of birth control
which informed the writings of one individual, George Drysdale.
Of course, there was no suggestion in that chapter that his
ideas were as unique as he himself originally believed them to
be, since he did not discover the existence of other birth-
control literature until after his 'Elements of Social Science'
was published. Nor was it suggested that this book, for all
its many editions, precipitated an organized social movement
for fertility reform. Rather was it implied that ideas, not very
different from his, had stimulated the imaginations of a number
of people, especially those who formed the Malthusian League
after the Bradlaugh-Besant trial of 1877. In that chapter, it
was concluded, however, that although a substantial proportion
of the Engish population was practising family limitation by
the 1870s very few of these 'pioneers' could have been influenced
positively, either directly or indirectly, by the propaganda of
the neo-Malthusians. The customs in question, therefore, most
probably consisted of the universal transmission and spread
of relatively new ideas which had their origin elsewhere than
in this source; and the circumstances which converted such
behavioural 'variability' into a new 'species' of customary
behaviour are not illuminated by too close a consideration of
the fortunes of the secularist Malthusians, old and new.

In this connection, because the Malthusian League and the
twentieth-century Family Planning organizations survived
beyond a single generation and might seem perhaps on this
account to be a socially viable 'variation', the case of France
may be used as a useful corrective, since there had been in
that country nothing which had even remotely resembled neo-
Malthusian propagandist groups, properly so-called, until as
late as 1896 when Paul Robin formed his Ligue de la
Régénération Humaine,[20] even if there is some evidence of a
small 'radical' neo-Malthusian 'fringe' in the French socialist
movement.[21] For this reason one French authoress has indeed
criticized Himes because he seemed 'to forget or not to know
that the "democratisation" of contraceptive practices began
in France almost a century before having made some headway
in England'.[22] Unless it can be shown that, in spite of the
similarities in family limitation practices in the two countries,
the underlying customs which became so 'democratised' were

very different in France as compared with Britain, it seems
reasonable to assume in the state of present knowledge that
the circumstances in question which favoured the spread of
the custom of having smaller families had very little to do with
propaganda of the organized neo-Malthusian sort, or for that
matter with Malthusian and neo-Malthusian doctrines generally.

Nevertheless, the emphasis in chapters 5, 6 and 8 above on
the similarity between the relevant future-time perspective
and the meritocratic career demands further consideration if
the French case is to be regarded as genuinely similar to the
British. Were the 'pioneers' of family limitation the same sort
of people in the two countries? Here the lack of anything
French as detailed as the Fertility Census of 1911 constitutes
a serious drawback, and the attempts to bridge the gap with
'reconstructions' of Census and other global data, and even
local registration information, have not as yet proved very
enlightening.[23] While it may have been the case that by 1780
or thereabouts 'the great contraceptive revolution had des-
cended from the superior classes in Parisian society down to
the peasants (rich and poor) of the fertile region near the
capital'[24] clear evidence of such diffusion is very sparse. The
'reconstitution' of families from parish registers provides
information for such inferences which itself is so small in proportion of the total population at any one point in time that its
representative characteristics are almost wholly speculative.
What is beyond question, of course, is the difference between
the two countries, which is demonstrated by Census statistics.
Whereas in England and Wales by 1851 the urban population
was recorded as constituting 50.2 per cent of the total, in
France it amounted to no more than 25.5 per cent; and by 1881
these proportions had increased to 67.9 per cent and no more
than 34.8 per cent respectively,[25] so that the persistence of
the traditional rural way of life in the latter case cannot be
ignored. Indeed, while in England and Wales the 16.1 per cent
of the total population, recorded as occupied agriculturally in
1851, had declined to 4.3 per cent by 1911,[26] in France the
figures were very much higher, being 53.0 per cent in 1850 and
still 40.3 per cent in 1911.[27] The problem, then, is how much
a persistence of the traditional emphasis on agriculture can be
reconciled with the possibility that family limitation is a
consequence of the meritocratic emphasis, granted that French
peasants were conservative about the education of their children and that compulsory education was not introduced into
France until 1882.[28]

One fairly common explanation which was current during the
second half of the nineteenth century was that:[29]

the Code Civil, as is well known, compels a man to divide
his land and other property equally among his children. The
French peasant regards the extreme partition of his possessions as an evil only to be avoided by limiting the number of
his descendants. He therefore restricts himself to two

children.
Such partage forcé, as Frederick Le Play called it,[30] was
universalized apparently by the law of 1793, although it had
been customary in some parts of France long before that date[31]
and was still not in fact universal by the end of the nineteenth
century.[32] To the degree, indeed, that the system did not
apparently result in the 'parcels' of land, owned by each
smallholder, becoming progressively smaller each generation,
partly because some children took their inheritance in money
rather than in land or sold their shares to one another,[33] le
partage merely resulted in their leaving the homestead for
another way of life, in much the same way as the younger
children under primogeniture sought a living elsewhere than
on the family estate. In brief, in France as in England, the
decline in child and adult mortality resulted in proportionately
more of the sons following an occupation different from that
of their fathers; and this, as was emphasized in the last
chapter, was a feature in the revaluation of children which
occurred rather widely eventually in late Victorian England.

This highly speculative and largely unsatisfactory examination of the French circumstances must for present purposes
suffice until detailed analyses of the relevant information
about France along lines similar to those employed in 'Prosperity
and Parenthood', 'Feminism and Family Planning' and this
present study are undertaken by French scholars in the
attempt to answer these questions, as well as those more
directly connected with the emergence of the meritocratic
emphasis, such as the efforts of Saint-Germain to abolish the
sale of commissions in the French army as early as 1775 and
their eventual abolition in 1790,[34] some eighty years before the
English set out to achieve a similar result. What, however,
this discussion of French practices has been introduced to
suggest is no more than the possibility that the general conclusions of the last and immediately preceding chapter of this
book may perhaps be generalized to explain the cause of the
decline in fertility in more countries than just Britain alone,
without any significant reference to the cause of mortality
decline beyond the emphasis that an ever-growing population
was impossible without the existence of opportunities to earn
a living elsewhere than on the land. For this reason the
applicability of these conclusions to policy-making may be
enhanced by reference to the likelihood that the socially
'natural' selection of customary ways of thinking and behaving,
conducive to family limitation, were the consequence of developments in the organization of such occupations from the middle
of the eighteenth century, inculcating a future-time perspective
associated with the notion of the career - originally a French
word - as the enduring feature in the lives of an increasing
number of men and, therefore, since these were very much
male-orientated societies, in the lives of their wives.

If a government, that is to say, wishes to persuade its

subjects to produce fewer children than they might otherwise
do, it is not sufficient for it merely to provide clinics and
family planning services and to publish birth-control advice,
although these are necessary. Nor is it sufficient for it to
preach a doctrine of the essential desirability of all its subjects
cultivating a long-term, future-time perspective, rather than
living for the moment. The burden of the present analysis is
that it must necessarily create the conditions, as willy-nilly
most governments already have in their educational examination
provisions, whereby men and women in their working lives can
experience the operation of the process of meritocratic achievement and advancement up a career and income hierarchy which
induces in them the conception of planning ahead over a
relatively long period. Needless to say, this conclusion rests
on the assumption that a fertility policy is desirable, not only
so that no unwanted children should be born as a simple consequence of the unthinking sexual urges of careless parents,
but also so that no wanted children should be born simply
because their parents believe it would be desirable for them
to have offspring, regardless of whether they can be provided
with opportunities for the cultivation of whatever potentialities
they have been born with. Governments, to be sure, often
have other objectives in mind in their population debates
beyond the welfare of such children themselves. They may,
indeed, favour pro-natalist policies, for the glory of God,
for the honour of the nation, to make their state the most
powerful in the world. At the present time the continuing process of declining mortality has, moreover, caused some to
eye askance what they interpret as an ever-growing burden
of dependent aged people, and to believe that only by increasing the size of the family will later generations be able to
maintain the level of living. Yet the paragraphs with which
this book began cannot be ignored. The population of the
world cannot keep on growing continuously, even in order to
maintain a high expectation of life at birth. Some other solution
for the 'burden' of the aged must be found, for otherwise the
problem will simply resolve itself in a return to the higher
mortality rates of the past.

NOTES

1 FERTILITY AND THE DECLINE IN RELIGIOUS BELIEF

1 United Nations, Department of Social Affairs, Population Division, 'The Determinants and Consequences of Population Trends', New York, 1953, Table 2, p.11.
2 United Kingdom, 'Report of the Population Panel', London, 1973, Cmnd 5258, Table I, p.19.
3 United Nations, 'The Determinants and Consequences of Population Trends: New Summary of Findings on Interaction of Demographic, Economic and Social Factors', vol.1, New York, 1973, Table III, p.10.
4 United Nations, Department of Economic and Social Affairs, 'The Future Growth of World Population', New York, 1958, p.v.
5 See, for example, Harold L. Geisert, 'World Population Pressures', Washington, 1958.
6 United Nations, Secretariat, Bureau of Social Affairs, 'Report on the World Social Situation', New York, 1957, p.27.
7 Richard Symonds and Michael Corder, 'The United Nations and the Population Question, 1945-1970', London, 1973, p.176.
8 United Nations, Department of Economic and Social Affairs, 'The World Population Situation in 1970', New York, 1971, p.77.
9 United Nations, Department of Economic and Social Affairs, 'Measures, Policies and Programmes Affecting Fertility, with particular reference to National Family Planning Programmes', New York, 1972, pp.57-73.
10 Joseph M. Stycos, 'Family and Fertility in Puerto Rico', New York, 1955, pp.7 and 183-4.
11 Reuben Hill, J.M. Stycos and K.W. Back, 'The Family and Population Control', Chapel Hill, 1959, p.24. Italics in the original.
12 Sripati Chandrasekhar, 'Population and Planned Parenthood in India', London, 1955, pp.75-87.
13 Sripati Chandrasekhar, Family Planning in Rural India, 'Antioch Review', vol.19, 1959, pp.399-411.
14 Sripati Chandrasekhar, 'Infant Mortality, Population Growth and Family Planning in India', London, 1972, pp.269-91.
15 R.A. Gopalaswami, How Japan Halved Her Birth Rate in Ten Years and the Lessons for India, 'Population Review: a Journal of Asian Demography', vol.3, 1959, pp.52-7; Y. Koya, Lessons from Contraceptive Failure, 'Population Studies', vol.16, 1962, pp.4-11.
16 For an example of this kind of assumption see Richard L. Meier, 'Modern Science and the Human Fertility Problem', New York, 1959.
17 Stycos, op. cit., p.21. Such a belief system he defined as 'the sum total of *consciously* held beliefs and attitudes common to a group which have *explicit* reference to fertility behaviour – for example, a belief that children bring good fortune'. Italics in the original.
18 W. Gibbons, The Catholic Value System in Relation to Human Fertility, in George F. Mair, ed., 'Studies in Population', Princeton, 1949.
19 Gerhard Lenski, 'The Religious Factor', New York, 1961, pp.229 and 232.
20 Ibid., p.252. See Ronald Freedman et al., 'Family Planning, Sterility and Population Growth', New York, 1958, pp.182-4.
21 Clyde Kiser and P.K. Whelpton, eds, 'Social and Psychological Factors

Affecting Fertility', Milbank Memorial Fund, 5 volumes, various dates,
reprinted from the 'Milbank Memorial Fund Quarterly', July 1942
(vol.21, no.3) to July 1958 (vol.36, no.3).
22 The Indianapolis Study of the Social and Psychological Factors affecting
Fertility (see note 21 p.150-1 above) was begun in 1938 under the
sponsorship of the Milbank Memorial Fund with a grant from the Carnegie
Corporation. The fieldwork was carried out in 1941-2 under the control
of a committee which included P.K. Whelpton as one of its members.
Whelpton was later responsible for inaugurating the Growth of American
Families Studies, conducted by the Survey Research Center at the
University of Michigan. They published 'Family Planning, Sterility and
Population Growth', by Freedman et al. (New York) in 1958 and Pascal
K. Whelpton et al., 'Fertility and Family Planning in the United States',
Princeton, 1966. The research was then retitled the National Fertility
Study which published two further reports (on the 1965 and a 1970 study),
namely, Norman B. Ryder and Charles F. Westoff, 'Reproduction in the
United States', Princeton, 1971, and by the same authors, Wanted and
Unwanted Fertility in the United States: 1965 and 1970 in Charles F.
Westoff and Robert Parke, eds, 'Demographic and Social Aspects of
Population Growth', Washington, 1972.
   The office of Population Research at Princeton has published many
papers on its research into fertility and four books, all by Charles F.
Westoff et al., namely, 'Family Growth in Metropolitan America', Princeton,
1963, 'The Third Child', Princeton, 1963, 'College Women and Fertility
Values', Princeton, 1967, and 'The Contraceptive Revolution', Princeton,
1977. The first of the Population Investigation Committee's surveys
- for 1959-60 - was published in the form of two articles by R.M. Pierce
and Griselda Rowntree, Birth Control in Britain, in the Committee's
journal, 'Population Studies', vol.15, 1961, pp.3-31, 121-60, and the
second - for 1967-8 - in C.M. Langford, 'Birth Control Practice and
Marital Fertility in Great Britain', London, 1976. The Institute of
Community Studies Report on 'Parents and Family Planning Services'
by Ann Cartwright was published by Routledge & Kegan Paul, London,
in 1970. They also published another study by her, this time for the
Institute for Social Studies in Medical Care, in 1976 - 'How Many Children?'.
Aberdeen's 'Fertility and Deprivation' by Janet Askham was published
by Cambridge University Press in 1975. The British Government's Office
of Population Censuses and Surveys has so far published three studies,
Myra Woolf, 'Family Intentions', London, 1971; Margaret Bone, 'Family
Planning Services in England and Wales', London, 1973; and Myra Woolf
and Sue Pegdon, 'Families Five Years On', London, 1976. Mention should
also be made of the first of a series of longitudinal studies planned by
John Peel, namely, John Peel and Griselda Carr, 'Conceptions and
Family Design', Edinburgh, 1975.
   In case the comments in the text might give the impression that modern
sociological surveys provide information on which highly reliable
predictions of future fertility may be made, it should perhaps be
emphasized that the only reliable knowledge is whether couples do or
do not practise birth control. See E.F. Borgatta and C.F. Westoff, The
Prediction of Total Fertility, 'Milbank Memorial Fund Quarterly', vol.32,
1954, pp.398-9. Even this information correlates only very partially with
attitudes to other aspects of a couple's life and to their circumstances,
such as the husband's annual earnings. 'Liking for children' correlated
most highly in the Indianapolis survey (+0.23) but mainly at the 'break'
between having children and remaining childless. See C.F. Westoff and
E.F. Borgatta, The Prediction of Planned Fertility, 'Milbank Memorial
Fund Quarterly', vol.33, 1955, pp.51-3, 56. Questions put to couples
at marriage about how many children they want to have leaves as much
as 90 per cent of the total variation in fertility unexplained - 98 per cent
in the case of those who do not plan their families and 80 per cent in the
case of family planners; C.W. Westoff, E.G. Mishler and E.C. Kelly,

Preferences in Size of Family and Eventual Fertility Twenty Years After,
'American Journal of Sociology', vol.62, 1957, p.494. Historical evidence
of this sort, which throws considerable doubt on the predictive value of
social surveys, lends further support to the claim for historical research
in this area. See also N.B. Ryder, A Critique of the National Fertility
Study, 'Demography', vol.10, 1973, p.505, where 'the wisdom of the
strategy of surveying individuals' is challenged, and C.F. Westoff and
N.B. Ryder, The Predictive Validity of Reproduction Intentions,
'Demography', vol.14, 1977, pp.432-7.

23 David V. Glass, Fertility and Birth Control in Developed Societies, and
Some Questions of Policy for Less Developed Societies, 'Malayan
Economic Review', vol.8, 1963, p.29.

24 Ibid., p.34.

25 R. Freedman, The Sociology of Human Fertility: a Trend Report and
Bibliography, 'Current Sociology', vols.X/XI, 1961-2, p.53.

26 Ibid., pp.53-7 for an account of the findings of research into some of
these points. A second, expanded edition of this trend report has been
published by Ronald Freedman under the title of 'The Sociology of
Fertility: an Annotated Bibliography', New York, 1975. For details of
surveys see pp.217-23.

27 Norman E. Himes, 'The Medical History of Contraception' (1936), New
York, 1963, p.392.

28 United Kingdom, Royal Commission on Population, 'Report', London,
1949, Cmnd 7695, 'Parliamentary Papers', London, 1948-9, vol.19,
para.96. The five common factors in the 'Report' and the 'Medical
History' are the decline of religious belief and the rise of rationalism
and science, urbanism, the growing emancipation of women, the widespread desire to advance economically, and social mobility and social
ambition. The Royal Commission also advanced the decline of agriculture
and the advance of industrialism, loss of security with competitive
individualism, the growth of popular education, and the spread of
humanitarianism, as compared with Himes's hedonism, utilitarianism and
materialism, the development of general and preventive medicine, fear
of over-population, improved methods of communicatory knowledge, and
army instruction in sexual prophylaxis during the First World War. Note
that elsewhere in his book Himes referred to industrialization as a
factor, op. cit., pp.100 and 209.

29 J. Hawkes, Prosperity and Parenthood, a review in 'Family Planning',
vol.3, 1954, p.6. Compare, Edward Shorter, Female Emancipation, Birth
Control, and Fertility in European History, 'American Historical Review',
vol.78, 1973, pp.605-40 for a similar, although more sophisticated,
rationalistic 'explanation', for example, 'A previous century of female
emancipation had created a large lower-class population of women who
were mentally prepared for small families, who desired ardently to curb
their own fertility, but who ... *had lacked the requisite sophistication
about reproductive biology*', p.631. Italics not in the original.

30 Himes, op. cit., p.100.

31 United Kingdom, Census of England and Wales, 1911, vol.XIII,
'Fertility and Marriage', pt I, London, 1917. John W. Innes, 'Class
Fertility Trends in England and Wales, 1876-1934', Princeton, 1938.
Using the technique of stable population analysis Hollingsworth has
estimated that the beginning of the decline in English fertility began
even earlier than these two sources imply, as early indeed as 1820,
Thomas H. Hollingsworth, 'Historical Demography', London, 1969,
pp.345-51.

32 J. Bourgeois-Pichat, Evolution Générale de la Population Française
depuis le XVIII Siècle, 'Population', vol.6, 1951, graph 6, p.654.
Hélène Bergues et al., 'La Prévention des Naissances dans la Famille',
Paris, 1960, pp.227, 317 and 319.

33 Himes, op. cit., p.423. Bernard Finch and H. Green, 'Contraception
Through the Ages', London, 1963, largely follow Himes apart from

including data from after 1936 when Himes's book was published.
34 Himes, op. cit., p.100 and the whole of pts 5 and 6, pp.209-420.
35 Henry H. Fyfe, 'Revolt of Women', London, 1933. Shorter argues that
female emancipation rather than conscious feminism was the crucial
factor and that therefore 'the Bankses should look as much to the lower
classes as to the middle for the social sources of female autonomy',
op. cit., p.629, n.36. The reference is to Joseph A. and Olive Banks,
'Feminism and Family Planning in Victorian England', Liverpool, 1964.
36 Ibid., especially chs 3, 4, and 9. For the view that this argument is
'simplistic' see Patricia Branca, 'Silent Sisterhood: Middle Class Women
in the Victorian Home', London, 1975, ch. 7.
37 Himes, op. cit., p.393.
38 Freedman, The Sociology of Human Fertility, pp.56-9. For the weaknesses
of the urbanization hypothesis see the summary of the studies in Sydney
H. Coontz, 'Population Theories and the Economic Interpretation',
London, 1957, pp.76-82.
39 Joseph A. Banks, 'Prosperity and Parenthood', London, 1954, ch. 12.
James Beshers, 'Population Processes in Social Systems', New York,
1967, ignores this point in developing what he refers to as the Weber-
Banks thesis of future-time orientations, p.86.
40 Joseph A. and Olive Banks, op. cit., ch. 6.
41 Banks, op. cit., p.202. Italics in the original.
42 J.A. and O. Banks, op. cit., p.7.
43 Bergues et al. op. cit., pp.311, 389-90.
44 F. Campbell, Birth Control and the Christian Churches, 'Population
Studies', vol.14, 1960, pp.131-47.
45 Census of Great Britain, 1851. 'Religious Worship, England and Wales,
Report and Tables', London, 1853, p. clviii.
46 Ibid., pp.cxix-cxxiv.
47 Ibid., p.cxxx. Italics in the original. See also Kenneth S. Inglis,
'Churches and the Working Classes in Victorian England', London,
1963, pp.1-20.
48 See the criticisms of 'Population and Parenthood' on this point in
Geoffrey Hawthorn, 'The Sociology of Fertility', London, 1970, p.127,
note in the bibliography on Banks, J.A. (1954) and (1968). See also,
Shorter, op. cit., n.36, p.629 where a Banks-Shorter hypothesis is
concluded to the effect that 'the Bradlaugh-Besant trial of 1877 rapidly
diffused news of birth-control practices, confined until then to decidedly
unliberated upper-middle-class families, among the eager but ignorant
popular classes'.
49 Census of Great Britain, 1851, 'Religious Worship', p.cxxx.

2 THE RELIGIOUS ROOTS OF THE MALTHUSIAN CONTROVERSY

1 [Thomas R. Malthus], 'An Essay on the Principle of Population, as it
affects the future improvement of society', London, 1798, reprinted
with notes by James Bonar, London, 1926, pp.15-16; reprinted with a
foreword by Kenneth E. Boulding, Ann Arbor, 1959, pp.5-6; reprinted
together with Malthus's 'A Summary View of the Principle of Populations',
London, 1830, and with an introduction and notes by Anthony Flew,
Harmondsworth, 1970, p.72.
2 Ibid., Preface, 1926, p.iv; 1959, p.xiv; 1970, p.62.
3 Ibid., 1926, p.6; 1959, p.2; 1970, p.68.
4 Ibid., 1926, p.16; 1959, p.6; 1970, p.72.
5 Ibid., 1926, p.349; 1959, p.122; 1970, p.200.
6 Ibid., 1926, p.353; 1959, p.123; 1970, p.202.
7 Patricia James, 'Biographical Sketches' in the 'Travel Diaries of
Thomas Robert Malthus', ed. Patricia James, Cambridge, 1966,
pp.3 and 6. See also her 'Population Malthus: his Life and Times',
London, 1979, pp.40-6, 332-4.

8 Bonar asserted this of Malthus; see James Bonar, 'Malthus and his
Work', London, 1885, pp.323-4. Paley acknowledged his debt to Tucker
in the Preface to his 'The Principles of Moral and Political Philosophy',
London, 1785, although there is some evidence that he was more indebted
to Thomas Rutherforth than to Tucker, and the usually cited source
for Paley's own watch analogy is Bernard Nieuweatyt's 'Religious
Philosopher', English translation, 1719. See D.L. Lemahieu, 'The Mind
of William Paley', University of Nebraska Press, Lincoln, 1976, pp.60-1,
and 124.

9 Abraham Tucker, 'The Light of Nature Pursued', 2nd edn, revised and
corrected, together with some account of the life of the author by
H.P. Mildmay, London, 1805, vol.4, ch.25, p.93. Note that the opening
chapter of Paley's 'Natural Theology', London, 1802, began with the
analogy of God as the watchmaker and the universe as the watch.

10 Tucker, op. cit., p.94.

11 Ibid., vol.3, ch.18, p.271.

12 Leslie Stephen, 'History of English Thought in the Eighteenth Century',
London, 1876, vol.2, pp.116-17.

13 Tucker, op. cit., vol.4, ch.31, p.505.

14 Ibid., p.498.

15 Malthus, op. cit., 1926, p.358; 1954, p.125 footnote. Ibid., 1926, p.361;
1959, p.126; 1970, p.203.

16 Ibid., 1926, p.391; 1959, p.137; 1970, p.216.

17 Ibid., 1926, p.392; 1959, p.138; 1970, p.217.

18 Ibid., 1926, pp.189-91; 1959, pp.66-7; 1970, pp.137-8.

19 William Godwin, 'Enquiry Concerning Political Justice and its Influence
on Morals and Happiness', 3rd edn, London, 1797, vol.2, book 8, ch.9,
pp.517-18.

20 A letter from Malthus to Godwin, 2 August 1798, reprinted in Charles
K. Paul, 'William Godwin, his Friends and Contemporaries', London,
1876, vol.1, pp.323-4. This letter is also reproduced in Bonar's edition
of Malthus's First Essay, op. cit., 1926, Notes, pp.vi-vii. Godwin's
letter to Malthus has, unfortunately, not survived.

21 William Godwin, 'Thoughts Occasioned by the Perusal of Dr Parr's
Spital Sermon', London, 1801, p.76. There is a useful summary in
Kenneth Smith, 'The Malthusian Controversy', London, 1951, pp.38-41.

22 Thomas R. Malthus, 'An Essay on the Principle of Population; or,
a View of its Past and Present Effects on Human Happiness', 'A New
Edition, very much enlarged', London, 1803, p.385; 4th edn, London,
1807, vol.2, p.55. In the 5th edition, London, 1817, and in subsequent
editions this reference to Godwin's reply was omitted.

23 Ibid., London, 1803, Preface, p.v. This passage did not appear in
subsequent editions.

24 See especially ibid., pp.484, 502-3. These passages appear in all the
later editions.

25 Bonar, op. cit., p.38.

26 William Empson, Life, Writings, and Character of Mr Malthus, 'Edinburgh
Review', January 1837, art.9, p.483, reprinted in Bernard Semmel,
'Occasional Papers of T.R. Malthus', New York, 1963, p.245.

27 From an unpublished manuscript, entitled, The Crisis, A View of
the Present Interesting State of Great Britain, by a Friend of the
Constitution, quoted in Empson, op. cit., p.482, Semmel, op. cit.,
p.244.

28 William Paley, 'The Principles of Moral and Political Philosophy', Book 6,
ch. 11. So many versions of Paley's work are extant that it seems
valueless to cite page references to any one.

29 William Paley, 'Natural Theology, or Evidence of the Existence and
Attributes of the Deity, Collected from the Appearances of Nature',
ch.26, The Goodness of the Deity. A footnote to the passage quoted
above reads: 'See statement of this subject, in a late treatise upon
population.'

30 The 'Principles' was first published in 1785 and appeared in 'corrected' editions until the 7th in 1790. Thereafter it appeared without any subtitle epithet until the 'new' (18th?) edition of 1809. From 1819 it seems largely to have been incorporated in 'Complete Works', new editions of which were published every five years or so until the 1860s. 'Natural Theology' ran through six 'editions' in one year and afterwards appeared not only in the 'Collected Works' but separately, right up to the 1880s and beyond. Both books, as well as Paley's other writings, were regularly studied at Cambridge during this period; but Oxford does not seem to have paid Paley much attention. See John M. Robertson, 'A History of Freethought in the Nineteenth Century', London, 1929, p.229. See also Lemahieu, op. cit., ch.6 Paley and the Nineteenth Century, passim. For an example of how mid-Victorian writers interpreted Paley and Malthus as being in opposite camps, see Henry Christmas, 'Christian Politics: an Essay on the Text of Paley', London, 1855; 'there are *two* theories concerning population: one, that of Paley which regards it in *all actual* cases as a good, and therefore to be encouraged; another, that of Malthus and his disciples, which regards it *under certain circumstances* as an evil, and requiring a check', p.306, italics in the original.
31 In his article on Paley in the 'Dictionary of National Biography', Leslie Stephen wrote that Paley 'spoke with great admiration of Malthus's essay on Population'.
32 Malthus, op. cit., 5th edn, London, vol.3, 1817, p.425.
33 Empson, op. cit., p.486; Semmel, op. cit., p.248. For the view that it was only after they had read Sumner's 'Records' that church leaders learned about Malthus and even then cited Sumner rather than Malthus when discussing the relationship between the church and the poverty stricken, see Richard A. Soloway, 'Prelates and People, Ecclesiastical Social Thought in England, 1783-1852', London, 1969, pp.92-3 and 101.
34 John B. Sumner, 'A Treatise on the Records of Creation and on the Moral Attributes of the Creator', London, 1816, 3rd edn, London, 1825, pp.157-60.
35 Malthus, op. cit., 5th edn, vol.3, p.426.
36 Malthus, op. cit., 4th edn, vol.2, p.430.
37 Ibid., vol.2, p.433.
38 Ibid., vol.2, p.431.
39 John B. Sumner, Review of the 5th edition of Malthus's 'Essay', in the 'Quarterly Review', July 1817, art.4, pp.381-2. Reprinted in Joseph J. Spengler, ed., 'Population Problems in the Victorian Age', vol.I, 'Theory', Farnborough, 1973.
40 Henry N. Brailsford, 'Shelley, Godwin and their Circle', London, 1913, pp.80-7.
41 'A Summons of Wakening, or the Evil Tendency and Danger of Speculative Philosophy', Hawick, 1807, quoted in Bonar, op. cit., p.365. See also James, 'Population Malthus', pp.117-18.
42 Stephen, 'History of English Thought', vol.1, p.411.
43 Vernon F. Starr, 'The Development of English Theology in the Nineteenth Century', London, 1913, p.61.
44 Horton Davies, 'Worship and Theology in England from Watts and Wesley to Maurice, 1760 to 1850', Princeton, 1961, p.238.
45 Thomas R. Malthus, 'A Summary View of the Principle of Population', London, 1830, reprinted in David V. Glass, ed., 'Introduction to Malthus', London, 1953, p.153, and in Flew op. cit., p.250. 'The Summary View' consisted of the larger part of 'Population', Malthus's contribution to the supplement to the 6th edition of the 'Encyclopaedia Britannica' in 1824. Malthus died in 1834. 'The Summary View' may, therefore, be fairly taken as his last words on the subject in spite of the fact that the 6th edition of his 'Essay' appeared in 1826.
46 Malthus, op. cit., 1926, p.19; 1959, p.10; 1970, p.76. This passage was retained in all later editions.

47 Malthus, op. cit., 1803, p.11.
48 This phrase first appeared in a footnote to the 4th edn, vol.1, p.19.
49 Malthus, op. cit., 1803, vol.2, p.499.
50 Ernst Troeltsch, 'The Social Teaching of the Christian Churches',
   trans. O. Wyon, London, 1931, vol.1, p.81.
51 Malthus, op. cit., 1803, p.501.
52 Ibid., p.501, 5th edn, vol.3, pp.98-9.
53 Ibid., 1803, vol.2, pp.505-6; 1817, vol.3, p.105.
54 Ibid., 1817, vol.3, p.179.
55 Ibid., 1817, vol.3, p.249.
56 Grahame's 'Inquiry into the Principle of Population' was published in
   Edinburgh in 1816.
57 Appendix to the 5th edn of the 'Essay', 1817, vol.3, pp.393-4.
58 Francis Place, 'Illustrations and Proof of the Principle of Population',
   London, 1822, p.165.
59 Graham Wallas, 'The Life of Francis Place, 1771-1854', London, 1918,
   p.169.
60 Norman E. Himes, Editor's Introduction to the annotated re-issue of
   Place's 'Illustrations and Proofs', London, 1930, p.47. See also
   Norman E. Himes, McCulloch's Relation to the Neo-Malthusian Propaganda
   of his time: and episode in the history of English Neo-Malthusianism,
   'Journal of Political Economy', vol.37, Chicago, 1929, pp.74-83; Peter
   Fryer, 'The Birth Controllers', London, 1965, pp.79-86.
61 Norman E. Himes, 'The Medical History of Contraception', New York,
   1963, p.230. The reference is to the years between the death of Malthus
   in 1834 and the Bradlaugh-Besant trial of 1877.
62 Gallery of Literary Characters, No.71, Francis Place, Esquire,
   'Fraser's Magazine for Town and Country', vol.13, London, 1836,
   p.427. For more details of working-class rejection of birth-control
   propaganda during this period see Angus McLaren, Contraception and
   the Working Class: the Social Ideology of the English Birth Control
   Movement in its Early Years, 'Comparative Studies in Society and History',
   vol.18, 1976, esp. pp.247-51. See also Angus McLaren, 'Birth Control
   in Nineteenth-Century England', London, 1978, pp.69-72.

3 THE SECULARIST CASE FOR BIRTH CONTROL

1 George J. Holyoake, 'Secularism, the Practical Philosophy of the
  People', London, 1854, p.4. Italics, capital letters and inverted commas
  in the original. Holyoake was much prone to the use of such emphatic
  devices. For a critical but not altogether unsympathetic account of the
  this-worldly morality of the secularists at this time, see Adam S. Farrar,
  'A Critical History of Free Thought in Reference to the Christian
  Religion', London, 1862, especially pp.432-3, 441-2.
2 Persona, 'Negative Article III' of a ten article series by different authors,
  five for, five against secularism, published under the general title:
  Is Secularism Consonant with the Highest Amount of Social Happiness?
  in 'The British Controversialist and Impartial Inquirer', vol.6, 1855,
  p.268.
3 John A. Langford, 'Christianity, not Secularism, the Practical
  Philosophy of the People', London, 1854, p.7.
4 George J. Holyoake, 'Sixty Years of an Agitator's Life', London, 1906,
  part I, ch.26. For the Owenite missionaries generally see John F.C.
  Harrison, 'Robert Owen and the Owenites in Britain and America',
  London, 1969, pp.219-24.
5 'World-makers,' he wrote, 'seems a more relevant term than Utopianists',
  George J. Holyoake, 'The History of Co-operation' Revised and Completed,
  London, 1908, p.15.
6 Letter to Holyoake, no date, quoted in Joseph McCabe, 'Life and Letters
  of George Jacob Holyoake', London, 1908, vol.1, pp.217-18.

Miss Collett published a pamphlet, 'George Jacob Holyoake and Modern Atheism' in 1855.

7 Reproduced in Robert Owen, 'A New View of Society and Other Writings', London, 1927, p.181.

8 Robert D. Owen, 'Moral Physiology; or, a brief and plain treatise on the population question', New Edition, London, 1832, p.16: 'complete withdrawal ... immediately previous to emission' is advocated as 'a complete control over this instinct', ibid., pp.46-7.

9 William Thompson, 'Practical Directions for the Speedy and Economical Establishment of Communities in the Principles of Mutual Co-operation, United Possessions and Equality of Exertions and the Means of Enjoyments', London, 1830, pp.229-48. See also Holyoake, 'History of Co-operation', p.47.

10 Edward Royle, 'Victorian Infidels, the Origins of the British Secularist Movement 1791-1866', Manchester, 1974, p.143. Another author claims that Holyoake 'advertised and sold contraceptive appliances in his shop', but gives no references to support his claim. F.B. Smith, The Atheist Mission, 1840-1900, in Robert Robson, ed., 'Ideas and Institutions of Victorian Britain', London, 1967, p.219.

11 G.J. Holyoake, letter to 'The Times', Monday, 5 March 1857, p.9.

12 Holyoake, 'Sixty Years', p.126.

13 Royle, op. cit., p.109.

14 Holyoake, 'Sixty Years', p.126.

15 This date is usually given as 1854 but the only extant copy of the first edition, apparently in the Library of Congress, is recorded in the National Union Catalog as 1855. The Preface is dated December 1854, so the book may well have not appeared until early in the following year. The second edition, similarly, is usually dated 1856 and it was advertised to appear in that year but 'The Political Economist, and Journal of Social Science', edited by the Author of 'Physical, Sexual, and Natural Religion' records it as having appeared on 1 March 1857; see no.15, April, 1857.

16 Preface. Peter Fryer, 'The Birth Controllers', London, 1965, p.110, reports that this relative was Drysdale's mother 'whose feelings would have been hurt by an avowal of heterodox opinions on theology and its traditional morality'.

17 In the Preface to the 3rd edition of 1860 Drysdale wrote that his 'chief reason for changing the title was that the Malthusian Principle and the laws of nature involved in it' were in his opinion 'incomparably *the most important* elements of social science' and that he was very desirous of directing attention to this science (italics in the original). He made no reference to Holyoake in this connection. But in any case, Holyoake's memory was notorious for its inaccuracies. As John Ludlow wrote to John Carter on 8 March 1904, 'his inaccuracy of statement is such that if he said he had dined off a mutton chop the chances would be ten to one that it was probably a beefsteak', quoted in Charles E. Raven, 'Christian Socialism, 1848-1854', London, 1920, p.62.

18 [George Drysdale], 'The Elements of Social Science: or Physical, Sexual, and Natural Religion', by a Graduate of Medicine, 3rd edn, enlarged, London, 1860, p.442. Italics and capitals in the original. Drysdale had been awarded his M.D. by the University of Edinburgh in 1855 and by 1860 was sharing an address, if not a practice, with his younger brother, Charles Robert (M.D. St Andrews, 1859) at 39, Southampton Row, London. 'The Medical Register', London, 1860, p.97.

19 [Drysdale], 'The Elements', 3rd edn, p.446.

20 Ibid., p.3.

21 Ibid., p.1.

22 Ibid., pp.49-50.

23 Ibid., p.451. Capital letters in the original.

24 Ibid., p.343. Italics in the original.

25 Ibid., p.346.
26 Ibid., p.335. Italics in the original.
27 Ibid., p.347. Capitals in the original.
28 Ibid., p.351. Italics in the original.
29 Ibid., p.352.
30 Ibid., p.273.
31 Ibid., p.11.
32 Review of the 3rd edn in the 'British Journal of Homeo-pathy', vol.18, January 1860, p.176.
33 Himes, 'The Medical History of Contraception', p.233. Glass estimated the total sales of 'The Elements' from 1854 to 1914 to have been about 100,000 copies, of which perhaps 20,000 were sold before 1877. David Glass, 'Population Policies and Movements in Europe', Oxford, 1940, p.40.
34 Letter to the editor from R.W., 'The Political Economist and Journal of Social Science', no.11, January 1857, p.86.
35 George K. Rickards, 'Population and Capital, being a Course of lectures delivered before the University of Oxford in 1853-4', London, 1854, p.195.
36 French Principles and English Quacks, the 'Weekly Dispatch', 22 January 1860. See also [George Drysdale], 'Population Fallacies: a Defence of the Malthusian or True Theory of Society: in Reply to the "Weekly Dispatch", "Times" and Others', by a graduate of Medicine, author of 'The Elements of Social Science', London, 1860, 2nd edn, London, 1867.
37 The origin of this term in the late 1870s has been attributed to Samuel Van Houten. See Glass, op. cit., p.425, note aa, and Rosanna Ledbetter, 'A History of the Malthusian League, 1877-1927', Columbus, 1976, p.xiv, and note 6, p.xxi. Certainly, Charles V. Drysdale made this claim in his evidence to the National Birth-Rate Commission on 24 October 1913. See the Commission's report, 'The Declining Birth-Rate, its Causes and Effects', 2nd edn, London, 1917, p.88.
38 For details, see J.A. Banks and D.V. Glass, A List of Books, Pamphlets and Articles on the Population Question, published in Britain in the period, 1793 to 1880, in D.V. Glass, ed., 'Introduction to Malthus', London, 1953, pp.106-10. The earlier books and pamphlets were not very well known, even to secularists. Drysdale confessed in 1857 that he had not known 'until lately ... how many cheap treatises and tracts have already been written on the subject of preventive intercourse; and how many others have pointed out this means, as the true remedy for the population evils'. Editor's comment on the letter from R.W., 'The Political Economist and Journal of Social Science', no.11, January 1857, p.87.
39 G.R. was, of course, George Drysdale, writing under the initials of his pseudonym, George Rex, which dated from the days of his rapid progress at the Circle Place School, Edinburgh. See Fryer, op. cit., p.110.
40 Royle, op. cit., p.277. The 'National Reformer' was begun under the joint editorship of Charles Bradlaugh and Joseph Barker in 1860 but the two men soon quarrelled over almost everything, including neo-Malthusianism. Hypatia B. Bonner, 'Charles Bradlaugh: a Record of his Life and Work by his daughter', London, 1908, part I, pp.120-6.
41 'National Reformer', 16 August 1862, quoted in David Tribe, 'President Charles Bradlaugh, M.P.', London, 1971, p.83.
42 United Kingdom, Census of England and Wales, 1911, vol.XIII, 'Fertility of Marriage', pt I, London, 1917. Innes's analysis of the completed families in this Report shows that the earliest signs of the change in this reproductive behaviour took place amongst the families of military and naval officers, clergymen, lawyers, doctors, authors, journalists and architects. Not far behind them were civil service officers and clerks, law clerks, dentists, schoolmasters, teachers,

professors, and lecturers, people employed in scientific pursuits and
accountants. Other groups of commercial men lagged some way behind
but all these three classes were easily distinguishable in their fertility
from textile workers, who of all sections of the working class showed
the earliest signs of family limitation. John W. Innes, 'Class Fertility
Trends in England and Wales, 1876-1934', Princeton, 1938, ch.3,
sections 1 and 2. For a different list of 'pioneers' see, however, the
text above, pp. 40-1, 98, and 99-100.

43 Royle, op. cit., p.241, and more generally, pp.233-44 and Appendix
IV, pp.304-5. Royle's analysis seems much more reliable than Susan
Budd's belief that it was the coal-mining and heavy-industry areas
of the country where secularism flourished. S. Budd, 'The Loss of
Faith; Reasons for Unbelief among Members of the Secular Movement
in England, 1850-1950, 'Past and Present', no.36, April 1967, p.107.
See, however, her more recent analysis of sources for the mid-
Victorian period in Susan Budd, 'Varieties of Unbelief: Atheists and
Agnostics in English Society, 1850-1960', London, 1977, p.95, no.29.

44 Royle, op. cit., p.239.

45 United Kingdom, Census of 1911, op. cit., pp.cxi-cxiii. Margaret
Hewitt, 'Wives and Mothers in Victorian Industry', London, 1958,
provides a very clear, summary table of the relevant comparisons, p.87.
Note that the Census Report did not comment on the fact that, apart
from domestic servants, there were seven Class III and one Class IV
occupations whose total, completed fertility by 1911 was below the
average for textile workers. These were college and club servants, tram
conductors, electricians (undefined), motor-car chassis-makers and
mechanics, printers, wig-makers and hairdressers, barmen and waiters
(not domestic). See table XLVIII, pp.cv-cvii - cases where the fertility
was lower for both the actual number of children born per 100 couples
and the standardized number, that is, taking into account the different
ages of the wives at marriage.

46 See W.S.F. Pickering, The 1851 religious census - a useless experiment?;
'British Journal of Sociology', vol.18, 1967, Map 1, p.397. Lancashire's
'weak' rate for maximum attendance - 27 per cent of the total population -
was surpassed by only two other areas, Cumberland (25 per cent) and
London (21 per cent). The area of highest attendance was Bedfordshire
with 57 per cent. See also D.M. Thompson, The 1851 Religious Census:
Problems and Possibilities, 'Victorian Studies', vol.17, 1967-8,
esp. pp.96-7, where conclusions about how to read the Census
information are underlined.

47 Hewitt, op. cit., pp.91-3.

48 G.B. Terry, Rival Explanations in the Work-Fertility Relationship,
'Population Studies', vol.29, 1975, pp.191-205.

49 Neil J. Smelser, 'Social Change in the Industrial Revolution', London,
1959, p.281. Smelser's reference to Hewitt's dissertation on which
her book (op. cit.) rests does not constitute support for his argument
as a general summary of the position.

4 THE EMANCIPATION OF WOMEN

1 George J. Holyoake, 'The History of Co-operation', Revised and
Completed, London, 1908, p.92.

2 William Thompson, 'An Inquiry into the Principles of the Distribution
of Wealth most Conducive to Human Happiness, applied to the newly
proposed System of Voluntary Equality of Wealth', London, 1824, p.430.

3 Ibid., p.390.

4 Robert Cooper, 'A Contrast between the New Moral World and the
Old Immoral World', Hulme, 1838, p.7.

5 Thompson, op. cit., p.431.

6 William Thompson, 'Appeal of one Half of the Human Race',

London, 1825, p.177.
7 Ibid., p.179. Italics in the original.
8 R.D. Owen, 'Moral Physiology; or, a brief and plain treatise on the population question', New Edition, London, 1832, p.31. Italics in the original.
9 [George Drysdale], 'The Elements of Social Science: or Physical, Sexual, and Natural Religion', by a Graduate of Medicine, 3rd edition, enlarged, London, 1860, p.328.
10 Ibid., p.351.
11 S. Budd, The Loss of Faith; Reasons for Unbelief among Members of the Secular Movement in England, 1850-1950', 'Past and Present', no.36, April 1967, p.107.
12 'Harriet Martineau's Autobiography, with memorials by Maria W. Chapman', 2nd edn, London, 1877, Period 6, Sections 3, 5 and 6; Vera Wheatley, 'The Life and Work of Harriet Martineau', London, 1957, ch.15; Robert K. Webb, 'Harriet Martineau: a Radical Victorian', New York, 1960, ch.1.
13 R.K.B. Pankhurst, Anna Wheeler: a Pioneer Socialist and Feminist, 'Political Quarterly', vol.25, 1954, pp.132-43.
14 Annie Besant, 'An Autobiography', 2nd edn, London, 1908, chs 4 and 5; Arthur H. Nethercott, 'The First Five Lives of Annie Besant', London, 1961, pts I and II.
15 Margaret Hewitt, 'Wives and Mothers in Victorian Industry', London, 1958, p.93.
16 Ivy Pinchbeck, 'Women Workers and the Industrial Revolution, 1750-1850', London, 1969, p.185.
17 Edward Shorter, Female Emancipation, Birth Control, and Fertility in European History, 'American Historical Review', vol.78, 1973, p.612. In his later, 'The Making of the Modern Family', London, 1976, Shorter has sought to locate this personal autonomy for the young men and women of the lower classes in the eighteenth century, regarding it as a consequence of the development of the capitalist market economy and its associated economic individualism; but he denies that this operated similarly for capitalists themselves 'because for them family values overrode everything else' (p.261). It is not clear why this should have been so for one class when it was not for the other.
18 Pinchbeck, op. cit., p.122. Note the complaint of journeymen, 'particularly among the weavers' that the factory system 'deprived them of the assistance of their wives and children', ibid., p.121.
19 M. Anderson, Household structure and the industrial revolution; mid-nineteenth century Preston in comparative perspective, in Peter Laslett and Richard Wall, eds, 'Household and Family in Past Time', Cambridge, 1972, p.230. Italics in the original.
20 Reported in the 'Manchester and Salford Advertiser', 8 June 1842, quoted in Pinchbeck, op. cit., p.200.
21 'Letter X', 8 October 1841, republished in William Dodd, 'The Factory System Illustrated, in a series of letters to the Right Hon. Lord Ashley', London, 1842, p.64. For doubts about whether Dodd had ever been a factory worker see the discussion in W.H. Chaloner, Introduction to the New Edition, of 'The Factory System', published together with Dodd's 'Narrative of the Experiences and Sufferings of William Dodd', (2nd edn, London, 1847), London, 1968.
22 Friedrich Engels, 'Die Lage der arbeitenden Klasse in England', Leipzig, 1845, reprinted in Karl Marx and Friedrich Engels, 'Werke', vol.2, Dietz, Berlin, 1962, p.369. The usual translations of 'The Condition of the Working Class' are made from the 1887 edition which was revised for publication in New York and was rewritten to omit the reference to what Henderson and Chaloner, in their translation of the first edition, call 'the righteous indignation of the workers at being virtually turned into eunuchs'. Engels, 'The Condition of the Working Class in England', trans. and ed. William O. Henderson and

W.H. Chaloner, Oxford, 1971, p.162.
23 Duncan Blythell, 'The Handloom Weavers', Cambridge, 1969, p.257.
24 Ibid., pp.252-4. See also Edward H. Hunt, 'Regional Wage Variations in Britain, 1850-1914', Oxford, 1973, p.116. 'The female cotton workers, well paid, well organized, and well protected, were a no less representative and far more enduring consequence of the industrial revolution than the much lamented handloom weavers.'
25 Bessie R. Parkes, A Year's Experience in Women's Work, 'Transactions of the National Association for the Promotion of Social Science', 1880, p.813.
26 Joseph A. and Olive Banks, 'Feminism and Family Planning in Victorian England', Liverpool, 1964, p.27 and the references cited.
27 See the attack on Mrs Lynn Linton's 'Woman's Place in Nature and Society' ('Belgravia', May, 1876) published in 'The Victoria Magazine', July, 1876.
28 See, for example, the couples described in Rhona and Robert Rapoport, 'Dual-Career Families', Harmondsworth, 1971.
29 William Landels, 'Woman's Sphere and Work, considered in the light of scripture', London, 1859, pp.32, 91 and 109. Italics in the original.
30 [Dinah Craik, née Mulock], 'A Woman's Thoughts about Women', reprinted from 'Chambers Journal', London, 1858, pp.149-50.
31 Duncan Crow, 'The Victorian Woman', London, 1971, p.155.
32 George J. Holyoake, 'Sixty Years of an Agitator's Life', London, 1906, p.16.
33 Hester Burton, 'Barbara Bodichon, 1827-1891', London, 1949, p.47.
34 Ibid., p.100. See also Barbara Smith's remark that slavery in America and injustice to women were both false beliefs, neither true to Christianity. Barbara L.S. Bodichon, 'An American Diary, 1857-8', ed. J.W. Reed, London, 1972, p.63.
35 Raymond V. Holt, 'The Unitarian Contribution to Social Progress in England', London, revised edition, 1952, ch.7. These views made the Unitarians socially unacceptable and this may in part have been why the two young ladies were in revolt against the conventions of their day.
36 Mrs Belloc Lowndes, '"I, too, have lived in Arcadia": a Record of Love and Childhood', London, 1941, p.3.
37 Sarah S. Ellis, 'The Women of England, their Social Duties and Domestic Habits', London, 1839, preface.
38 Sarah S. Ellis, 'The Daughters of England, their Position in Society, Character and Responsibilities', London, n.d. (1843?), p.318. Italics and quotations in the original.
39 Patricia Branca Uttrachi and Peter N. Stearns, 'Modernization of Women in the 19th Century', Missouri, 1973, p.318. See also Patricia Branca, 'Silent Sisterhood: Middle Class Women in the Victorian Home', London, 1975, ch.8.
40 Ibid., p.117. Both with her colleague, Stearns, and in her own book Branca rejects the argument that these women were uninfluenced by birth-control propaganda. In support of her position she quotes from writers like Francis Place (1823), Richard Carlile (1825), George Drysdale (1854) and Henry Allbut (1887) on the assumption that because they published birth-control arguments and described birth-control techniques their work must have been read and acted upon by the women to whom their works were addressed who were also the women whose families were restricted just about this time.
41 United Kingdom, Census of England and Wales, 1911, vol.XIII, 'Fertility of Marriage' pt II, London, 1923, pp.98-146.
42 David V. Glass and E. Grebenick, 'On the Trend and Pattern of Fertility in Great Britain', Papers of the Royal Commission on Population, 1954, vol.6, pt 1, Table 2, p.70.
43 United Kingdom, Census of 1911, op. cit., Report, p.lxxvi.
44 Ibid., p.lxxvii.

45 Only three Class I occupations had more children born to them in both
marriage periods at this time, compared with the mean numbers in
Class II. These were coal and shale mine owners, agents and managers
(8.92 for marriages contracted before 1861, 7.64 for those 1861-71),
builders (8.09 for before 1861, 7.12 for 1861-71), and students (9.00
for before 1861 and 9.14 for 1861-71). This last category should perhaps
be ignored because they were so classified in 1911 when two couples
only amongst them had been married for over 50 years and seven for
40 to 50 years.
46 'The Fertility of Marriage' report, in discussing the rates for shopkeepers as a whole emphasized that tobacconists in distribution
employed 'the largest proportion of married female to married male
labour - 42 per cent', p.cxiii.
47 Albert V. Dicey, 'Lectures on the Relation between Law and Public
Opinion in England during the Nineteenth Century', 2nd edn, London,
1914, p.376. See also L. Holcombe, Victorian Wives and Property.
Reform of the Married Women's Property Law, 1857-1882, in Martha
Vicinus, ed., 'A Widening Sphere, Changing Roles of Victorian
Women', Bloomington, 1977, pp.7-8, where it is claimed that one married
woman in ten 'had separate property in equity secured to her'.
Fitzjames Stephen claimed that amongst 'the comfortable and moderately
wealthy classes' the marriage settlement was 'as much a part of the
business as the wedding breakfast, or anything else connected with
the transaction'. Marriage Settlements, 'The Cornhill Magazine', vol.8,
December 1863, p.668.
48 Peter Laslett, Introduction: the history of the family, in Laslett and
Wall et al., op. cit., p.26.
49 Alice Clark, 'Working Life of Women in the Seventeenth Century',
London, 1919, p.294.
50 Emily Davies, 'The Higher Education of Women', London, 1866, p.110.
51 Branca, op. cit., p.16. The source of her reference is Eliza Warren's
'How I Managed My Home on Two Hundred Pounds a Year', London,
1864, which she maintains is a better guide than Isabella Beeton's
'Book of Household Management', London, 1861, to the world of that
silent sisterhood whose 'modern' outlook resulted in birth control
because these women were 'active moulders of their personal situation',
p.62. Strangely enough she fails to show that they were, in fact,
the 'pioneers' of the smaller family. As the text above argues, they
were not.
52 Harold Perkin, 'The Origins of Modern English Society, 1780-1886',
London, 1969, p.252. The reference is to the early nineteenth century.
53 Ibid., pp.254 and 256.
54 William J. Reader, 'Professional Men: the Rise of the Professional
Class in Nineteenth-Century England', London, 1966, Appendix I,
p.208. Physicians, surgeons and solicitors formed exceptions to this
general pattern of growth.
55 What these incomes actually were is very difficult to ascertain. See
Joseph A. Banks, 'Prosperity and Parenthood', London, 1954, ch.7.
For likely increases in the separate professions see Reader, op. cit.,
pp.200-2.
56 Banks, op. cit., p.83 provides Tables of numbers and percentage
growths, 1851, 1861 and 1871.
57 Hilda Hookham, The Class Structure of Society as illustrated by the
Novels of Jane Austen, unpublished prize essay in the Library of
the London School of Economics, 1938, p.43. See also Banks, op. cit.,
ch.6.
58 Banks, op. cit., chs 4-6, provides details.
59 Leonore Davidoff, 'The Best Circles', London, 1973, p.36.
60 Branca, op. cit., p.53.
61 Angus McLaren, 'Birth Control in Nineteenth-Century England', London,
1978, p.95. The term 'domestic feminism' was taken by McLaren from

D.S.Smith, Family Limitation, Sexual Control and Domestic Feminism in Victorian America, 'Feminist Studies', vol.1, 1973, reprinted in Mary Hartmann and Lois W. Banner, 'Clio's Consciousness Raised: New Perspectives on the History of Women', New York, 1974, pp.128-33, where a distinction but eventual convergence between domestic and public families is drawn from the literature, even if Smith admits that 'there are serious questions about the applicability of this literary evidence to actual behaviour'.

62 T. McBride, 'As the Twig is Bent': The Victorian Nanny, in Anthony S. Wohl, ed., 'The Victorian Family, Structures and Stresses', London, 1978, p.52. Jonathan Gathorne-Hardy, 'The Rise and Fall of the British Nanny', London, 1972, p.66, provides details of advertisements in 'The Times', for, and by, nurses, increasing regularly from 1822 to 1882.

63 Letter from Beau Jolais, 'The Times', 28 June 1861.

64 Royal Commission on Population, 'Report', op. cit., table XIII and discussion, pp.21-3.

5 HOSTAGES TO FORTUNE

1 Letter to Malthus, 9 April 1829, reprinted in Nassau W. Senior, 'Two Lectures on Population, delivered before the University of Oxford, 1828, to which is added a correspondence between the author and the Rev. T.R. Malthus', London, 1829, p.89.

2 John R. McCulloch, 'The Principles of Political Economy', 2nd edn, corrected and greatly enlarged, Edinburgh, 1830, p.212. The first edition of this work, which had appeared in 1825 was much more pessimistic in the neo-Malthusian sense.

3 Ibid., 3rd edn, enlarged and corrected throughout, Edinburgh, 1843, p.222.

4 Ibid., pp.227-8.

5 N.W. Senior, letter to Malthus, 15 March 1829, reprinted in Senior, op. cit., p.58.

6 Joseph A. Banks, 'Prosperity and Parenthood', London, 1954, ch.3, See especially p.37, where it is claimed that there occurred in the 1840s, or thereabouts, a 'changed attitude towards matrimony'. See also p.198 where the curious argument is proffered, that the middle classes came to apply the notion of control as 'a definitely moral obligation' to themselves as a consequence of 'attempting to persuade the working classes to cure their poverty by self-restraint'.

7 J. Hajnal, European Marriage Patterns in Perspective, in David V. Glass and D.E.C. Eversley, eds, 'Population in History', London, 1965, p.101. Since Hajnal wrote this paper, a number of studies have been published which tend to confirm his analysis. See the summary in Rudolf Andorka, 'Determinants of Fertility in Advanced Societies', London, 1978, pp.66-9. Some of the evidence, however, is open to different interpretations. R.M. Smith, Some Reflections on the Evidence for the Origins of the 'European Marriage Pattern' in England, in Chris Harris, ed., 'The Sociology of the Family: New Directions for Britain', Sociological Review Monograph, 28 June 1979.

8 As was emphasized above (p.39 and chapter 4, note 42), the couples married before 1871 and still living in 1911 represent only a relatively small proportion of all those married in those years. Hence the couples whose reproductive behaviour is summarized on pp.39-41 were likely to have been married at much younger ages than couples generally in the same occupational categories. The 1911 Census, unfortunately, did not report on the groom's age at marriage; but the median ages of the brides ranged from 21.9 years for wives of army officers to 24.4 years for wives of hospital, etc. servants (marriages contracted before 1861) and from 22.6 again for the wives of army officers to

24.2 years for the wives of ministers of religion, other than the Church
of England, for marriages contracted between 1861 and 1871. These last
averages should perhaps be contrasted with the mean age at marriage
of spinsters generally between 1861 and 1870, namely, 24.3 years
(all brides, 25.6) to further emphasize the point that the couples in
the text above clearly limited their families within marriage. See the
Census of England and Wales, 1871, vol.IV, 'General Report', p.xvii.

9 Morals and Manners, 'Guardian', 27 January 1858. For further details
of the proper time to marry see Banks, op. cit., ch.4.

10 William Logan, 'The Great Social Evil: its causes, extent, results
and remedies', London, 1871, p.97. This book was very much a
revised version of his 'An Exposure, from personal observation, of
Female Prostitution in London, Leeds and Rochdale, and especially
in the City of Glasgow, with remarks on the cause, extent, results
and remedy of the evil', Glasgow, 1843.

11 Banks, op. cit., chs 4-6, J.A. Banks and O. Banks, 'Feminism and
Family Planning in Victorian England', Liverpool, 1964, chs 5 and 6.

12 Banks, op. cit., pp.170-3 and the evidence cited.

13 Ibid., pp.71-2, 80-3, and 111.

14 [M. Burrows], Female Education, 'Quarterly Review', vol.126, April,
1869, pp.466-7. See also T.D. Acland, On the Education of the
Middle Classes, 'Transactions of the National Association for the
Promotion of Social Science', 1859, p.301. 'University and professional
training commonly extend beyond the age of 21 - involving an expense
in the whole between £1500 and £2000, or more.'

15 'A New System of Practical Domestic Economy', new edn, London,
1824, p.448. The author allowed 4 per cent for education, which
at the incomes given in the text above meant in 1824 an expenditure
of £300 to £600 a year, or £100 to £200 per boy, that is, £1000 to
£2000 for ten years' education each. The 'New System's' estimates
were used as a point of departure for examining the relevant patterns
of expenditure in Banks, op. cit., pp.55-6. They have also been
highly recommended by Patricia Branca, 'Silent Sisterhood: Middle
Class Women in the Victorian Home', London, 1975, pp.26-8.

16 'Report of Her Majesty's Commissioners Appointed to Inquire into the
Revenues and Management of Certain Colleges and Schools', vol.1,
'Parliamentary Papers', 1964, vol.29, p.13.

17 Eton's annual charges at this time were £144 plus extras (ibid., p.100),
Harrow's £144 to £205 plus extras (ibid., p.225), while Winchester
charged £115 (ibid., p.154), Charterhouse £80 to £90 (p.129), Rugby
£90 plus extras (p.260) and Shrewsbury £100 (p.310).

18 The Schools Inquiry Commission, 'Report', vol.1, 'Parliamentary Papers',
1867-8, vol.28, pp.16-18.

19 T.W. Bamford, 'Rise of the Public Schools', London, 1967, tables,
pp.18 and 270. See also Banks, op. cit., pp.189-90. The calculations
in these pages are based on the information taken from 'The Public
and Preparatory Schools' Year Book', 1947, as summarized in note R,
pp.228-9. This list has been subjected to very pertinent criticism
by John R. de S. Honey, 'Tom Brown's Universe', Millington, 1977,
p.395, no.10, since some of the schools which were regarded as 'public'
or 'preparatory' in 1947 were not so regarded in the nineteenth century.
See also Bamford, op. cit., pp.188-91.

20 Figures calculated from table 3 of T.W. Bamford, Public Schools and
Social Class, 1800-1850, 'British Journal of Sociology', vol.12, 1961,
p.229.

21 Compare, for example, Harriet Martineau's remark that 'physicians,
surgeons, solicitors, Army and Navy officers, clergymen and
Dissenting ministers in the provinces, can rarely afford to send
their boys to any of the great public schools', 'The Cornhill Magazine',
October 1864, Middle-class Education in England: Boys, vol.10,
p.411.

22 Hermann Levy, 'Large and Small Holdings', translated and revised, Cambridge, 1911, p.91. No gentleman farmer, of course, had a small holding, although some working farmers had large ones. The difference between them in this latter case was social not economic.
23 Rupert Wilkinson, 'The Prefects: British Leadership and the Public School Tradition', London, 1964, ch.6.
24 Lawrence Stone, Literacy and Education in England, 1640-1900, 'Past and Present', no.42, February, 1969, pp.92-3.
25 Between 1680 and 1729 of 100 male children born to ducal families 27 had died by age five and 37 by age twenty. The comparable figures for 1730 to 1779 were 20 and 27, for 1780 to 1829 were 18 and 26, and for 1830 to 1879 were 14 and 18, respectively. T.H. Hollingsworth, A Demographic Study of the British Ducal Families, reproduced in Glass and Eversley, ed, op. cit., table 10, p.362. Obviously the striking feature of these figures is the decline in child mortality over the whole period which of itself must necessarily have increased the cost of child-rearing, to age twenty, by about 30 per cent.
26 Nicholas Hans, 'New Trends on Education in the Eighteenth Century', London, 1951, p.184.
27 Percentages calculated from ibid., Table III, pp.26-7.
28 In the 1790s the Duke of Rutland paid £300 a year for a tutor and in the 1820s Lord Verulam paid £150, at a time when Eton cost £175 to £250. Francis L. Thompson, 'English Landed Society in the Nineteenth Century', London, 1963, p.84. Clearly, the range in the cost of private tutors was likely to have been similar to that of boarding-school education and just about as expensive.
29 F. Musgrove, Middle Class Families and Schools, 1780-1850: interaction and exchange of function between institutions, 'Sociological Review', vol.7, 1959, p.175. The argument that educational facilities expanded more rapidly than professional openings developed was dealt with in greater detail in his Middle-class Education and Employment in the Nineteenth Century, 'Economic History Review',vol.12, 1959-60, pp.99 et seq. This argument was challenged by H.J. Perkin, Middle-Class Education and Employment in the Nineteenth Century: a Critical Note, and defended in F. Musgrove, Middle-Class Education and Employment in the Nineteenth Century: a Rejoinder, 'Economic History Review', vol.14, 1961-2, pp.122-30, 320-9.
30 Census of England and Wales, 1871, 'Population Abstracts', vol.III, p.liv.
31 George C. Brodrick, 'English Land and English Landlords', London, 1881, p.118.
32 F.R. Crane, Family Settlements and Succession, ch.10 of Ronald H. Graveson and F.R. Crane, eds, '1857-1957, A Century of Family Law', London, 1957, pp.234-5.
33 For details in support of this argument, albeit for ducal families only, see Hollingsworth, op. cit., tables 32 and 35, pp.374 and 376.
34 Crane, op. cit., p.233,
35 Speech by Sir Charles Burrell, 'Hansard', vol.6, 1822, p.1179.
36 Speech by Colonel S.A. Dickson in a debate on a motion to abolish army purchase, 6 March 1860, 'Hansard', vol.157, 1860, pp.33-4.
37 William J. Reader, 'Professional Men: the Rise of the Professional Class in Nineteenth-Century England', London, 1966, p.8. See also P.E. Razzell, Social Origins of Officers in the Indian and British Home Army, 1758-1962, 'British Journal of Sociology', vol.14, 1963, p.258.
38 'Report of Her Majesty's Commissioners', vol.1, 'Parliamentary Papers', 1864, vol.29, p.56.
39 Gordon E. Mingay, 'English Landed Society in the Eighteenth Century', London, 1963, ch.3. Mingay estimates that some 400 families, owning about 20.25 per cent of the cultivated land in England and Wales, and receiving a range of income from £5000 to £50,000 a year (p.26) provided nearly 300 peers by the end of the century (p.6).

40 In 1820 it was estimated that the Crown possessed the gift of 1,000
livings, while a further 5,700 were 'in the nomination of the
Aristocracy and Country Gentlemen', the remainder being in the gift
of the bishops themselves, the cathedrals, the two Universities and
'the Colleges of Eton and Winchester', [John Wade], 'The Black Book;
or Corruption Unmasked', London, 1820, p.311.
41 Gerrit P. Judd, IV, 'Members of Parliament, 1734-1832', New Haven,
1955, Appendix I, p.79.
42 Norman Gash, 'Politics in the Age of Peel', London, 1953, pp.193 et seq.
Family boroughs were those which invariably returned a member of the
same family, whatever the reason; proprietary boroughs were those
so much under the control of a man of property that they returned
him, or a member of his family, or anyone else he chose to nominate.
43 Ibid., Appendix D, pp.438-9.
44 Mingay, op. cit., p.123.
45 Wade, op. cit., p.411.
46 Ibid., pp.12-91.
47 Edward C. Mack, 'Public Schools and British Opinion, 1780 to 1860',
London, 1938, pp.26-7.
48 'Report of Her Majesty's Commissioners', vol.1, 'Parliamentary Papers',
1864, vol.29, p.56.
49 Howard Staunton, 'The Great Schools of England', London, 1865, p.xx.
'The Great Endowed Schools are less to be considered as educational
agencies, in the intellectual sense, than as social agencies', p.xix.
50 Mingay, op. cit., p.141, points out that towards the end of the
eighteenth century daughters began to be sent to boarding schools.
51 Percentages calculated from Judd, op. cit., pp.79-81.
52 Mingay, op. cit., p.26.
53 For details of the number and proportion of 'newcomers' between 1840
and 1873 see Francis Thompson, op. cit., pp.122-3.
54 Mingay's figure of 400 families at the end of the eighteenth century
(op. cit., p.10) may be contrasted with Francis Thompson's 300
(op. cit., p.25), not however to suggest an actual decrease but
the great difficulty of arriving at reliable figures.
55 Hollingsworth, op. cit., table 22, p.367. His figures are, of course,
for ducal families only, while the text above assumes that the figures
for all landed families were the same as these. Note that the comparable
rate for 1830-79 was 1.16. The generation reproduction rate is the
total number of children born to the parents of a generation, divided
by the original number of individuals in the parental generation,
whether they had children or not.
56 Ibid., table 10, p.362 gives survival rates for this age-group of
women as 62 per 100 for those born between 1730 and 1779, and 69
for those born 1780-1829, but many of these would have completed
their families by the age of forty so that a mortality rate of 30 per
100 would not seem to overstate the increase.
57 J. Habbakkuk, The Rise and Fall of English Landed Families, 1600-1800,
'Transactions of the Royal Historical Society', fifth series, vol.29,
1979, p.189.
58 Jonathan R.T. Hughes, 'Fluctuations in Trade, Industry and Finance;
a study of British Economic Development, 1850-1860', Oxford, 1960,
p.288.
59 D. Cannadine, Aristocratic Indebtedness in the Nineteenth Century:
the Case Re-opened, 'Economic History Review', vol.30, 1977, p.634.
60 Census of Great Britain, 1851, vol.1, 'Summary Tables', p.ccxviii,
England and Wales figures only. Census of England and Wales, 1871,
'Population Abstracts', vol.III, table XVII, p.xxxv. According to
the latter source, the number of persons in the category 'is not so
great in such a society as ours, and it is probable that a considerable
number of the men have been engaged in professions or businesses
from which they have retired', ibid., 'General Report', vol.IV, p.liii.

61 [T.E. Kebbel], Country Gentlemen, 'Cornhill Magazine', vol.9, 1864,
   pp.618-26 emphasized that 'young squires' after university and a
   'year or two of travel' usually chose the army, parliament, the bar -
   'a comparatively rare case' - or sat down at home with their
   families, p.621.
62 Henry Labouchere, contributing to the debate on the Committee Stage
   of the Public Schools' Bill, 7 July 1868, 'Hansard', vol.193, p.820.
63 Mack, op. cit., pp.35-6, 40-1, 105-6, 272, see also Wilkinson, op. cit.,
   pp.17-36, and E.G. Dunning, Power and Authority in the Public
   Schools (1700-1850), in Peter R. Gleichmann et. al., eds, 'Human
   Figurations, Essays for Norbert Elias', Amsterdam, 1977, pp.231-50.
64 William F. Lloyd, 'Two Lectures on the Checks to Population, delivered
   before the University of Oxford in Michaelmass Term, 1832', Oxford,
   1833, pp.21 and 62-3. Lloyd himself took holy orders but held no
   preferment, choosing to live off his property. He was an only son.

6 THE MERITOCRATIC EMPHASIS

1 'Report of the Commissioners Appointed to Inquire into Over-Regulation
  Payments in Promotion in the Army', 'Parliamentary Papers', 1870,
  vol.12, p.xi. For details, 1719 to 1866, see pp.v-xi. See also
  H. Biddulph, The Era of Army Purchase, 'Journal of the Society of
  Army Historical Research', vol.12, 1932, pp.222-7, and E. Robson,
  Purchase and Promotion in the British Army in the 18th Century,
  'History', vol.36, 1951, pp.57-72.
2 Colonel S.A. Dickson (MP for Limerick), speaking in the House of
  Commons debate on a motion by Lt.-General Sir De Lacy Evans
  (Westminster) praying the Queen 'to order the gradual abolition,
  as soon as practicable, of the Sale and Purchase of Commissions in
  the Army ...', 6 March 1860, 'Hansard', vol.157, 1860, pp.32-3.
3 Brian Bond, 'The Victorian Army and the Staff College, 1854-1914',
  London, 1972, p.44.
4 John W. Fortescue, 'A History of the British Army', vol.13, 1852-70,
  London, 1930, p.576.
5 For details see the 'Report of the Select Committee on Army and Navy
  Appointments', 'Parliamentary Papers', 1833, vol.7, pp.v et seq.,
  where it was proposed that the allowances should be abolished and
  the Colonel's pay increased to cover the loss to him of this
  perquisite. The Select Committee decided that the provision of
  clothing should be left in the hands of the colonels and it was not
  until 1853-5 that the army itself took over this task through public
  contract. See Lord Panmure's evidence to the 'Select Committee
  on Military Organization', 'Parliamentary Papers', 1860, vol.7,
  Q.274, pp.95-6. Panmure thought that the soldier now got 'better
  clothing at less expense to the nation'. Q.276, p.96. On moving the
  vote on the army estimates on 19 February 1855, Frederick Peel said
  that this change in the system of providing clothing had been
  introduced 'in consequence of its condemnation by public opinion',
  'Hansard', 1854-5, vol.136, p.1550. See also Robert Biddulph,
  'Lord Cardwell at the War Office, a History of his Administration,
  1868 1874', London, 1904, pp.9 and 12.
6 Elizabeth Longford, 'Wellington; the Years of the Sword', London,
  1969, p.67.
7 Letter to his brother, 13 September 1809, reproduced in C. Webster,
  ed., Some letters of the Duke of Wellington to his brother William
  Wellesley-Pole, 'Camden Miscellany', vol.18, 1948, p.24.
8 Longford, op. cit., p.22.
9 Owen Wheeler, 'The War Office, Past and Present', London, 1914,
  p.199.
10 Carole Owen, 'Nelson', London, 1947, pp.30 and 49.

11 Michael Lewis, 'A Social History of the Navy, 1793-1815', London,
   1960, pp.318-23. A Royal Proclamation of 3 February 1836 extended
   the redistribution of prize money, reducing the captain's, or
   captains', share to one-third of what it had been before 1808 and
   increasing the lower ranks accordingly. 'Parliamentary Papers'
   1837-8, vol.37, pp.255-6.
12 Communication from the Duke of Wellington, Appendix I of the 'Report
   from the Select Committee on Army and Navy Appointments', p.278.
13 Geoffrey Best, 'Temporal Pillars: Queen Anne's Bounty, the
   Ecclesiastical Commissioners, and the Church of England', Cambridge,
   1964, p.189.
14 John S. Brewer, 'The Endowments and Establishments of the Church of
   England', London, 1873, ed. Lewis T. Dibdin, London, 1885,
   pp.20 and 126.
15 C.Y. Sturge, Reform of Patronage, in Charles Gore, ed., 'Essays
   in Aid of the Reform of the Church', London, 1898, p.224.
16 Henry Parris, 'Constitutional Bureaucracy: the development of British
   Central Administration since the Eighteenth Century', London, 1969,
   pp.22-3. See also E. Jones-Parry, Under Secretaries of State for
   Foreign Affairs, 1782-1855, 'English Historical Review', vol.49,
   1934, pp.311 and 317.
17 'Report of Commissioners for Inquiry into Naval and Military Promotion
   and Retirement', 'Parliamentary Papers', vol.22, 1840, pp.22-9 and 64.
18 [G.R. Gleig], Army Reform, 'The Edinburgh Review', vol.101, 1855,
   p.543 referred to the entrance examination as 'the caricature of an
   examination' which was 'never so constituted as to furnish any safe
   test of the talents or acquirements of candidates'. Gleig was Chaplain-
   General of the Forces at this time. See also Gwyn Harries-Jenkins,
   'The Army in Victorian Society', London, 1977, p.124, where it is
   pointed out that the army examiners adjusted the qualifying
   examinations when they found that they were too difficult for
   candidates.
19 Letter from Sidney Herbert to Viscount Hardinge, January 1954,
   reproduced as Appendix 5 to the 'Report from the Select Committee
   on Sandhurst Royal Military College', 'Parliamentary Papers', 1854-5,
   vol.12.
20 'Hansard', vol.157, 1860, p.66.
21 'Report of the Commissioners appointed to inquire into the System of
   Purchase and Sales of Commissions in the Army', 'Parliamentary Papers',
   1857, vol.18, p.xxx. It should perhaps be noticed that although
   De Lacy Evans signed this report he added a demurrer to the end of it.
22 Ibid., p.xxi.
23 'Report of the Royal Commission on Army Promotion and Retirement,
   Minutes of Evidence', 'Parliamentary Papers', 1876, vol.15, q.2212
   p.110, and qq.3872-3 pp.191-2. The session with the Duke of
   Cambridge, his second, took place on 23 July 1875.
24 Colonel C.W. White's speech in the debate of 6 March 1871, seconding
   Colonel Lloyd Lindsay's amendment to the Bill for the better
   Regulations of the Regular and Auxiliary Land Forces of the Crown,
   'Hansard', 1871, vol.204, pp.1397 and 1411-12. The 'other officer'
   in the text was a full-time captain, Lord Talbot de Malahide, ibid.,
   p.1473.
25 R. Biddulph, op. cit., pp.149-51. Biddulph was Private Secretary
   to Cardwell at the War Office from October 1877 to January, 1873
   ibid., pp.xi-xii.
26 'Report of the Royal Commission on Army Promotion and Retirement',
   pp.xxxiii and appendices D, p.231 and F, p.168.
27 Ibid., Appendix C, p.274. The year of most rapid promotions of
   the six dates included in this Appendix - 1840, 1846, 1852, 1858,
   1864 and 1870 - was 1858.
28 Olive Anderson, 'A Liberal State at War: English Politics and

Economics during the Crimean War', London, 1967, p.52.

29 Meritocracy: government by the meritorious. This neologism was
coined by Michael Young in his 'The Rise of the Meritocracy, 1870-1933',
London, 1958. Young emphasized as crucial the introduction of
compulsory education in Britain and the abolition of patronage in
the civil service, but the concept is capable of wider application.

30 The Northcote-Trevelyan Report, 1854, reproduced in 'Public
Administration', vol.32, 1954, pp.3-4, and in the 'Report of the
Committee on the Civil Service', vol.1, 1968, 'Parliamentary Papers',
1967-8, vol.18, pp.246-7.

31 R.J. Moore, The Abolition of Patronage in the Indian Civil Service
and the closure of Haileybury College, 'Historical Journal', vol.7,
1964, p.246.

32 For details see Richard A. Chapman, 'The Higher Civil Service in
Britain', London, 1970, pp.23-32. See also J. Hart, Sir Charles
Trevelyan at the Treasury, 'English Historical Review', vol.75, 1960,
pp.103-4.

33 'Report of the Royal Commission', op. cit., 'Parliamentary Papers',
1876, vol.15, p.xxxiii.

34 'Report from the Select Committee on Navy (Promotion and Retirement)',
'Parliamentary Papers', 1863, vol.10, p.96 and the evidence of the
Duke of Somerset, First Lord, qq.4841 to 4860, pp.387-9.

35 The quotations are from speeches made by Sir John Ramsden and Sidney
Herbert in the debate on Sir De Lacy Evans's motion on military
instruction and competitive examinations for officers 'desiring to
qualify for the Staff', 28 July, 1857, 'Hansard', 1857, vol.147,
pp.577-8, 589 and 596.

36 'Hansard', 1871, vol.204, pp.136-7.

37 Harries-Jenkins's interpretation of the statistics he presents,
op. cit., pp.138-9, as indicating that 'relatively few officers were
drawn from the Clarendon schools' fails to distinguish between
direct entrants from those schools and candidates who sat the army
examinations after a period at university, without obtaining a degree,
or after coaching elsewhere. The statistics provided by the Public
Schools Commission, for example, distinguish between direct entrants
(thirty-eight cases of direct commissions straight from school) and
those with less than a two years' gap only (fifty-eight cases), op. cit.,
Appendix E, Section D, p.38.

38 [James F. Stephen], Gentlemen, 'Cornhill Magazine', March 1862,
vol.5, p.332.

39 'Hansard', vol.157, 1860, p.49.

40 '"Knowledge is Power" was a favourite dictum of the age', J.F.C.
Harrison, The Victorian Gospel of Success, 'Victorian Studies', vol.1,
1957, p.162.

41 C. Barnett, The Education of Military Elites, 'Journal of Contemporary
History', vol.2, 1967, p.15.

42 Statement on the education of officers for the army by Sidney Herbert
in the House of Commons, 5 June 1854, 'Hansard', vol.162, pp.989 and
991. See also [G.R. Gleig], Military Education, 'Blackwood's Edinburgh
Magazine', vol.82, 1857, a review of the 'Report of the Commissioners
appointed to consider the best mode of Reorganizing the System
for training Officers for the Scientific Corps', Gleig claimed that the
stress on public school education and the literature of Greece and
Rome made army officers into 'something more than accomplished
soldiers'. The British system 'thinks of the army not as an instrument
of repression over the people, but as a rational institution, and is
therefore disinclined to encourage such an excessive esprit de corps
among its officers, as would separate them in feeling and in social
habits from the rest of the community', p.269.

43 John Smyth, 'Sandhurst', London, 1961, pp.75 and 90.

44 'Reports of Commissioners on Military Education', 'Parliamentary Papers',

1870, vol.24, Appendix iv, p.lvix. For details of the Regulations
from 1849 onwards, see pp.lxix-lxxi.

45 Recent interpretations of the British 'revolution' in government
have taken their point of departure from criticisms of Dicey's 'Lectures
on the Relations between Law and Public Opinion in England', first
published in 1905. As Dicey himself pointed out, these lectures,
'reconsidered and rewritten' over some six or seven years, presented
the 'mere outline' of the topics with which they dealt. His book,
therefore, did not 'claim to be a work of research'. Rather it was
'a work of reference or reflection'. Nevertheless, as one of Dicey's
critics has emphasized, the book has commonly been taken to offer a
comprehensive explanation of the changes which have taken place in
the nature of the British state since the beginning of the nineteenth
century (Dicey, Preface to the First Editions, p.viii; Oliver
MacDonagh, 'A Pattern of Government Growth, 1800-60', London,
1961, pp.324-5). Dicey identified three periods in the nineteenth
century: (1) 1800-30, a period of Old Toryism, or legislative
quiescence, (2) 1825-70, a period of Benthamism, or individualism,
and (3) 1865-1900, a period of collectivism (chs 4, 5, 6 and 8); but
he did not hesitate to point out that the collectivists of the third
period owed a 'heavy debt' to the 'utilitarian reformers' of the second.
'From Benthamism the socialists of today have inherited a legislative
dogma, a legislative instrument, and a legislative tendency.' The
dogma was 'the celebrated principle of utility'; the instrument was
'the active use of parliamentary sovereignty'; and the tendency was
'the constant extension and improvement of the mechanism of
government' (ch.9). Thus the main issue of contention between
historians of these periods has been the extent to which the
development of administration has been nothing more than a response
to legislation, initiated mainly by persons influenced by utilitarian
doctrines, or has been a self-generating process leading from time
to time to amending legislation. On the whole MacDonagh, Lambert
and Roberts have taken the latter view (see O. MacDonagh, The
Nineteenth-Century Revolution in Government: a Reappraisal,
'Historical Journal', vol.1, 1958, pp.56-67, Delegated Legislation and
Administrative Discretion in the 1850's: a Particular Study, 'Victorian
Studies', vol.2, 1958-9, pp.28-44, Royston Lambert, 'Sir John Simon,
1816-1904, and English Social Administration', London, 1963, and
D. Roberts, Jeremy Bentham and the Victorian Administrative State,
'Victorian Studies', vol.2, 1958-9, pp.193-210, and David Roberts,
'Victorian Origins of the Welfare State', New Haven, 1960), while
Parris and Finer have championed the former (H. Parris, The
Nineteenth-Century Revolution in Government: a Reappraisal
Reappraised, 'Historical Journal', vol.3, 1960, pp.17-37, and S.E.
Finer, The Transmission of Benthamite Ideas, 1820-1850, in Sutherland,
ed., op. cit., pp.11-32. Samuel Finer, 'The Life and Times of
Sir Edwin Chadwick', London, 1952). See also the papers reprinted
in Peter Stansky, ed., 'The Victorian Revolution', New York, 1973,
V. Cromwell, Interpretations of Nineteenth-Century Administration:
an Analysis, 'Victorian Studies', vol.9, 1965-6, pp.245-54, and Wilham
C. Lubenow, 'The Politics of Government Growth', Newton Abbot, 1971.

46 'Report of the Committee on the Civil Service', 1968, p.245. See
also J. Hart, The genesis of the Northcote-Trevelyan Report, in
Gillian Sutherland, ed., 'Studies in the Growth of Nineteenth-Century
Government', London, 1972, pp.72-3, where it is argued that a
desire to cut down government expenditure and at the same time to
increase administrative efficiency is what motivated Trevelyan at
the time of the Report, not a desire 'to provide outlets for the
over-educated sons of the middle classes'. See also the proposals of
the Assistant Secretary to the Treasury - 'startling and novel
propositions', as Sir Benjamin Howes called them in a letter to

Major O'Brien, 17 July 1857, 'Parliamentary Papers', 1857, vol.18, p.536.

47 Percentages calculated from the Census of Great Britain, 1851, vol.1, 'Summary Tables', p.ccxviii, and pt I, vol.1, pp.cccxlv and cccxlvii, and the Census of England and Wales, 1871, vol.III, 'Population Abstracts', pp.xxxv and 133, 135 and 1371.

48 R. Biddulph, op. cit., p.x. He added elsewhere that 'judging by the debates on the army estimates, the troops seemed to be looked upon merely as a reserved police for the preservation of internal tranquillity at home and abroad', ibid., p.43.

49 Fortescue, op. cit., chs 48-58. For details of earlier campaigns in these areas and in Afghanistan, Nepal, Kashmir, Burma, Ceylon, Australia and Africa see his 'History of the British Army', vol.11, 1815-38, London, 1923, chs 5-18 and vol.12, 1839-52, London, 1927, chs 22-30, 32-4, 36-40.

50 Edgar N. Gladden, 'Civil Services of the United Kingdom 1855-1870', London, 1967. Chart facing p.10, figures for 1851 and 1870. Similar fluctuations occurred in the civil as in the military services, the figures for 1860 being 32,000 and for 1880, 51,000.

51 A.P. Donazgrodski, New roles for old: the Northcote-Trevelyan Report and the clerks of the Home Office, 1822-48 in Sutherland, ed., op. cit., p.94.

52 Peter G. Richards, 'Patronage in British Government', London, 1963, pp.40-1.

53 Reproduced in Elizabeth Longford, 'Wellington: Pillar of State', London, 1972, p.352. Capitals in the original.

54 Brian Simon, Introduction to Brian Simon and Ian Bradley, eds, 'The Victorian Public School', London, 1975, pp.11-12. For some details of family and old-boy connections see T.W. Bamford, 'Rise of the Public Schools', London, 1967, ch.6.

55 For a discussion of the alternative view that civil service reforms were a consequence of 'middle-class' pressure for job opportunities and its rejection in favour of a concern with costs and efficiency, see J. Hart, The genesis ..., pp.68-73.

56 Thomas J.H. Bishop, in collaboration with Rupert Wilkinson, 'Winchester and the Public School Elite', London, 1967, tables 5 and 10, pp.65 and 105.

57 See the reference to income rather than wealth in the advice to young women on the 'proper' time to marry in Joseph A. Banks, 'Prosperity and Parenthood', London, 1954, pp.35-6 et seq.

58 Patricia Branca, 'Silent Sisterhood: Middle Class Women in the Victorian Home', London, 1975, p.147. Branca tells her readers to look at this question 'from the Victorian woman's point of view' but from the context it does not seem likely that she means by this 'from the point of view that Victorian women actually held'. Rather does she mean us to look sympathetically on the Victorian woman's child-bearing and child-rearing functions.

59 Ibid., p.62.

60 Ibid., p.89.

61 Charles Ansell, Jr, 'On the Rate of Mortality at Early Periods of Life, the Age at Marriage, the Number of Children to a Marriage in the Upper and Professional Classes', London, 1874. Ansell's data came from the replies to a postal survey covering 25,276 men of the Church, Legal and Medical Professions and 'Members of the Aristocracy, Merchants, Bankers and Manufacturers, etc.', pp.10-11.

62 Ibid., p.87. Figures of means and modes, calculated from Ansell's table XI. He did not provide details for the fourth, sixth, seventh children, etc. Note that compared with the birth of 6,035 first children, there were 1,595 eighth children, 86 fourteenth and 11 seventeenth.

63 Ansell was very careful about this, counting as having arrived at

their menopause wives under 44 who had had no children for ten years together with the wives of 44 who had had none for eight years, wives of 45 who had had none for six, and so on down to those over 48 who had had none for two years. Ibid., p.50.

64 Ibid., p.52. The average ranged from 4.82 in the case of medical men to 5.39 for the aristocracy etc. Ibid., p.52.

65 H. Hyrenius, Fertility and Reproduction in a Swedish Population Group without Family Limitation, 'Population Studies', vol.12, 1958-9, p.120. Figures calculated from the table on p.126, amalgamating the periods to make them more comparable with Ansell's data.

66 Ibid., table, p.60. For a comparison with a 'demographic laboratory' see the means given for all except fourth births in table 15 of T.E. Smith, The Cocos-Keeling Islands: a Demographic laboratory in 'Population Studies', vol.14, 1960-1, p.15, where the comparable figures are 2.17, 2.38, 2.43, 2.54 and 2.68 years.

67 By 'natural fertility' is meant 'fertility which exists or has existed in the absence of deliberate birth control' but which may nevertheless be below a couple's potential fertility because of the operation of social factors, such as sexual taboos. Louis Henry, Some Data on Natural Fertility, 'Eugenics Quarterly', vol.8, 1961, p.81. The English term, 'birth control', with its association of contraception, is perhaps not the best way for him to have referred in English to his alternative description of natural fertility, namely, 'la fécondité, en l'absence de limitation des naissances', Louis Henry, La Fécondité Naturelle, Observation, Théorie, Resultats, 'Population', vol.16, 1961, p.625. Fécondité must, of course, be translated by the English term 'fertility' not 'fecundity' which is equivalent to potential fertility.

68 John Knodel, Family Limitation and the Fertility Transition: Evidence from the Age Patterns of Fertility in Europe and Asia, 'Population Studies', vol.31, 1977, p.220.

69 Ansell, op. cit., p.63 and table XIII, p.89. Nine per cent of the couples were childless (percentages, calculated from table X, p.86, amalgamating columns A, B, C and D). From his Edinburgh and Glasgow statistics, Duncan concluded that as many as one marriage in eight was 'sterile'. See James M. Duncan, 'Fecundity, Fertility, Sterility and Allied Topics', 2nd edn, Edinburgh, 1871, p.196. Although it is not possible to identify the occupations of the fathers of the children in his statistics, the general analysis of fertile marriages in ch.6 of this book is very similar to Ansell's.

70 Knodel's references to pre-industrial societies demonstrates how 'modern' spacing really is, op. cit., p.220 et seq.

71 Arthur C. Benson and Viscount Esher, eds, 'The Letters of Queen Victoria', vol.1, 1837-43, London, 1907, p.321. Letter of 5 January 1841. Italics in the original.

7 THE APOSTASY OF THE PATERFAMILIAS

1 F.W. Newman, Malthusianism, true and false, 'Fraser's Magazine', May, 1871, vol.83, pp.584-98. Although he was not an Anglican leader, Francis Newman clearly expressed the dilemma for 'Malthusians', who did not wish to make their marriages 'unholy' by following the precepts of the 'Neo-Malthusians'. In 1889 the Church of England's Moral Reform Union, indeed, published a book by him on this very same subject: 'The Corruption Called Neo-Malthusianism'.

2 William Wilberforce, 'A Practical View of the Prevailing Religious System of Professed Christians in the Higher and Middle Classes in this Country, contrasted with Real Christians', London, 1797, p.12.

3 Edward Miall, 'The British Churches in Relation to the British People', London, 1850, pp.255-6. By 'middle-classes' Miall had in mind

'bankers, merchants, members of the liberal professions, manufacturers, farmers, and tradesmen'. His reference to the Establishment is an indication of his religious pluralism: he was one of the leaders of the Anti-State Church Association which had been set up in 1844 to Disestablish the Anglican church. Middle-class non-conformists, outside the pale of the Establishment, were taken to be sympathetic to 'the main purport of Christ's spiritual kingdom'. Miall described this minority as being 'in the main, devout and faithful'.

4 Owen Chadwick, 'The Victorian Church', pt 1, 3rd edn, London, 1971, p.127.

5 John R.H. Moorman, 'A History of the Church of England', London, 1953, p.390. Wilberforce's 'Practical View' was emphasized by Moorman as 'very popular and did much to influence those whom its author had in mind', pp.318-19. See also Ford K. Brown, 'Fathers of the Victorians', Cambridge, 1961, especially pp.235 and 538; and George M. Young, 'Victorian England: Portrait of an Age', Oxford, 1936, p.84 no.2. 'Lord Hatherton used to say that in 1810 only two gentlemen in Staffordshire had family prayers; in 1850 only two did not.' Davies made the point that Henry Thornton's 'Family Prayers', first published in 1834, reached its 31st edition in 1854. Horton Davies, 'Worship and Theology in England from Watts and Wesley to Maurice, 1760 to 1850', Princeton, 1961, p.221.

6 Desmond Bowen, 'The Idea of the Victorian Church', Montreal, 1968, p.140.

7 George K. Clark, 'The Making of Victorian England', London, 1962, p.286.

8 Bamford, op. cit., ch.3. David Newsome, 'Godliness and Good Learning', London, 1961, esp. ch.1.

9 Quoted in Margaret A. Crowther, 'Church Embattled: Religious Controversy in Mid-Victorian England', Newton Abbot, 1970, p.555. See also her justification for the conclusion that 'in the mid-century many able churchmen spent their time in rarefied arguments over obscure points of theology', p.243.

10 Letter to William Channing, undated, but between 18 July and 7 September 1840, reproduced in Joseph E. Carpenter, 'James Martineau: Theologian and Teacher', London, 1905, p.185. Italics in the original.

11 Margaret M. Maison, 'Search Your Soul, Eustace: a Survey of the Religious Novel in the Victorian Age', London, 1961, ch.10. Note her comment on how difficult it is for the twentieth-century reader to understand, still less enjoy, the 'incomprehensible battles' of this period, ibid., p.240.

12 Reproduced in Frederick W. Maitland, 'The Life and Letters of Leslie Stephen', London, 1906, pp.144-5.

13 Ibid., p.146. Maitland added, 'of this he said nothing to the public' and asserted that he, Maitland, had read 'many letters by Stephen between 1866 and 1904; many too in which he speaks of religion; but not one word of regret; only words that tell of relief'.

14 Ibid., quotation from a letter to his biographer from one of Stephen's friends 'who was intimate with him from about 1859 onwards and whose memory may be confidently trusted'.

15 Gertrude Himmelfarb, 'Victorian Minds', London, 1968, p.203. See also Neol G. Annan, 'Leslie Stephen: his thought and character in his Time', Cambridge, Mass., 1952, pp.20-1. Eton was 'free from moral uplift', 'free from cant'.

16 Alan D. Gilbert, 'Religion and Society in Industrial England', London, 1976, pp.176-87.

17 James Martineau, 'Studies of Christianity', London, 1858, p.356. Martineau attributed this claim to 'a distinguished foreigner' said to be 'conversant' with European society whose remarks on this head he had heard quoted!

18 Gilbert, op. cit., table 2.1, p.28.

19 For yearly figures from 1850 to 1868 and for 1874 see Frederick W.B. Bullock, 'A History of Training for the Ministry of the Church of England in England and Wales', St Leonards-on-Sea, 1955, pp.75 and 100.

20 Thomas J.H. Bishop, in collaboration with Rupert Wilkinson, 'Winchester and the Public School Elite', London, 1967, table 10, pp.64-5. See also Bamford, op. cit., fig.3, p.214, Harrow and Rugby. Bamford also dates the 'significant number of lay appointments for Eton, Harrow and Rugby' as occurring in the 1850's and relates it to changes 'in attitudes to sport and the utilization of the boys' leisure time. Both trends were in full swing long before the schools began to tackle the aridity of the curriculum and the advent of science', ibid., pp.54-5.

21 Leslie Stephen, 'Life of Sir James Fitzjames Stephen', London, 1895, p.113, quoted in Maitland, op. cit., p.132, where two other reasons were given, namely, that Stephen was very attached to Cambridge and that he wished to please his father who had always wanted one of his sons to become a clergyman and would have been very disappointed if the third and last of them had refused to take this step. Leslie Stephen senior died in 1859. This seems to have been a more important event for his youngest son's eventual career as a professional agnostic than the publication of the 'Origin of Species' which Annan (op. cit., p.162) asserted to be the significant fact. See also David D. Zink, 'Leslie Stephen', New York, 1972, pp.28-9, where Darwin's influence is discounted in favour of Mill's. Both views are probably examples of the intellectual's inability to see any influences other than the impact of other intellectuals as paramount in human experience.

22 For details of the family background and education of bishops, 1860-79, 1880-99, etc., see D.H.J. Morgan, The Social and Educational Background of Anglican Bishops - Continuities and Changes, 'British Journal of Sociology', vol.20, 1969, tables 1 and 2, pp.297-8.

23 [W. Sewell], Training of the Clergy, 'Quarterly Review', vol.III, Jan.-Apr. 1862, p.401.

24 D. Newsome, Newman and the Oxford Movement in Anthony Symondson, ed., 'The Victorian Crisis of Faith', London, 1970, p.99.

25 See above, p.10.

26 Francis W. Newman, 'Phases of Faith', 6th edn, London, 1860, p.169. See also H.R. Murphy, The Ethical Revolt against Christian Orthodoxy in Early Victorian England, 'American Historical Review', vol.60, 1955, pp.800-17.

27 Quoted in Geoffrey Rowell, 'Hell and the Victorians', Oxford, 1974, p.130.

28 The full text of what is usually referred to as the Oxford Declaration read as follows: 'We the undersigned Presbyters and Deacons in Holy Orders of the Church of England and Ireland, hold it to be our bounden duty to the Church and to the souls of men, to declare our firm belief that the Church of England and Ireland, in common with the whole Catholic Church, maintains without reserve or qualification, the Inspiration and Divine Authority of the whole Canonical Scriptures, as not only containing but being the Word of God; and further teaches, in the Words of our Blessed Lord, that the "punishment" of the "cursed" equally with the "life" of the "righteous" is "everlasting", quoted in Henry P. Liddon, 'The Life of Edward Bouverie Pusey', vol.4 (1860-82), London, 1897, p.54.

29 Alan M.G. Stephenson, 'The First Lambeth Conference, 1867', London, 1967, p.115.

30 H.B. Wilson, Scéances Historique de Génève. The National Church, in Frederick Temple, et al., 'Essays and Reviews', London, 1860, p.206. This was the last volume in a series, entitled Oxford Essays and Cambridge Essays, begun in 1854 and terminating with this volume. See [A. Stanley], Essays and Reviews, 'Edinburgh Review', vol.113,

1861, p.463. Temple was not the editor of the book; his essay was merely the first contribution to it. If anyone acted as editor it was probably Wilson. See Geoffrey Faber, 'Jowett, a Portrait with Background', London, 1957, pp.229-34.

31 [S. Wilberforce], Essays and Reviews, 'Quarterly Review', vol.109, 1861, p.273. Earlier he had referred to 'the open scepticism and laxity of Mr. Wilson', ibid., p.251. Note that Stanley in his 'Edinburgh Review' article asserted that the 'Quarterly' reviewer had 'displayed or affected the most astonishing ignorance ... of all that had passed in theological literature, in this and other countries, since the beginning of the century', op. cit., p.466.

32 Stephenson, op. cit., pp.111-15. Stephenson asserted that 'it was Wilberforce who stirred up the other bishops to action' but Standish Meacham has put forward a rather different view of the part played by the Bishop of Oxford. See his 'Lord Bishop, the Life of Samuel Wilberforce, 1805-1873, Cambridge, Mass., 1970, pp.247-50.

33 Wilson, op. cit., p.126.

34 B. Jowett, On the Interpretation of Scripture, in Temple et al., op. cit., p.377.

35 [S. Wilberforce], op. cit., pp.255-8.

36 Jowett, op. cit., p.337. Compare Stanley's comment that the Essayists had emphatically asserted or constantly implied the Bible to be 'unlike all other books', Stanley, op. cit., p.484.

37 F. Temple, The Education of the World, in Temple et al., op. cit., pp.12-13, 17-18 and 27.

38 Wilson, op. cit., pp.152-3. Wilson did not himself refer to the Greeks and the pre-Christian Romans in this connection, but to the teeming millions of the Far East who had lived long before 'the historic records of the West' but what he had to say about them also applied to the populations of the classical period.

39 [S. Wilberforce], op. cit., p.256.

40 Joseph E. Carpenter, 'The Bible in the Nineteenth Century', London, 1903, p.287.

41 G. Clark, op. cit., pp.147-8.

42 William Thompson, 'Appeal of One Half of the Human Race', London, 1825, p.35. For Bentham's own view on the subject see M. Williford, Bentham on the Rights of Women, 'Journal of the History of Ideas', vol.36, 1975, esp. pp.171-2, 174-5.

43 [J. Armstrong], Female Penitentiaries, 'Quarterly Review', vol.83, 1848, pp.360-1.

44 Grantley Berkeley, 'My Life and Recollections', London, 1865, vol.1, pp.30-2.

45 The Vices of the Streets, 'Meliora, a Quarterly Review of Social Science', vol.1, 1859, pp.73-4. In his attempt to account for the history of prostitution in terms of an oscillation between periods of prudery and periods of fashion Trudgill has taken 1830 as the watershed, largely because the evidence from novels and other such literature would suggest this date. See Eric Trudgill, 'Madonnas and Magdalens: the Origins and Development of Victorian Sexual Attitudes', London, 1976, chs 8 and 9.

46 'Social Versus Political Reform. The Sin of Great Cities; or, The Great Social Evil, a National Sin', London, 1859, p.4.

47 For the difficulties of statistical analysis in the assessment of the incidence of prostitution, see E.M. Sigsworth and T.J. Wyke, A Study of Victorian Prostitutes and Venereal Disease in Martha Vicinus, ed., 'Suffer and Be Still, Women in the Victorian Age', Bloomington, 1972, pp.78-80.

48 The Vices of the Streets, p.71.

49 Oliver R. McGregor, 'Divorce in England', London, 1957, pp.71 and 75-81.

50 W.R. Greg, Why are Women Redundant?, 'National Review', April 1862,

reprinted in William R. Greg, 'Literary and Social Judgments', London, 1868, pp.357-8, 364-5. See also his 'Enigmas of Life', London, 1851, 18th edn, 1891, where he attributed 'that sad blot upon our civilization which we have got to call THE SOCIAL EVIL, par excellence' to, among other things, 'our vast population of idle men', pp.24-30, footnote, capitals in the original.

51 See the letter from Beau Jolais from his Club to 'The Times', 28 June 1861. Although only half serious, perhaps, this letter contrasted the expectations of 'soul's idols' he might have married with the mistress of one of his friends. This letter was one of a number published in 'The Times' in the summer of 1861 on the themes of bachelorhood and the cost of marriage. See Joseph A. Banks, 'Prosperity and Parenthood', London, 1854, p.45 and the references given. See also Greg, Why are Women Redundant?, p.366: 'as wives become less expensive and less *exigeantes*, men will learn to prefer them to mistresses. Ladies themselves are far from guiltless in this matter; and though this truth has been somewhat rudely told lately, it *is* a truth, and it is one they would do well to lay to heart.' Italics in the original.

52 B. Hemyng, Prostitutes in London, in Henry Mayhew, 'London Labour and the London Poor', vol.4, London, 1862, pp.215-16.

53 Hyppolyte Taine, 'Notes sur l'Angleterre', 2nd edn, Paris, 1872, p.126: 'this is a closed book the mere mention of which is shocking', the reference in the 'Notes' is to June 1862.

54 'My Secret Life', New York, 1967, vol.1, pp.30 and 36. For more details about Walter see Steven Marcus, 'The Other Victorians', New York, 1966, chs 3 and 4. Marcus estimates that Walter was born between 1820 and 1825, ibid., p.87.

55 Hemyng, op. cit., p.258.

56 William Logan, 'The Great Social Evil: its causes, extent, results and remedies', London, 1871, p.53.

57 William Acton, 'Prostitution considered in its moral, social and sanitary aspects', London, 1857, p.175. 'My Secret Life' provides numerous examples of what trifling sums, from Walter's point of view, it cost him to engage in such seductions.

58 [W.R. Greg], Prostitution, 'Westminster Review', vol.53, p.457. Italics in the original. This article, 'being a reprint by request', was published separately, although still anonymously, in 1853 under the title 'The Great Sin of Great Cities'.

59 1 February 1859, quoted in Derek Hudson, 'Mumby: Man of Two Worlds', London, 1972, p.19. Italics in the original.

60 P. Cominos, Innocent 'Feminina Sensualis' in Unconscious Conflict, in Vicinus, op. cit., pp.155-72. J. L'Espérance, Doctors and Women in Nineteenth-Century Society: Sexuality and Role, in John Woodward and D. Richards, eds, 'Health Care and Popular Medicine in Nineteenth Century England', London, 1977, esp. pp.113-15.

61 William Acton, 'The Functions and Disorders of the Reproductive Organs in Youth, in Adult Age, and in Advanced Life', London, 1857, 2nd edn, 1862, pp.102-3, quoted in P.T. Cominos, Late Victorian Sexual Respectability and the Social System, 'International Review of Social History', vol.8, 1963, p.47.

62 [George Drysdale], 'The Elements of Social Science: or Physical, Sexual, and Natural Religion', by a Graduate of Medicine, 3rd edn, London, 1860, p.172. This passage occurs in a section on chlorosis, but see also his discussion of amenorrhoea, dysmenorrhoea, menorrhagia, leucorrhoea and other female disorders.

63 See the arguments of C.N. Degler in What ought to be and what was: Women's Sexuality in the Nineteenth Century, 'The American Historical Review', vol.79, 1974, p.1471. Much of Degler's supporting evidence is American and late Victorian at that.

64 [Drysdale], op. cit., pp.176-7 and 180. Italics in the original.

By 'hysterical counterfeits' Drysdale had in mind various symptoms
which were 'spurious', that is, only apparently organic or
physiological. See also R.B. Todd, Clinical Lectures in Cases of
Diseases of the Nervous System, Lecture III, Hysteria, the 'Lancet',
8 July 1843, vol.II, pp.470-91. 'In men the phenomena are not
generally so prominent as in women, nor are they so numerous. The
disease, as in woman, is frequently connected with the sexual
function.'

65 'My Secret Life', pp.26 and 38. Walter's godfather had been a
surgeon-major in the army. Later Walter got hold of a book on the
'diseases caused by sacrificing to Venus' which gave 'terrible
accounts of people dying through it, and being put in straight
waistcoats, etc.', p.46. See also E.H. Hare, Masturbatory Insanity:
the History of an Idea, 'Journal of Mental Science', vol.8, 1962,
pp.1-25.

66 P.II. MacDonald, The Frightful Consequences of Onanism. Notes on
the history of a delusion, 'Journal of the History of Ideas', vol.28,
1967, p.428. The reference here is to Hunter's 'Treatise on Venereal
Disease', 2nd edn, 1818.

67 [Drysdale], op. cit., p.87. Compare the letter by T.C. Lewis to the
'Lancet', 19 December 1843, p.438. 'I was once consulted by a
clergyman, for constipation, who practised masturbation. He had
never copulated but had a great wish to be married: the res augusta
domi prevented. He defended the practice of onanism, and urged
that a man who did not enjoy sexual union was led to it instinctively.'

68 A.N. Gilbert, Doctors, Patient and Onanist Diseases in the Nineteenth
Century, 'Journal of the History of Medicine and Allied Sciences',
vol.30, 1975, p.220.

69 The 'Lancet', 1843-4, vol.1, p.329. He was answered on 6 January
1844 by a letter from W.W. Morgan who exclaimed: 'the reply is
obvious: in the apostle's advice, "Rather than burn, marry"', loc. cit.,
p.478. See also Dangerfield's letter of 23 December in which he
protested that he had never said that sexual intercourse should be
illicit, p.399.

70 The 'Lancet', loc. cit., p.399. Bull's answer and repudiation appeared
in the 'Lancet' on 6 January 1844, loc. cit., p.480.

71 Letter of 23 December 1843, the 'Lancet', loc. cit., p.401.

72 Ibid., p.478.

73 Ibid., pp.440-2.

74 H. Thompson, Nitrate of Silver in Spermatorrhoea and a New Instrument
for Applying it, the 'Lancet', 24 January 1852, vol.1, p.89.

75 The 'Lancet', 10 February 1844, vol.1, p.663. Italics in the original.

76 Claude F. Lallemand, 'Les Pertes Séminales Involuntaires', Paris,
3 vols, 1836-42, trans. H.J. MacDougall under the title, 'A
Practical Treatise on the Causes, Symptoms, and Treatment of
Spermatorrhoea, London, 1847, 2nd edn, 1851.

77 [Drysdale], op. cit., p.100.

78 Thompson, op. cit., p.89.

79 'Night discharges ... seldom require much treatment, unless in excess',
J.L. Milton, On the Nature and Treatment of Spermatorrhoea, the
'Lancet', 11 March 1854, p.244. Milton wrote four articles on the
subject for the 'Lancet', on 4 March, 11 March, 2 April and 3
January, 1854. He collected these together into a book, published
in London in 1855, 'Practical Remarks on the Treatment of Spermatorrhoea
and Some Forms of Impotence'. On its 6th edition in 1862 he revised
it as 'On Spermatorrhoea and its Complications', and in its 12th edition
in 1887 as 'On the Pathology and Treatment of Spermatorrhoea'. What
was 'in excess' appears to have meant what was not subject to mild
treatment.

80 John S. Haller and R.M. Haller, 'The Physician and Sexuality in
Victorian America', Urbana, 1974, pp.x and 214.

81 A.N. Gilbert, op. cit., p.231.
82 Benjamin Scott, 'A State Iniquity. Its Rise, Extension and Overthrow',
    London, 1890, p.83.
83 Section 32 of the Association's Report, quoted in John Simon,
    Eleventh Report of the Medical Officer of the Privy Council,
    'Parliamentary Papers', 1868-9, vol.32, p.11.
84 P. Fryer, Notes to William Acton, 'Prostitution, edited with an
    Introduction and Notes', by Peter Fryer, London, 1968, note 47,
    p.239. The Association 'had in 1868 a membership of about 400,
    including about thirty M.P.s and two bishops'. The Council of the
    National Association for the Promotion of Social Science seems to have
    been influenced initially by the doctors of its Health Department.
    'Transactions of the National Association for the Promotion of Social
    Science', London, 1868, pp.xli-ii. At its Birmingham meeting, once
    again on the prompting of its Health Department, a resolution was
    passed recommending the Council to continue its efforts along the
    same lines. 'Transactions', London, 1869, pp.xxxiv and 509. But
    at the Bristol meeting in the following year a reaction, led by a
    clergyman, resulted in a resolution, deploring the extension of the
    Acts, 'Transactions', London, 1870, pp.449-51; and at Newcastle
    in 1870 the policy was completely reversed by a resolution, requiring
    the Council to 'take into its earliest consideration the best means
    of impressing on the Government of the country the urgent necessity
    for the immediate and complete repeal of the Acts', 'Transactions',
    London, 1871, p.234.
85 Eleventh Report, pp.11-12.
86 Speech by J.W. Henley, 'Hansard', 1866, vol.182, p.815. Following
    him the Member for Tower Hamlets, A.S. Ayrtoun took a very similar
    line, calling the Bill 'a disgrace to the country', ibid., p.815. In an
    address in Edinburgh on 24 February 1871, Josephine Butler said
    that she was one of the very few people who had read this account
    of the protest by Henley and Ayrtoun. 'It was in that year that the
    knowledge first broke upon me that this system, which I had so
    long regarded with horror, had actually found a footing in our
    England', quoted in Scott, op. cit., p.106.
87 Report from the 'Select Committee on Contagious Diseases Act' (1866),
    Minutes of Evidence, 'Parliamentary Papers', 1868-9, vol.7,
    Evidence of Dr E.K. Parsons, q.q.262, 287 and 369, pp.14, 15 and
    18-19, see also the evidence of Dr W.H. Sloggett q.q. 100, 116-17,
    pp.6-7, Dr P. Leonard, q.563, p.27, and Dr J.C. Barr, q.q.577-9
    and 592, pp.28 and 31.
88 See the return of the year ending March 1869. Of 4,748 prostitutes
    hospitalized under the Acts 4,284 (90.2 per cent) returned to
    prostitution after a period in hospital, 177 (3.7 per cent) went into
    Houses, etc., 214 (4.5 per cent) returned to 'friends', and 73
    (1.5 per cent) were discharged as incurable. Ibid., p.94.
89 Reply of Dr Lyon Playfair to the Motion by W. Fowler (Cambridge)
    to request leave to bring in a Bill to repeal the Contagious Diseases
    Acts, 24 May 1870, 'Hansard', 1870, vol.201, pp.1329-30.
90 'Ibid'., p.1325.
91 Letter to her Liverpool Associates for the repeal of the Acts, no date
    given, but probably about this time and quoted in Glen Petrie,
    'A Singular Iniquity: the Campaigns of Josephine Butler', London,
    1971, pp.122-3.
92 Speech of W. Fowler, 24 May 1870, 'Hansard', loc. cit., p.1322.

8 THE 1870s AND AFTER

1 Peter R. Cox, 'Demography', 4th edn, Cambridge, 1970, table 20.17,
   p.345.

2 D.V. Glass, A Note on the Under-Registration of Births in Britain
   in the Nineteenth Century, 'Population Studies', vol.5, 1951, table 12,
   p.85.
3 M.S. Teitelbaum, British Underregistration in the Constituent Counties
   of England and Wales, 1841-1901, 'Population Studies', vol.28, 1974,
   table 4, p.337. Note the error in the 1881-90 figure in this table,
   corrected by Rosalind Mitchison, 'British Population Change Since
   1860', London, 1977, table 1, p.24.
4 See, for example, J. Matras, Social Strategies of Family Formation:
   Data for British Female Cohorts born 1831-1906, 'Population Studies',
   vol.19, 1965, table 1, 168, where 19.5 per cent of all women born
   between 1831 and 1845 are estimated as 'controllers' on the basis
   of the 1911 Family Census information. See also Thomas H. Hollingsworth,
   'Historical Demography', London, 1969, Appendix I where, using
   stable population analysis, he concludes that the major fall in fertility
   occurred between 1818 and 1836.
5 United Kingdom, Royal Commission on Population, 'Report', op. cit.,
   paras. 58-73, pp.24-30.
6 John W. Innes, 'Class Fertility Trends in England and Wales 1876-1934',
   Princeton, 1938, table XVIII, p.60. Note that his means of children
   born cannot be compared directly with those in the text above because
   he has standardized for age differences in order to identify the
   effect of contraception, whereas in the text postponement of marriage
   and/or contraception are not separately discussed as techniques of
   limitation.
7 A comparison of the means of the means for all occupations in Class I,
   and of the standard deviation for those means, indicates a slight
   movement towards uniformity in that class over the period.

Marriage dates	Mean for Class I	Mean of occupational Means	s. d.	error
Before 1861	6.41	6.60	1.00	0.17
1861-71	5.90	6.06	0.87	0.15
1871-81	4.79	4.64	0.75	0.13
1881-91	3.46	3.40	0.77	0.13

8 Joseph A. Banks, 'Prosperity and Parenthood', London, 1954, pp.12-13,
   129-33.
9 See Samuel B. Saul, 'The Myth of the Great Depression, 1873-1896',
   London, 1969, where the conclusion is well maintained that the
   striking feature of these years was a loss of confidence on the part
   of British businessmen. See also the collection of reprinted articles
   on the question in Derek H. Aldcroft and Peter Fearon, eds, 'British
   Economic Fluctuations, 1870-1939', London, 1972.
10 Joseph A. Banks, 'Prosperity and Parenthood', London, 1954, p.133.
   Italics in the original.
11 Patricia Branca, 'Silent Sisterhood: Middle Class Women in the
   Victorian Home', London, 1975, pp.15-18, 116-17; Teresa M. McBride,
   'The Domestic Revolution', London, 1976, pp.18-21. See also her
   'As the Twig is Bent': the Victorian Nanny, in Anthony S. Wohl, ed.,
   'The Victorian Family, Structures and Stresses', London, 1978,
   pp.44 5.
12 Banks, op. cit., p.138. As is clear from this passage, 'Prosperity
   and Parenthood' failed to maintain a consistent usage of the term
   'middle class' or 'middle classes'. In the first chapter of the book the
   reference had been to those ranges of occupation classified as I and II
   by the Registrar-General. In the second and third chapters it had been

used even less precisely, meaning apparently all those writers of books
on population and kindred subjects, unless there was clear indication
to the contrary, as in the case of Francis Place, journeyman tailor.
In the fourth chapter income was the criterion; those people were
middle class who could afford to live in the manner described as
prescribed by middle-class standards; and this was also true of the
seventh chapter where the term 'middle-income range' was used as
equivalent to 'middle-class'. Finally, in the fifth chapter middle-class
equalled servant-employing class. Of course, the presumption of
the last chapter was that all these usages were not incompatible with
each other, but this is not at all the same thing as a clearly worked-
out conception of the relevant class characteristics.

Probably the most enduring difficulty to be faced in interpreting
the descriptions and analyses of social class in the eighteenth, nineteenth and twentieth centuries, whether written by historians or
sociologists, is to make sense of what the term is intended to denote.
At least two different concepts are regularly employed under the same
label and controversies between scholars have often been bedevilled
in consequence by their failure to realize that they have been writing
past one another. The first of these concepts is that which is most
commonly associated with the 'Communist Manifesto'. This connotes
the classification of human beings into groups which are bound
together in a relationship, referred to as 'contradictory' but perhaps
better labelled 'oppositional' or 'non-symmetrical'. The history of all
human society, according to the writers of the 'Manifesto', was the
history of class struggles. 'Freeman and slave, patrician and plebeian,
baron and serf, guildmaster and journeyman – in short, oppressor
and oppressed – stood in constant opposition [Gegenstand] to one
another, carried on an uninterrupted, now hidden, now open struggle ....
The modern bourgeois society, which has resulted from the collapse
of feudal society, has not abolished class oppositions. It has set up
only new classes, new conditions of oppression, new forms of the
struggle in place of the old.' ('Manifest der Kommunistischen Partei',
reprinted in Karl Marx and Friedrich Engels, 'Werke', vol.4, Berlin,
1959, pp.462-3). The other concept, which is also to be found in the
writings of Marx, is that which entails the notion of groups of people
living 'in economic conditions of existence which separate their mode of
life, their interests and their culture [Bildung] from those of other
classes, and oppose them in hostility'. On this occasion he was not
writing about the bourgeoisie or the proletariat, or classes more
generally, but about the French smallholders (Parzellenbauern); and
having asserted that they formed a class in this sense of possessing
a distinctive way of life, he went on immediately to qualify it by the
remark that 'insofar as only local coherence prevails between the
smallholders, the identity of their interests begets no community, no
national union [Verbindung] and no political organization amongst
them' (Karl Marx, Der achtzehnte Brumaire de Louis Bonaparte,
'Die Revolution', December 1851, to March 1852, revised and published
in book form in Hamburg in 1869 and reproduced in Marx and Engels,
'Werke', vol.8, Berlin, 1960, pp.198-9). Obviously, this is not the
place to consider the difficulties bequeathed by Marx to his disciples
on the question of what is necessary only and what is both necessary
and sufficient for class formation. What seems reasonably clear, however,
is that a conception of social stratification which identifies groups of
human beings, whether they are in a relationship of oppression to one
another or not, as possessing distinct and even, possibly, hostile ways
of life may be used to identify rather more classes (or are they strata?)
– such as, the landed leisured, the professional, the commercial and
industrial employing, the clerical and managerial employed, the urban
skilled 'aristocratic', the urban underprivileged, the rural labouring,
etc. – than is the case with that concept which identifies them in terms

of an unsymmetrical relationship of economic or political oppression
or manipulation, such as the employing, the self-employed and the
employed classes tout court, or the ruling class and its subjects. The
analysis of Victorian England in the text above by reference to a lateral
movement by members of the ruling class from a landed leisured
existence increasingly into officering the army, the navy, the civil
service, into the professions, etc. implies the use of the relational
concept because, although following distinct ways of life, they remain
members of the same ruling class vis-à-vis those whom they command
at work and in the home, whom they tax to provide the resources for
their various ways of life, and in general whom they use as means
merely for purposes which they, and only they, decide. The analysis
of these same people in their families, contrasted with others, labelled
middle, lower-middle, and working class, by reference not merely to
their manner of earning a living but also to the standard which they
severally deem appropriate for *their* way of life, which includes their
attitudes to family limitation, implies the use of stratification into
separate rather than related classes. Most research into the decline
in fertility has classified people according to the father's occupation
as indicating 'class' in this separate strata sense and much of the
present book has been written in this framework. From time to time,
however, the relational conceptualization has intruded, indicated
by the use of the term 'ruling class' rather than upper or upper-
middle, but it is not always possible to identify the differences in
the sources.
13 The term, relative deprivation, appears to have been first used by
Stouffer and his colleagues in their studies of the American soldier
during the Second World War. They used it to refer to the standards
which these soldiers used in comparing their promotion and other
prospects with what they assumed to be the prospects of others.
(Samuel A. Stouffer et al., 'The American Soldier', vol.1,
'Adjustment during Army Life', Princeton, 1949, pp.125-30.) A
sharper emphasis on the feeling of being relatively deprived was
subsequently developed by Walter G. Runciman, 'Relative Deprivation
and Social Justice', London, 1966, ch.2.
14 'Voyages en Angleterre', London, 7 September 1833, reproduced in
Alexis de Tocqueville, 'Oeuvres Complètes', 2nd edn, Paris, 1958,
vol.5, p.37.
15 Gordon E. Mingay, 'The Gentry: the Rise and Fall of a Ruling Class',
London, 1976, p.10. The whole of chapter 1 of this book is devoted
to a discussion of the importance of the process whereby 'new'
landed families were a commonplace of English history.
16 Compare Perkin's remark that many of the new men buying land in the
eighteenth century, 'were themselves younger sons striving to outdo
their elder brothers', 'The Origins of Modern English Society, 1780-1886',
London, 1969, p.60. See also his argument that one of the reasons for
the openness of British society was because the landlords had to make
room for younger sons to buy their way up into the gentry. Harold
Perkin, 'The Age of the Railway', Newton Abbot, 1971, pp.50-1.
17 W.L. Arnstein, The Survival of the Victorian Aristocracy, in Frederick
C. Jaher, ed., 'The Rich, the Well-born, and the Powerful', Urbana,
1973, pp.203-57.
18 Banks, op. cit., pp.192-3 and references cited.
19 Percentages of 227.25 per cent, 27.33 per cent, 25.0 per cent, and
24.71 per cent for each of these occupations respectively have been
calculated from the figures in Appendix A(1) of C. Booth, Occupations
of the People of the United Kingdom, 1801-91, 'Journal of the
Statistical Society', vol.49, 1886, pp.351-71. Booth's figures are
estimates derived from his attempt to achieve comparability between
censuses. Because of the changes in classification etc. crude
measures of growth have been used in the text to which this note

refers in preference to the more precise, but possibly misleading, percentages in this note.

20 Percentages of 141.96 per cent, 20.77 per cent, 19.13 per cent and 49.00 per cent respectively have been calculated for these occupations from Appendix VI of J.A. Banks, The Social Structure of Nineteenth Century England as seen through the Census, in Richard Lawton, ed., 'The Census and Social Structure', London, 1978, Class IA, p.203 and IE, p.205. The same considerations apply to this attempt at comparability as to Booth's.

21 Mean number of births by marriage dates

	Before 1861	1861-71	1871-81	1881-91
Commercial and business clerks	7.05	6.09	4.84	3.55
Civil service officers and clerks	6.66	6.53	4.89	3.57

22 Barry Supple, 'The Royal Exchange Assurance, a History of British Insurance, 1720-1970', Cambridge, 1970, pp.378-80.

23 Ibid., pp.298-9, 386-9.

24 Ibid., p.392.

25 Banks, 'Prosperity and Parenthood', pp.190-1.

26 David Lockwood, 'The Blackcoated Worker', London, 1958, pp.22-9. For more detailed treatment of various types of clerks in banking, etc. between 1840 and 1900, including demands at various times in the earlier part of this period that clerks should be located on salary scales and have pensions, see Francis D. Klingender, 'The Condition of Clerical Labour in Britain', London, 1935, ch. I, especially pp.6-16. Compare, however, Gregory Anderson, 'Victorian Clerks', Manchester, 1976, pp.20-4.

27 The growth of the population in England and Wales amounted to about 29 per cent between 1861 and 1881, and about 25 per cent between 1881 and 1901.

28 Michael Robbins, 'The Railway Age', London, 1962, p.83.

29 T.R. Gourvish, A British Business Elite: the Chief Executive Managers of the Railway Industry, 1850-1922, 'Business History Review', vol.47, 1973, p.307 no.64.

30 Ibid., tables 5, 14, 15, 16 and 17, pp.301, 310-12 and p.306. For details of salaries see table 11, p.307. The mean salaries of these executive managers rose from £1,370 per annum in 1850-69 to £1,900 in 1870-89, to £2,910 in 1890-1909.

31 Ibid., p.292 n.18.

32 Peter W. Kingsford, 'Victorian Railwaymen', London, 1970, table III, p.3. For the effect of expansion through amalgamation decreasing the mobility of individuals among clerks generally, see G.L. Anderson, The Social Economy of Late-Victorian Clerks, in Geoffrey Crossick, ed., 'The Lower Middle Class in Britain, 1870-1914', London, 1977, pp.115-17.

33 P.L. Payne, The Emergence of the Large-scale Company in Great Britain, 1870-1914, 'Economic History Review', vol.20, 1967, p.526.

34 Roger V. Clements, 'Managers: a Study of their Careers in Industry', London, 1958, p.24.

35 Kingsford, op. cit., pp.88-9. Details of such rates are given for the early 1830s to the early 1860s in ch.6 of this book.

36 See also David V. Glass and E. Grebenick, 'On the Trend and Pattern of Fertility in Great Britain', Papers of the Royal Commission on Population, vol.6, 1954, table 15, p.86, where the number of live births per woman in this country shows the following steady decline by the mother's date of birth: 1870-9: 5.8, 1880-6: 5.3, 1890-9: 4.3, 1900-9: 3.4, 1910-19: 2.7, 1920-4: 2.4. These figures, it should be

understood, have been weighted by the age of the woman and are thus
not comparable with the figures in the text above which have not been
weighted in order to allow the effect of variations in age at marriage
to be shown in the comparisons.

37 One estimate gives the decline in the number of male indoor domestic
servants as from 68,300 in 1871 to 47,900 in 1901 while the number of
females continue to increase from 1,204,500 to 1,285,000. See M. Ebery
and B. Preston, Domestic Service in Late Victorian and Edwardian
England, 1871-1914, 'Reading Geographical Papers', no.42, 1976,
table 2, Appendix, p.112; but there are considerable difficulties in
obtaining reliable estimates and another author has not attempted a
1901 figure for the men and has a different estimate for the women.
See J. Franklin, Troops of Servants: Labour and Planning in the
Country House, 1840-1914, 'Victorian Studies', vol.19, 1975, pp.220-1.
The 1871 Census figures included 'retired' domestic servants, while
later Censuses did not. The 1901 Census included non-resident waiters
in boarding houses and colleges in its number of male domestics,
although the earlier Censuses had not.

38 Ebery and Preston, op. cit., table 3c, p.21.

39 Angus McLaren, 'Birth Control in Nineteenth-Century England', London,
1978, pp.95 and 101. His argument is applied to middle-class women
before this time and emphasizes an 'articulated doctrine' which he
assumes these women accepted; but in principle this argument is open
to extension to working-class women, at least in so far as some of them
may have become familiar with such a doctrine. The term 'domestic
feminism' seems to have been invented by Daniel Smith who used it
in contrast to what he called 'public feminism' in an attempt to argue
that 'Feminism and Family Planning' ignored 'women's increasing
autonomy within the family'. D.S. Smith, Family Limitation, Sexual
Control and Domestic Feminism in Victorian America, 'Feminist Studies',
vol.1, 1973, reprinted in Mary Hartmann and Lois W. Banner,
'Clio's Consciousness Raised: New Perspectives on the History of
Women', New York, 1974, p.131. Yet Smith in his turn concentrated
on domestic feminism as a 'revolt' of women and ignored that other
kind of growth of autonomy which 'Feminism and Family Planning'
referred to as 'the emancipation of women'. See Joseph A. and Olive
Banks, 'Feminism and Family Planning in Victorian England',
Liverpool, 1964, pp.11-13, 54-7, 67-70, 104-5, 123-5.

40 L. Davidoff, Mastered for Life: Servant and Wife in Victorian and
Edwardian England, 'Journal of Social History', vol.7, 1974, p.409.
Notice also Diana Gittins's argument from the ignorance of her
working-class interviewees about sexual matters that the Banks's
'diffusion' theory might thus be discounted because 'even if a young
domestic servant knew that her mistress had only two children, how,
given no knowledge of reproduction or the existence of birth control,
could she put this into practice in her own future family-building?'
D.G. Gittins, Married Life and Birth Control Between the Wars,
'Oral History', vol.3, 1975, p.55. Gittins's assumption of a
mistress/servant taboo on sexual discussion, derived by analogy
from her evidence of a mother/daughter taboo, is too plausible to
be lightly dismissed.

41 R. Lawton, Rural Depopulation in Nineteenth Century England, in
Robert W. Steel and Richard Lawton, eds, 'Liverpool Essays in
Geography', London, 1967, p.233. For the argument, however, that
some of the movement to the towns, even on the part of women,
constituted a striving for independence, at least from their parents,
see J.A. Banks, The Contagion of Numbers, in Harold J. Dyos and
Michael Wolff, eds, 'The Victorian City: Images and Realities', vol.1,
London, 1973, pp.113-14.

42 P.N. Stearns, Working Class Women in Britain, 1890-1914, in Vicinus,
ed., 'Suffer and be Still, Women in the Victorian Age', Bloomington,

1972, p.110. Stearns claims that working-class women breast-fed babies for two years or more 'partly to save money on food, but more to delay the next pregnancy'. He does not mention abortion and emphasizes that 'many women among the poor were resigned to their lot', ibid., pp.104-5.

43 Standish Meacham, 'A Life Apart: the English Working Class, 1890-1914', London, 1977, especially ch.4. Meacham has made use of the archive of taped interviews, built up by Paul Thompson and Thea Vigne. See also L. Oren, The Welfare of Women in Labouring Families: England, 1860-1950, in Hartmann and Banner, op. cit., pp.229-30.

44 McLaren, op. cit., p.221.

45 These prices are taken from what John Peel has called 'a typical illustrated retail list' of the day. See J. Peel, The Manufacture and Retailing of Contraceptives in England, 'Population Studies', vol.18, 1962, p.116.

46 E. Hobsbawm, The Labour Aristocracy in Nineteenth-Century Britain, 1954, reprinted in Eric Hobsbawm, 'Labouring Men', London, 1964, tables II and III for 1906, pp.284 and 286. For a discussion of wages generally see Hugh A. Clegg et al., 'A History of British Trade Unions since 1889', Oxford, 1964, pp.478-83.

47 Meacham, op. cit., p.75.

48 The 'late age of marriage and not infrequently long engagements of the Edwardian years' has led one author to conclude that 'there cannot be any doubt that as a whole this was a time of striking sexual restraint among young adults'. Paul Thompson, 'The Edwardians', London, 1975, p.71.

49 Norman E. Himes, 'The Medical History of Contraception' (1936), New York, 1963, pts one and two. George Devereux, 'A Study of Abortion in Primitive Societies', London, 1960, especially chs 2, 3 and 10. Moni Nag, 'Factors affecting Human Fertility in Non-industrial Societies', New Haven, 1962, pp.135-9 and table 73, p.219.

50 G. Greaves, Observations on Some of the Causes of Infanticide, 'Transactions of the Manchester Statistical Society', Session 1862-3, p.14. It made one 'almost tremble', he thought, 'to contemplate the mischief which such laxity of principle, on the part of those who ought to be the leaders of society, must produce on their inferiors and dependents, and especially on the class of female domestic servants'. See also Banks, 'Prosperity and Parenthood', pp.142-4, and for the later concern at the time of the Chrimes brothers' blackmail case, pp.157-9. This case is dealt with in more detail in A. McLaren, Abortion in England, 1890-1914, 'Victorian Studies', vol.20, 1976-7, pp.381-7 and in a slightly revised version in his 'Birth Control', pp.232-8.

51 Ernest Lewis-Faning, Report on an Enquiry into Family Limitation and its Influence on Human Fertility during the past fifty years, 'Papers of the Royal Commission on Population', vol.1, London, 1949, table 115, p.166 and text p.167. Lewis-Faning himself used the more cautious estimate of 10 per cent for abortions and stillbirths, p.14. From the 386 letters, written to the Women's Co-operative Guild in 1914, of which only 160 were published, a miscarriage and still-birth ratio of 17 per cent is ascertainable from the figures published, calculated as 21.5 per 100 live births. 'Maternity: Letters from Working Women, collected by the Women's Co-operative Guild', London, 1915, p.194. Meacham incorrectly reproduces this last figure as 21.3 per cent, op. cit., pp.67-8 where he makes the comment that this evidence came from 'literate, educated working-class women who may have been reared in severely "respectable" households'. Did 'rough' working-class women have more - or less - abortions? For a list of the occupations of Guild members' husbands see 'Maternity', op. cit., pp.192-3. See also David Glass, 'Population Policies and Movements in Europe', Oxford, 1940, pp.51-5 where the

attempt to consider the statistics in terms of induced and spontaneous abortions leads to the conclusion that 16 per cent is about the right figure even if 'it would be unjustifiable to draw more definite conclusions'.

52 Malcolm Potts et al., 'Abortion', Cambridge, 1977, pp.257-261.

53 R. Sauer, Infanticide and Abortion in Nineteenth-century Britain, 'Population Studies', vol.32, 1978, p.92. Sauer believes that this medical development 'probably contributed to the rise in the number of abortions'.

54 Potts et al., op. cit., pp.278-83.

55 T.J.B. Buckingham, The Trade in Questionable Rubber Goods, 'The India Rubber World', 15 March 1892, p.164. Buckingham was, of course, writing from American experience but there is no reason to believe the situation any different in England.

56 For details of the Allbut case see Banks, op. cit., pp.156-7 and Rosanna Ledbetter, 'A History of the Malthusian League, 1877-1927', Columbus, 1976, pp.131-41.

57 The Persecution of Dr Henry Allbut, 'The Malthusian', December 1887, p.89, quoted in Ledbetter, op. cit., pp.138 and 164, notes 46 and 47.

58 'British Medical Journal', 28 May 1887, p.1177. On 2 April the 'Journal' had published a letter from Allbut about this proposed action by the Fellows but had declined to publish a petition from the Malthusian League on his behalf on the ground that it was 'too lengthy for insertion', ibid., p.754.

59 Ibid., 14 December 1895, p.1509. Most of the 'female pills' advertised, it claimed, were 'mere swindles', for, 'although some of them undoubtedly contain injurious and poisonous substances, the majority contain nothing more than a little aperient'. The incidence of such advertisements, it seems, is more an indication of the possible recognition by those who placed them in the newspapers that there was a greater desire at this time for few pregnancies than it is of the effectiveness of abortifacients in satisfying this desire. See P.S. Brown, Female Pills and the Reputation of Iron as an Abortifacient, 'Medical History', vol.21, 1977, esp. pp.300-3.

60 'British Medical Journal', 14 January 1899, p.111. This comment was inspired by the trial of the Chimes brothers for attempted blackmail on the purchasers of abortifacients. See note 50 above, p.186. See also the article, The French and English Birth-Rates, 'British Medical Journal', 29 June 1901, p.1630, where the decline which it deplored, was attributed mainly to contraceptives, even if abortion, 'it is to be feared, is more prevalent than is commonly imagined'.

61 National Birth-Rate Commission, 'The Declining Birth-Rate', 2nd edn, London, 1917, pp.178-82. The other questioner was Dr A.T. Schofield.

62 J. Peel, Contraception and the Medical Profession, 'Population Studies', vol.18, 1964, p.136.

63 A. McLaren, The Early Birth Control Movement: an Example of Medical Self-Help, in John Woodward and D. Richards, eds, 'Health Care and Popular Medicine in Nineteenth Century England', London, 1977, pp.92-7. See also his 'Birth Control', pp.81-4.

64 Ibid., p.119.

65 Ledbetter, op. cit., pp.208-9. They were then sent a pamphlet, 'Hygienic Methods of Family Limitation', which recommended coitus interruptus, douching, and the condom.

66 'The Malthusian', February 1891, quoted in F. D'Arcy, The Malthusian League and the Resistance to Birth Control Propaganda in Late Victorian England, 'Population Studies', vol.31, 1977, p.435. In the text the year is printed as 1896.

67 For details of the trial and its immediate aftermath see Banks,

op. cit., pp.150-4, Peter Fryer, 'The Birth Controllers', London,
1965, pp.162-4, 173-4, Ledbetter, op. cit., pp.33-7.
68 Ledbetter, op. cit., pp.229-30.
69 Glass, 'Population Movements', p.42. 'Prosperity and Parenthood',
incorrectly alleged that over one third of these gave details of
contraception, p.154.
70 J.A. and O. Banks, op. cit., pp.100-5, 111-13, 118-21.
71 Ledbetter, op. cit., ch.4, McLaren, 'Birth Control', chs 9 and 10,
D'Arcy, op. cit., pp.439-48.
72 For details see McLaren, 'Birth Control', pp.224-5.
73 In a working-class area like Stepney more children attended the
Church of England on Sunday mornings than all the men and women
added together, and more children than men, although less than
women, attended evening services. In an area like Marylebone,
by contrast, more women than men and children, added together,
attended both morning and evening services, and more men attended
evening services than children. Robert Mudie-Smith, ed., 'The
Religious Life of London', London, 1904, pp.53 and 97.
74 McLaren, 'Birth Control', pp.218 and 220.
75 Benjamin S. Rowntree, 'Poverty: a Study of Town Life', 3rd edn,
London, 1902, pp.136-7. Thus, 'the 7,230 persons shown by this
enquiry to be in a state of "primary" poverty, *represent merely
that section who happened to be in one of these poverty periods
at the time the enquiry was made'*. Quotation marks and italics in
the original.
76 Ibid., p.120. These percentages are for those below the primary
poverty line only. For a comparative study of village life, in
Ridgmount near Woburn, see P.H. Mann, Life in an Agricultural
Village in England, in the Sociological Society's 'Sociological Papers',
London, 1905. Ten per cent of Mann's poverty-stricken villagers
had large families, averaging 8.2, and 27.5 per cent earned wages
below a level comparable to Rowntree's primary poverty line. These
had an average family size of 5.0. In Ridgmount the chief cause
of primary poverty was the illness or old age of the wage-earner
(35 per cent), although the average family size in this category was
only 1.9; pp.177-83.
77 Booth wrote at the end of the century that 'nowadays the home tie
is broken early .... The growing independence on the part of the
children is frequently spoken of.' Charles Booth, 'Life and Labour
of the People in London', final volume, 1903, p.43.
78 Margaret Hewitt, 'Wives and Mothers in Victorian Industry', London,
1958, p.17. For the difficulties involved in attempting to arrive at
relevant statistics, see her ch.2.
79 D.V. Glass, Marriage Frequency and Economic Fluctuations in England
and Wales, 1851 to 1934, in Lancelot Hogben, ed., 'Political
Arithmetic: a Symposium of Population Studies', London, 1938,
p.280. See also figure 10, p.264.

9 THE REVALUATION OF CHILDREN

1 George A.N. Lowndes, 'The Silent Social Revolution', London,
1937, p.3.
2 Census of Great Britain, 1851, 'Education Report and Tables', London,
1854, pp.xxiii, xxix and xl. Italics in the original.
3 Frederick Keeling, 'Child Labour in the United Kingdom', London, 1914.
Details of the Factory Acts' provisions on education are provided in
chart forms on pp.xlv-xvll of this book.
4 1851 Census, 'Education Report', p.xl. Italics in the original.
5 'Final Report of the Royal Commission on the Working of the Education
Acts, England and Wales', 'Parliamentary Papers', 1888, vol.25,

pp. 103-4, 110.

6 David Rubinstein, 'School Attendance in London, 1870-1904, a Social History', Hull, 1969, pp.37 and 51, and table III, p.112. Note Lancashire's 93,969 half-timers, as compared with Yorkshire's 44,791.

7 D. Rubinstein, Socialization and the London School Board, 1870-1914: aims, methods and public opinion, in Phillip McCann, ed., 'Popular Education and Socialization in the Nineteenth Century', London, 1977, p.258.

8 Compare Rubinstein, 'School Attendance', p.13 - 'By the later 1860's working-class demands for universal elementary education were widespread and were instrumental in securing the passage of the Elementary Act of 1870' - with Eric E. Rich, 'The Education Act, 1870: a Study of Public Opinion', London, 1870, p.ix - 'so far as I have been able to discover there was no effective working-class opinion which influenced the development of law-making opinion'.

9 James Kay-Shuttleworth, 'Four Periods of Public Education as Reviewed in 1832, 1839, 1846, 1862', London, 1862, p.590. These were the children of 'dissolute, or rude parents'.

10 T.H. Laqueur, Working-class demand and the growth of English Elementary Education, 1750-1850, in Lawrence Stone, ed., 'Schooling and Society', Baltimore, 1976, pp.195-7.

11 Report of the Schools Inquiry Commission, vol.7, 'General Reports, Parliamentary Papers', 1867-8, vol.28, p.14.

12 In Joseph A. Banks, 'Prosperity and Parenthood', London, 1954, pp.194-5 this argument was referred to in a comparison of the older Ansell's figures for the clergy in 1830 with his son's figures for gentlemen generally in 1871, i.e., 5 more children per 100 born had reached the age of 20 in the later period.

13 L.A.Tilly, et al., Women's Work and European Fertility Patterns, 'Journal of Interdisciplinary History', vol.6, 1975-6, p.472.

14 J. Knodel, European Populations in the Past: Family-level Relations, in Samuel H. Preston, ed., 'The Effects of Infant and Child Mortality on Fertility', New York, 1978. The evidence of deliberate strategy is much less conclusive than that on the physiological effect of breast-feeding on the mother's ability to conceive. A nursing infant prevents an early conception. For further details on this point see the references cited in E.L.R. Laduire, Feminine Amenorrhoea (Seventeenth-Twentieth Century) in Robert Foster and O. Ranum, eds, 'Biology of Man in History', Baltimore, 1975, pp.172-8.

15 C.E. Taylor et al., The Child Survival Hypothesis, 'Population Studies', vol.30, 1976, p.286 refers to a study of Taylor's own in India in the late 1960s where less than one in ten of the respondents were so motivated.

16 David Yaukey, 'Fertility Differences in a Modernizing Country: a Study of Lebanese Couples', Princeton, 1961, p.161. John B. Wyan and J.E. Gordon, 'The Khanna Study: Population Problems in Rural Punjab', Cambridge, Mass., 1971, pp.83 and 231. Angela Molnos, 'Attitudes Towards Family Planning in East Africa', Munich, 1968, p.118.

17 'Involuntary Childlessness', 'Report of the Biological and Medical Committee to the Royal Commission on Population, Parliamentary Papers', vol.4, pp.37-9.

18 J.E. Cohen, Childhood Mortality, Family Size and Birth Order in Pre-Industrial Europe, 'Demography', vol.12, 1975, p.43.

19 In one study of East African families it has been reported that 87 per cent of the respondents regarded barrenness in wives as a tragedy but nevertheless less than 1 per cent advocated adoption as the remedy. Molnos, op. cit., pp.108-9.

20 Brian R. Mitchell and P. Deane, 'Abstract of British Historical

Statistics', Cambridge, 1962, Tables 12 and 13, pp.36–42, and the
Registrar-General's 'Statistical Review of England and Wales' for the
year, 1973, Part 1 (A) Tables, Medical, Table 4, pp.6–8.

21 R. Leete and J. Fox, Registrar General's Social Classes: Origins
and Uses, 'Population Trends', no.8, 1977, table 2, p.2. The
slope from 76 per 1,000 live births in Class I to 153 in Class V is
almost linear across the five classes.

22 Banks, op. cit., pp.187–9.

23 W.S. (William Sewell), 'A Speech at the Annual Dinner of Old
Radleians', London, 1873, p.59, quoted in John R. de S. Honey,
'Tom Brown's Universe', Millington, 1977, pp.228–9.

24 Grace Leybourne and Kenneth White, 'Education and the Birth-Rate,
a Social Dilemma', London, 1940, p.34.

25 The description of the late nineteenth century as marked by a
'struggle for security and social promotion' is taken from the 'Report
of the Royal Commission on Population', op. cit., p.39.

26 Arsène Dumont, 'Dépopulation et Civilisation', Paris, 1890, p.110.
'Prosperity and Parenthood' can be read as mainly concerned with this
theme, as one author has assumed in his reference to the Dumont-
Banks Model, see William Petersen, 'Population', 2nd edn, London,
1969, pp.500–6. See also his p.6n. where he correctly pointed out
that the theme was anticipated by Malthus.

27 [G.T. Chesney], Army Promotion and Retirement, 'Blackwood's
Edinburgh Magazine', vol.120, 1876, p.603.

28 J.A. Banks, The Social Structure of Nineteenth Century England
as seen through the Census, in Richard Lawton, ed., 'The Census
and Social Structure', London, 1978, table 6.14, p.197. The
conclusion in the text above stands whichever system of classification
is accepted, that of 1911 or that of 1951, and the difference between
the two systems is reflected in the lower and higher figures of mobility
into Classes II and III. For a discussion of the structural changes
in the economy, which possibly produced these mobility changes,
such as the decline of agriculture, the decline of textile and clothing
manufacture, large industries with low productivity, the advance of
public-service employment, of the professions and quasi-professions
and of industries with high productivity, especially metals,
engineering, mining and shipbuilding, see W. Ashworth, Changes in
the Industrial Structure, 1870–1914, 'Yorkshire Bulletin of Economic
and Social Research', vol.17, 1965, pp.62, 64, 66–7.

29 A. Poole and A. Kuhn, Family Size and Ordinal Position: correlates
of academic success, 'Journal of Biosocial Science', vol.5, 1973,
pp.51–9, and the references cited.

30 C. Clay, Marriage, Inheritance, and the Rise of Large Estates in
England, 1660–1815, 'Economic History Review', vol.21, 1968,
pp.504–5, 510–11.

31 M.B. Rose, The Role of the Family in Providing Capital and
Managerial Talent in Samuel Greg and Company, 1784–1840, 'Business
History', vol.19, 1977. Because it was 'quite usual for an
entrepreneur's sons to follow him into the family business ...
Samuel Greg's sons had little choice but to enter his business',
pp.42 and 50. Even when the prosperous entrepreneur bought land
which his oldest son inherited, it was assumed that the younger
sons would follow their father into the business which had made this
land purchase possible. See, for example, William G. Rimmer,
'Marshalls of Leeds, Flax Spinners, 1788–1886', Cambridge, 1960,
pp.114–15.

32 Musgrove, Middle Class Families and Schools, 1780–1850: interaction
and exchange of function, between institutions, 'Sociological Review',
vol.7, 1959, pp.173–4.

33 Rudolf Trumbach, 'The Rise of the Egalitarian Family', New York,
1978, p.188. An earlier writer on this same point referred to the

'habit of calling a number of boys in succession by the same name, as happened in the family of Edward Gibbon, each of whom died after a short time and was at once replaced by another Edward, (which sc.) shows an absence of individual recognition based clearly on failure to survive', David E.C. Eversley, 'Social Theories of Fertility and the Malthusian Debate', Oxford, 1959, p.80. See also the examples given in Lawrence Stone, 'The Family, Sex and Marriage in England, 1500-1800', London, 1977, pp.70 and 409.

34 Shorter, 'The Making of the Modern Family', London, 1976, p.204.

35 F. Musgrove, Population Changes and the Status of the Young in England since the Eighteenth Century, 'Sociological Review', vol.11, 1963, p.72.

36 T.H. Hollingsworth, The Demography of the British Peerage, 'Population Studies', vol.18, 1964, pp.68-9.

37 Thomas McKeown, 'The Modern Rise of Population', London, 1976, pp.138-142. A possible confusion over his use of the term 'exposure' has been cleared up in T. McKeown, Fertility, Mortality and the Cause of Death: an examination of issues related to the modern rise of population, 'Population Studies', vol.32, 1978, pp.539-42.

38 P.E. Razzell, An Interpretation of the Modern Rise of Population in Europe - a Critique, 'Population Studies', vol.28, 1974, pp.13-17.

39 Jack C. Drummond and Anne Wilbraham, 'The Englishman's Food', London, 1939, pp.245-50, 288-94 and 97. It has been estimated that 'the quantity of food exported from agriculture to the urban sector increased by something like 265 per cent between 1701 and 1815' P.K. O'Brien, Agriculture and the Industrial Revolution, 'Economic History Review', vol.30, 1977, p.176. Razzell, who had rejected the argument about a general increase in the consumption of food by the working class, has nevertheless referred to the possibility that land drainage had some effect on improving its health, op. cit., pp.7-11.

40 Hollingsworth, op. cit., table 32, p.42 provides the following figures of mean family size for marriages of completed fertility: birth dates of the children, 1725-49: 4.51, 1750-74: 4.93, 1775-99: 5.02, 1800-24: 4.60, 1825-49: 4.06, 1850-74: 2.75, 1875-99: 2.49. Hollingsworth is not altogether clear about what these figures stand for but if they are for the mean number of children born per family, the nearest comparable figures to these last two for gentlemen of private means from the 1911 Fertility Census are 5.14 births to marriages contracted before 1871 and 2.84 to marriages contracted between 1871 and 1891. There can hardly be any doubt that the advance vanguard of the 'pioneers' of family limitation was composed of the families of the peers of the realm.

41 Frank Musgrove, 'Youth and the Social Order', London, 1964, pp.43 and 61 and the references cited. See also Peter Coveney, 'The Image of Childhood', Harmondsworth, 1967, p.29. 'Until the last decades of the eighteenth century the child did not exist as an important and continuous theme in English literature.'

42 Trumbach, op. cit., p.120. For his part, Shorter has attributed such 'domesticity' to the French bourgeoisie at about this time. Shorter, op. cit., pp.228-30.

43 L. de Mause, The Evolution of Childhood, in Lloyd de Mause, ed., 'The History of Childhood', London, 1976, p.40. See also his claim that 'the further back in history one goes, the lower the level of child care, and the more likely children are to be killed, abandoned, beaten, terrorized, and sexually abused', ibid., p.1.

44 J.H. Plumb, The New World of Children in Eighteenth-Century England, 'Past and Present', no.67, 1975, p.65.

45 Honey, op. cit., p.196 and pp.164-229 passim. For details of the flogging of boys by masters see Jonathan Gathorne-Hardy, 'The Public School Phenomenon', London, 1977, pp.108-12. For home and

school beating generally and the use of the birch at Eton in the
nineteenth and twentieth centuries, see Ian Gibson, 'The English Vice',
London, 1978, chs 2 and 3. One answer given to the question why
ruling-class Victorian fathers sent their boys away from home to school
was because 'many fathers cared little for their children'. D. Roberts,
The Paterfamilias of the Victorian Governing Classes, in Anthony S.
Wohl, ed., 'The Victorian Family, Structures and Stresses', London,
1978, p.62.

46 B.M. Berry, The First English Pediatricians and Tudor Attitudes
Toward Children, 'Journal of the History of Ideas', vol.35, 1974,
pp.563-4. Olive Banks and Douglas Findlayson, 'Success and Failure
in the Secondary Schools', London, 1973, pp.82-90.

47 R.V. Schnucker, Elizabethan Birth Control and Puritan Attitudes,
'Journal of Interdisciplinary History', vol.5, 1975, pp.665-7; Ann
Cartwright, 'How Many Children?', London, 1976, p.45.

48 Norman E. Himes, 'The Medical History of Contraception' (1936), New
York, 1963, pp.209 and 211. Italics in the original.

49 George F. McCleary, 'The Maternity and Child Welfare Movement',
London, 1935, p.3, dated the rise of this movement as from about
1870 and the passing of the Infant Life Protection Act of 1872.

50 Norbert Elias, 'The Civilizing Process', Oxford, 1978, p.137.

51 For clarification on the use of inverted commas in this context see
Joseph A. Banks, 'The Sociology of Social Movements', London,
1972, pp.7-16.

52 Francis L. Thompson, 'English Landed Society in the Nineteenth
Century', London, 1963, p.126.

53 John Roach, 'Public Examinations in England, 1850-1900', Cambridge,
1971, p.3.

54 Charles E. Mallet, 'A History of the University of Oxford', vol.3,
London, 1927, pp.162-7.

55 Robert J. Montgomery, 'Examinations, an account of their evolution
as administrative devices in England', London, 1965, pp.7-8.

56 Quoted from the Charter of Incorporation, 1849, by the Secretary
of the College to the Schools Inquiry Commissioners, vol.4,
'Minutes of Evidence', Part I, 'Parliamentary Papers', 1867-8, vol.28,
Q.7, p.1.

57 Schools Inquiry Commission, 'General Reports', p.331.

58 Matthew Arnold, 'Reports on Elementary Schools, 1852-1882', New
Edition, London, 1908, 'General Report for the Year, 1863', pp.91-3.
The Revised Code is reproduced in Appendix K of this volume,
ibid., pp.331-66. It was also published in the 'Report of the Committee
of Council on Education, 1861-62', pp.xvi-xliv, 'Parliamentary Papers',
1862, vol.XLII.

59 Montgomery, op. cit., p.41. For complaints between 1870 and 1902
that the majority of government inspectors of the state schools were
mainly Oxford and Cambridge graduates, taking an inappropriate
view of the problems of the schools they inspected see Asher Tropp,
'The School Teachers', London, 1957, pp.118-20.

60 A. Rogers, Churches and Children - a Study in the Controversy over
the 1902 Education Act, 'British Journal of Educational Studies',
vol.8, 1959-60, p.41, and references.

61 B.S. Cane, Scientific and Technical Subjects in the Curriculum of
English Secondary Schools at the Turn of the Century, ibid.,
tables I, and II, pp.54 and 56. It was not, however, very popular
with those who sat the London Matriculation Examination, table III,
p.58.

62 See note 73 on p.186 above.

63 Charles Booth, 'Life and Labour of the People in London', 3rd series,
'Religious Influences', vol.7, Summary, London, 1903, pp.423-4.

64 Charles F.G. Masterman, 'The Condition of England', London, 1909,
reset London, 1960, pp.207-8. Masterman attributed family

limitation to the 'considerable undermining process which suburban
religion has undergone', that is, 'weakening supernatural sanctions',
ibid., pp.69-70. For much earlier statistics, exemplifying how
unsuccessful the Sunday schools were as a source of recruitment to
church and chapel between 1800 and 1850, see Thomas W. Laqueur,
'Religion and Respectability: Sunday Schools and Working Class Culture,
1780-1850', New Haven, 1976, pp.79-81.
65 F.B. Smith, The Atheist Mission, 1840-1900, in Robert Robson, ed.,
'Ideas and Institutions of Victorian Britain', London, 1967, p.234.
Hugh McCleod, 'Class and Religion in the Late Victorian City', London,
1974, p.224.
66 Quoted in E. Sandford, Exeter Memoir, 1869-1885, in E. Sandford
et al., 'Memoirs of Archbishop Temple by Seven Friends', 2nd edn,
London, 1906, vol.2, p.281. For further details of the opposition
to Temple's appointment at Exeter, see pp.283-91. Note, however,
Sandford's appraisal of Temple that 'he did not follow his contribution
to 'Essays and Reviews' by appearing as a prophet of progressive
theology; he did not lead an advanced wing of political Churchmen',
ibid., p.406. For details of the Exeter case before the Court of the
Vicar-General, 8 December 1869, see Robert Phillimore, 'The
Ecclesiastical Law of the Church of England', London, 1873, vol.1,
pp.51-5.
67 Banks, 'Prosperity and Parenthood', pp.160-1, F. Campbell, Birth
Control and the Christian Churches, 'Population Studies', vol.14,
1960, pp.134-5.
68 Christabel Pankhurst, 'The Great Scourge and How to End it', London,
1913, pp.v-vi.
69 'Final Report of the Royal Commission on Venereal Diseases', 1916,
p.23, 'Parliamentary Papers', 1916, vol.XVI. The Royal Commission
launched a number of special enquiries and studies to obtain more
accurate information but concluded that because people were so
unwilling to admit to having venereal diseases it was virtually
impossible to estimate their incidence in the civilian population,
ibid., pp.16-22.
70 James Hinton, 'The First Shop Stewards' Movement', London, 1973,
pp.336 explicitly recognizes that 'this was what workers' control
meant to most workers - not wild schemes of general nationalization',
although much of the book is devoted to ideological controversies
between minority groups of workers and economic changes within
different industries, as though working-class consciousness has
its roots in either or both of these phenomena alone.

10 TOWARDS A FERTILITY POLICY

1 The term 'demographic transition' has been claimed to have been first
used by the demographer, Frank Notestein in 1945. J.C. Caldwell,
Towards a Restatement of Demographic Transition Theory, 'Population
and Development Review', 1976, p.359, no.4. In the present context
it should be emphasized that Notestein himself complained about the
disposition of population forecasters 'to treat population growth as
an independent variable, to view growth as a dynamic response to
laws of nature moving irresistibly toward an inevitable goal'. F.W.
Notestein, Population - The Long View, in Theodore W. Schultz, ed.,
'Food for the World', Chicago, 1945, p.36. The terms 'transitional
growth' and 'demographic transition' appeared on pp.41 and 48 of
this paper.
2 Thomas R. Malthus, 'An Essay on the Principle of Population, as it
affects the future improvement of society', London, 1798, reprinted
with notes by James Bonar, London, 1926, pp.101-2 and 106-7;
reprinted with a foreword by Kenneth E. Boulding, Ann Arbor, 1959,

pp.36 and 38; reprinted together with A Summary View of the Principle of Populations, London, 1830, and with an introduction and notes by Anthony Flew, Harmondsworth, 1970, pp.104 and 106.

3 Ibid., 1926, pp.63, 67 and 150; 1954, pp.22-3 and 53; 1970, pp.89-91 and 123.

4 In his original essay and in all subsequent editions Malthus used a very simple illustration of the nature of the difference between a geometric and an arithmetic progression, namely, 1, 2, 4, 8, 16, etc. as compared with 1, 2, 3, 4, 5, etc. This simplistic differentiation unfortunately blinded him and many of his subsequent readers to the possibility that population growth and food production could vary thus differentially although on the basis of different multipliers or additives. Granted that sterility and sub-fecundity prevent some couples from doubling themselves, while others may have only mild sexual drives and some no interest sexually in members of the other sex, the growth of population, while still geometric, might be at less than the doubling rate, assumed by Malthus. Hence the geometric sequence, 1, 1.75, 3.06, etc. implies that the middle generations of three will live in comparative affluence, assuming an increase in food production at no more than unit ratio - 1, 2, 3, 4, etc. The geometric sequence 1, 1.5, 2.25, 3.37, 5.07, etc., on this same assumption, would result in three generations of affluence, that is, 90 years, or thereabouts, 1, 1.25, 1.56, 1.95, 2.44, etc. promise centuries of affluence. Obviously if the arithmetic ratio of food production is increased more generously to 1, 2.25, 3.5, 4.75, etc., or to 1, 2.5, 4.0, 5.5, etc., similar considerations apply, although in the comparison of any of these progressions the geometric will always eventually outstrip the arithmetic. Their failure to understand the principle of Malthus's argument led many of his early critics to argue irrelevantly about the accuracy of his figures, which were merely illustrative. See the examples referred to in Kenneth Smith, 'The Malthusian Controversy', London, 1951, Book III, chs 1-3. As against these compare the sophistication of Malthus's analysis of the doubling of the American population in twenty-five years or less, as set out in A.J. Coale, The Use of Modern Analytical Demography by T.R. Malthus, 'Population Studies', vol.33, 1979, pp.329-32.

5 M.S. Teitelbaum, Fertility Effects of the Abolition of Legal Abortion in Romania, 'Population Studies', vol.26, 1972, pp.405-7. The crude birth-rate, and total fertility rate, and the gross and net reproduction rates doubled approximately in one year, from 1966-7, as a consequence of this change of policy; but see also B. Berelson, Romania's 1966 Anti-Abortion Decree: the Demographic Experience of the First Decade, 'Population Studies', vol.33, 1979, pp.209-22. After 1967 the crude birth rate fell in 1976 to a figure of only 36 per cent above that of 1966, so that although there was no clear sign of a return to the fertility level of 1966, it is nevertheless apparent that traditional methods of birth control, such as abstinence and coitus interruptus, had been employed - in defiance? - of the policy-makers' intentions.

6 D.V. Glass, Fertility Trends in Europe since the Second World War, 'Population Studies', vol.22, 1968, p.126.

7 Even Campbell, who compared the fertility rates of eighteen selected countries in the 1930s with those of the early 1950s, late 1950s and 1960s, and early 1970s, to draw the conclusion that they had gone beyond the demographic transition to enter a new demographic era, nevertheless confessed that it was 'still difficult to estimate the extent to which the postwar rise in fertility was brought about by increases in completed fertility rates, that is, in the average number of children per 1,000 women that a cohort has borne by age 50'. A.A. Campbell, Beyond the Demographic Transition, 'Demography', vol.II, 1974, p.553. The details are provided in Table I, pp.550-1.

8 Alexander M. Carr-Saunders, 'The Population Problem - A Study in Human Evolution', Oxford, 1922, pp.200-1, 213 and 233. For a brief account of the earlier optimum population 'theorists', see Edward P. Hutchinson, 'The Population Debate: the Development of Conflicting Theories up to 1900', Boston, 1967, ch.13.
Almost completely independently of Carr-Saunders a 'theory' of the 'homeostatic' control of population density in animals has been based on the concept of the optimum number to the point of claiming that some animal populations 'contrive' to inflict mortality on themselves and others to control fertility. Vero C. Wynne-Edwards, 'Animal Dispersion in Relation to Social Behaviour', Edinburgh, 1962, esp. chs 21 and 22. For his debt to Carr-Saunders see p.493. This homeostatic 'theory' has been attacked for its lack of information about prudential restraint amongst animals and for its failure to consider adequately the degree to which the upper limit to survival, set by the food supply, is not reached because of the action of predators and parasites. David Lack, 'Population Studies of Birds', Oxford, 1966, pp.275 and 301-2. Wynne-Edwards's vaguely teleological reference to the fact that 'uncontrollable mortality is chancy and fluctuating' so that 'especially versatile and flexible adaptations are required at this stage to complement it, so as still to come out at the end with the optimal quota of recruits' (op. cit., p.555) stands as his conclusion to a very brief discussion of predators and disease near the end of his book. For a discussion of these points see C. Perrins, Bird Populations, in Anthony Allison, ed., 'Population Control', Harmondsworth, 1970, pp.76-81. For an application of the Wynne-Edwards's thesis to human populations, see Edward Wrigley, 'Population and History', London, 1969, pp.112-15, and for a criticism, G. Hawthorne, Explaining Human Fertility, 'Sociology', vol.2, 1968, pp.67-70.
9 J. Hajnal, European Marriage Patterns in Perspective, in David V. Glass and D.E.C. Eversley, eds, 'Population in History', London, 1965, pp.110-11 and 115.
10 Probably the most quoted recent source of information about the French situation is The General Development of the Population of France since the Eighteenth Century, by J. Bourgeois-Pichat, published in 'Population', 1951-2, and in translation in Glass and Eversley, op. cit., pp.474-506. Table 3 on p.506 provides gross and net reproduction rates per 100 women from 1771-5 to 1950. Note that the gross rate falls consistently from 1771-5, but the net rate does not fall consistently below the 1771-5 figure until 1836-40. To use the gross rate only, as Alfred Sauvy has done in his 'Présentation' to Hélène Bergues et al., 'La Prévention des Naissances dans la Famille', Paris, 1960, p.14, can be very misleading. The problem is that no French government has ever produced the kind of information which was made available about Britain through the Fertility Census of 1911, so that all the information about eighteenth and nineteenth century France is shot through with speculative inferences about what is implied by the rather sparse statistics. See the discussion of sources in L. Henry, 'The Population of France in the Eighteenth Century' in Glass and Eversley, op. cit., pp.436-40. An example of the considerable degree of speculative inference involved may be seen in M. Lachiver, Fécondité Légitime et Contraception dans la Région Parisienne, in André Armengaud et al., 'Sur la Population Française au XVIII et au XIX Siecles', Paris, 1973. Despite the work done in this area since 1945, Spengler's pre-war judgment still stands. 'While it is not determinable whether or not French natality fell prior to the French Revolution, it is evident that a socio-psychological attitude favourable to birth limitation existed already in the early eighteenth century, if not prior to that time.' Joseph J. Spengler, 'France Faces Depopulation', Durham, N.C., 1938, p.65. The current conviction

that the origins of birth control are to be found in France rests on this combination of partial evidence of favourable attitudes and partial statistics. See also the discussion in A. Armengaud, La population française a la vieille de la Revolution, in Fernand Brandel and Ernest Labrousse, ed., 'Histoire Economique et Sociale de la France', Book III, vol.I, Paris, 1976, pp.162-4, where he concludes that it is impossible to conclude whether there was any difference at the end as compared with the beginning of the eighteenth century.

11 Julian L. Simon, 'The Economics of Population Growth', Princeton, 1977, p.44.

12 Charles P. Kindleberger, 'Economic Growth in France and Britain, 1851-1950', Cambridge, Mass., 1964, pp.69-82. F. Crouzet, French Economic Growth in the Nineteenth Century Reconsidered, 'History', vol.59, 1974, especially pp.169-70, 175-6.

13 The following figures of the people aged 20-64, expressed as a percentage of the total population, have been calculated from Bourgeois-Pichat, Appendix II, table 1, op. cit., p.498: 52.8 per cent in 1776, 52.5 per cent in 1801, 54.9 per cent in 1851, 57.2 per cent in 1901, 58.6 per cent in 1951. The corresponding percentages for people aged 65 and over are: 4.4 per cent, 5.6 per cent, 6.6 per cent, 8.5 per cent and 11.5 per cent, so that the dependent population was decreased solely by the drop in the percentage of people aged under twenty, namely: from 42.8 per cent through 41.9 per cent, 38.5 per cent, 34.3 per cent to 29.9 per cent.

14 Simon Kuznets, 'Economic Growth of Nations', Cambridge, Mass., 1971, Table 1, pp.11-14.

15 Simon's very elaborate analysis of more developed and less developed countries leads to the conclusion that 'after an initial period of lower per-worker output, the higher birth-rate variations come to show higher per-worker output after anywhere from less than half a century to somewhat more than a century'; but the evidence in favour of this anti-Carr-Saunders argument is based on rather crude approximations, as even a quick glance at a figure like that on economic growth rates, related to population density, 1960-5, will confirm. Simon, op. cit., pp.141 and 480.

16 Rosanna Ledbetter, 'A History of the Malthusian League, 1877-1927', Columbus, 1976, pp.87-9.

17 The comparable figures for increases per decade are:

Decades	Great Britain Occupied Males	United Kingdom Income over £150
1851-61	10.9	23.4
1861-71	12.5	44.9
1871-81	8.1	33.2
1881-91	13.2	16.4
1891-1901	15.4	26.0
1901-11	12.0	24.0

The percentages in the first column have been calculated from Table 102 of the Department of Employment's 'British Labour Statistics, Historical Abstract, 1886-1968', London, 1971, p.102. Those in the second have been taken from Joseph A. Banks, 'Prosperity and Parenthood', London, 1954, p.132. For a discussion of the difficulties on using taxation returns see ibid., pp.103-8.

18 'If I had to rewrite my book, I would use "natural preservation" or "naturally preserved".' Letter from Charles Darwin to William Harvey, August 1860, reproduced in Francis Darwin, 'More Letters of Charles Darwin', vol.1, London, 1903, p.161.

19 'I have over and over again said in the *Origin* that Natural Selection does nothing without variability.' Letter from Charles Darwin to

Charles Lyell, 21 August 1861, ibid., p.193. In the very first chapter of the 'Origin', entitled Variation under Domestication, Darwin wrote that he suspected variability to be caused by male and female 'reproductive elements having been affected prior to the act of conception', but, he added a little further on, 'the laws governing inheritance are quite unknown'. Morse Peckham, ed., 'The Origin of Species by Charles Darwin: a Variorum Text', Philadelphia, 1959, pp.79 and 86.

20 Ledbetter, op. cit., p.182.
21 A. McLaren, Sex and Socialism: the Opposition of the French Left to Birth Control in the Nineteenth Century, 'Journal of the History of Ideas', vol.37, 1976, p.491.
22 Bergues, op. cit., p.52.
23 For an example of the considerable difficulties, and therefore 'inspired guesses' involved, see Colin Foster and G.-S.L. Tucker, 'Economic Opportunity and White American Fertility Ratios, 1800-1860', New Haven, 1972. The conclusion that a plentiful supply of fertile land is the key to fertility and its disappearance to family limitation is one such 'guess'. See also Etienne van de Walle, 'The Female Population of France in the Nineteenth Century', Princeton, 1974.
24 P. Goubert, Révolution Démographique au XVII Siècle, in Braudel and Labrousse, op. cit., Book II, Paris, 1970, pp.82-3.
25 R. Lawton, Rural Depopulation in Nineteenth Century England, in Robert W. Steel and Richard Lawton, eds, 'Liverpool Essays in Geography', London, 1967, p.195. A. Armengaud, Les Nouvelles Repartitions in Brandel and Labrousse, op. cit., Book III, vol.1, p.230.
26 Percentages calculated from the Census of 1851, 'Summary Tables', p.ccxix, for persons aged twenty and over, and from the Census of 1911 vol.10, 'Occupations and Industries', Pt I, Table I, pp.2-3, for persons aged ten and over.
27 Percentages calculated from Brian Mitchell, 'European Historical Statistics', London, 1975, Table C1, p.15.
28 Antoine Prost, 'Histoire de l'Enseignement en France, 1800-1967', 2nd edn, Paris, 1968, pp.99 and 101.
29 [Henry Reeve], France, the 'Edinburgh Review', January 1871, p.21. See also his 'Census of France in 1872', ibid., October 1874, p.383. Malthus, although cautious on the grounds that the law in his day had not been in existence long enough for him to decide, thought that it would probably discourage prudence in marriage and that therefore there would be an upsurge of births, leading to poverty and distress in France. Thomas R. Malthus, 'Principles of Political Economy', London, 1820, pp.433-4.
30 Pierre F. Le Play, 'La Réforme Sociale en France', Paris, 1867, vol.I, pp.229-30. Le Play claimed that the law made marriages sterile, ibid., pp.242, 363, and 396.
31 Armengaud, Les Nouvelles Repartitions, p.194.
32 See the map reproduced from the French translation of A. von Brandt's 'Law and Customs of the Rural Population of France' in F. Mendel, La composition du ménage paysan en France au XIX siècle, 'Annales, E.S.C.', vol.33, 1978, p.799.
33 T.E.C. Leslie, The Land System of France in John W. Probyn, ed., 'Systems of Land Tenure in Various Countries', New Edition, London, 1881, pp.304-5.
34 Spencer Wilkinson, 'The French Army before Napoleon', Oxford, 1915, pp.90 and 107.

INDEX TO SOURCES

GENERAL INDEX